We Are As Gods

We Are As Gods

BACK TO THE LAND in the 1970s on the Quest for a New America

KATE DALOZ

PUBLICAFFAIRS

New York

Published in the United States by PublicAffairs™, a Member of the Perseus
Books Group

PublicAffairs books are available at special discounts for bulk purchases
in the U.S. by corporations, institutions, and other organizations. For more
information, please contact the Special Markets Department at the Perseus
Books Group, 2300 Chestnut Street, Suite 200, Philadelphia, PA 19103, call
(800) 810-4145, ext. 5000, or e-mail special.markets@perseusbooks.com.

Book Design by Amnet

Library of Congress Cataloging-in-Publication Data

Names: Daloz, Kate, author.
Title: We are as gods : back to the land in the 1970s on the quest for a new
    America / Kate Daloz.
Description: First Edition. | New York : PublicAffairs, 2016.
Identifiers: LCCN 2016002225 (print) | LCCN 2016004849 (ebook) |
    ISBN 9781610392259 (hardback) | ISBN 9781610392266 (ebook)
Subjects: LCSH: United States—Social conditions—20th century. | Land
    settlement—United States—History—20th century. | Farm ownership—
    United States—History—20th century. | Sustainable living—
    United States—History—20th century. | BISAC: HISTORY / United States /
    20th Century. | SOCIAL SCIENCE / Sociology / Rural. | HOUSE & HOME /
    Sustainable Living.
Classification: LCC HN57 .D25 2016 (print) | LCC HN57 (ebook) | DDC
    306.0973—dc23
LC record available at http://lccn.loc.gov/2016002225

ISBN 978-1-61039-225-9 (HC)
ISBN 978-1-61039-226-6 (EB)

First Edition
10 9 8 7 6 5 4 3 2 1

For Mom and Dad
And in memory of Nash

"We *are* as gods and might as well get good at it. So far remotely done power and glory—as via government, big business, formal education, church—has succeeded to point where gross defects obscure actual gains. In response to this dilemma and to these gains a realm of intimate, personal power is developing—power of the individual to conduct his own education, find his own inspiration, shape his own environment, and share his adventure with whoever is interested."

—"Purpose," *Whole Earth Catalog*, Fall 1968

"We are <u>as</u> gods, and may as well get good at it. This might include losing the pride that went before the fall we are in the process of taking. Rolling with such a fall is our present lesson—learning whatever resilience, ingenuity, basic skills, and enthused detachment that survival requires. And learning perhaps to reverence some Gods who are not <u>as</u> us."

—"Purpose," *Whole Earth Epilog*, October 1974

Prologue

The land had been, most recently, a potato farm.

Or more accurately, of the three adjoining fields carved into the woody hillside, the middle one had spent the last several summers planted in a cash crop of spuds. Freeman Brooks' actual farm lay a few miles away. He was getting older and it was getting harder to get around, plus the rough tractor road that connected the fields was in terrible condition. It was no longer worth the hassle, he decided; the land would be worth more to him in cash. The whole lot—a 116-acre square, including all three fields and surrounding woods—was now for sale.

His neighbors weren't interested. The lower field was too soggy and the upper one too sloped and the hillside woods went directly from rocky and steep to marshy. The lot included no buildings, though this hadn't always been the case. Some years past, a family had lived up there, raising turkeys. One autumn, the farmer, accompanied by his sons, had taken the turkeys into the city to sell. While he was gone, his wife had an affair with the hired man. When the husband came back, he found out and killed them both. The land had passed out of the family after that, and now, in April 1970, it was Freeman Brooks' turn to pass it on to whoever would own it next.

One afternoon, a battered car came to a stop near the entrance of the tractor road. It was an overcast day. Spring would not arrive for weeks, but the bitterness had gone out of the wind and the light fell gently over the hills. The thick snow still blanketing the open fields had begun to leak away into rivulets, softening even the well-graded main road into slippery ruts.

Just as they'd been warned, the tractor road was a hopeless morass, so the prospective buyers were preparing to enter the land on foot. Loraine emerged from the car's backseat and looked around. To the right lay a large, well-maintained hayfield, clearly belonging to the neighboring farm. The field's high rolls obscured the horizon, but its steepest point, Loraine noticed, would make an excellent toboggan hill; a good run on fast snow might bring you all the way down to the main road in an exhilarated rush.

Ahead of her, the others had already started up the narrow, muddy track, and Loraine followed them. To the left, the spruce crowded close together, their spiny branches so thick and dark it was hard to tell how far back they went. To the right stood the hayfield's hedgerow of elegant old maples, their shaggy trunks hung with sap buckets. Their branches reached across the road, almost touching the needles on the other side. With the sky low and gray overhead, it felt a little like walking into a tunnel.

This was Loraine's first time joining the men on a land-scouting expedition. For weeks, they'd been coming back from each trip with a reason why the property they'd seen wouldn't work: it was too close to a big road, or within sight of neighbors, or included a house with the modern amenities (electricity, running water) that were exactly what they were trying to get away from. Loraine wondered how this one would compare. Underfoot, the mud gave way in voluptuous rolls, everyone's boots slipping sideways as they picked their way around the biggest puddles. The guys had noticed the sap buckets and begun discussing the possibilities of syrup as a cash crop. Normally Loraine would have joined in, or tried to—she'd helped sugar before and she had a sense of how much work it would take—but this time her attention was focused elsewhere. She had a different set of questions for the land.

They passed the hayfield and entered onto a long, straight stretch of road where the trees clung thick on both sides; overhead, the gray sky hung close above the leafless tangle. The men's voices came floating back to Loraine hushed, though they were speaking in normal tones. She was concentrating. From the stillness of the woods came a low, steady, rushing sound—snowmelt, pure water, coursing away from under the gritty crusts beneath the trees. Back in the woods somewhere, a crow gave a hoarse grok.

As she walked along, holding her long wool skirt out of the mud, Loraine silently hummed her questions like a mantra: *Will I be safe here? Will I learn here? Will I grow here? Will I be safe here?* She listened—or not listened, exactly, as much as attuned her whole body—for a response.

Up ahead, the men had paused. On the left side of the road the trees continued unbroken, but on the other side they ended abruptly. When Loraine caught up, she found herself standing at the short edge of a long, open, gently sloping rectangle. The field was still mostly covered in snow, but thin yellow stalks poked through here and there, the thawing earth filling the air with a muddy, intoxicating, crushed-grass stink.

The visitors stood for a moment, taking it in. A thick border of spruce ran along each side of the field; directly across from them at the field's far edge rose a low hill, covered in empty maples. The white backdrop of the snowy ground, visible through the bare branches, highlighted the maple forest's dreamy mauve. All around them, the hillsides that had looked gray at first glance actually wore a subtle but electric shade of purple.

From where she stood looking across the field, Loraine could not see over the ridge to whatever vista lay beyond. So on the one hand, no view. But on the other, the forest-encircled field felt like a jewel box of a space, close and enclosed, secret from everywhere but the sky.

They walked on. Just in the corner of the field, a pool of clear water revealed itself as one of the springs they'd been told to look for. Small flakes danced in the eddies at the bottom of the pool as the water rose up from the silty depths.

Past the spring, the road began to climb slightly uphill. In the woods to the left, Loraine suddenly noticed an old stone wall running parallel to the road. The trees directly behind it, she saw, were not the same scrubby tangle as elsewhere, but a graceful row of immense, elderly maples, wider and older than any other trees around. They must have been a hedgerow once, she realized. The woods behind them was actually an overgrown field, some long-gone settler's work undone by the eager press of trees. On the near side of the maples, where Loraine stood, the field remained open. She and the others stopped again to look around.

The big, square, open space was actually two fields, they realized. At the row of maples, the road suddenly broke away from the wall, hooking sharply to the right and cutting the field in half before disappearing into the trees on the far side. Above the road, the sloped upper field was bordered by the wall and the ancient maples on the left and a stand of dark, scrubby brush along the long top and right side. Below the road lay a flatter middle field, also bordered by trees. Dead in its center lay the perfectly square indentation of an old cellar hole.

They were just about to start walking again when they heard it: snapping twigs and a heavy body pushing through the trees. Everyone froze.

From the dense underbrush at the top of the high field thirty yards away, a buck deer appeared. He stepped out of the woods and stood, staring at them. His muscled, regal neck had started to shed its shaggy winter coat, but he had not yet dropped that year's antlers. The pale, bony branches balanced improbably atop his slender head. He fixed them with his gaze.

No one moved. The moment stretched until suddenly—Loraine wasn't sure later what had broken the spell; someone got restless or the wind shifted imperceptibly—the buck kicked away into the woods and vanished.

Another moment passed. Then Fletcher broke the silence. "Well," he said with a grin, "that's that!"

As they walked back down the muddy road to the car, Craig and Fletcher were already eagerly making plans. Loraine only half-listened. Her heart was still racing with adrenaline, but with excitement now, her ears alert to every crack in the woods. She gazed around with new eyes, taking in every contour of her new home.

It seemed too good to be true. Everything was possible, now that they had land.

CHAPTER 1

The summer before Loraine left the city, the weather was humid and sticky. But what Loraine remembered decades later was not the heat, but the mood. A restless energy ran through Cambridge that year, the same prickly, electric tension that builds before a thunderstorm—everyone walking around a little wild-eyed, waiting for the flash and the crack and the sudden wind before the deluge.

For more than a year, the bad news had been relentless. First King was shot and then a few weeks later Robert Kennedy too. Every day you woke up expecting to hear who was next. All over the country frustration and anger exploded into riots, downtowns erupting into flame. In Chicago, police beat protesters with billy clubs and the news showed crowds of people running through the streets choking on tear gas.

Loraine and her two-year-old daughter were living in a rented bedroom in a friend's second-floor walk-up. The apartment was not on a particularly busy street, but Loraine never got used to the drone of traffic or the smell of exhaust. At night, ambulances wailed by, red light ricocheting off windows.

Loraine had a job in a cafe near Harvard Square; she'd found a woman down the street who agreed to watch her daughter while she was at work. In the evenings, after Amelia was tucked in bed, Loraine's roommate sometimes stayed in so that Loraine could go out to the coffeehouses and hear music: Judy Collins, Van Morrison, Joan Baez.

Loraine was a musician too. She had taught herself ukulele in high school, enough to pick out the songs she was constantly writing in her head. Sometimes she built up the courage to sing them for friends, looking down at her hands, a curtain of wavy brown hair half hiding her face. When she glanced up, her huge, blue eyes were wide behind her thick glasses.

In Boston, she met a guy who was on his way to India to learn the sitar and was giving up all his worldly belongings. He agreed to sell her his guitar for $50. The Martin was scarred but beautiful and fit her perfectly. It was her first and only guitar, her most prized possession for the rest of her life. She would have loved to perform at the coffeehouse open mic nights but she was far too shy.

The Hare Krishnas were offering free meals you could share even if you didn't feel like joining in the chanting—macrobiotic curries with brown rice and strange, salty sea vegetables. Loraine had never tasted curry before but the blonde women stirring the big pots in their long pastel saris were patient with her questions. One day at the cafe, the girl who made the soup called in sick and Loraine offered to do it even though she had no cooking experience. Her mother had hated kitchen work but felt strongly that it was the mother's duty alone to prepare the family's meals. She had never let Loraine graduate past opening cans of asparagus or scooping dollops of mayonnaise onto iceberg lettuce. Loraine had learned to satisfy her curiosity by checking cookbooks out of the library to read for pleasure. The soup she invented at the cafe was delicious. Just like that, she became a cook.

In Harvard Square there were fewer guys burning their draft cards now, but the protests were getting bigger. Loraine joined in sometimes but she preferred when the chanting crowds ebbed to reveal pools of young people sitting on the asphalt, listening to a guitarist or nodding along as a young man shouted, his fist in the air. Her favorite was a Peruvian band who played folk music in between political lectures. Once she was listening to them play and some children started dancing nearby. When Loraine joined them, swishing her long skirt and shaking her hair, their mother grabbed their hands and pulled them away.

Loraine didn't have a television but you didn't need one to find out what was happening with the war. Everyone was talking about it. Somehow the images crept in and stayed: news anchors in helmets in front of burning thatch houses, soldiers pointing guns at women and children and all those flag-draped coffins lined up, rows and rows of them. An unstoppable torrent of death and destruction, all for no reason. She couldn't wrap her head around it, but she couldn't look away.

Her brother was over there, she wasn't sure exactly where. He had wanted to drop out of college without risking the draft but he'd made the dire miscalculation of joining the state Reserves just before they were called up. Rather than run to Canada, he ducked his head and shipped out. Loraine couldn't tell how safe he was. Her previous apartment had been near a rifle range and she'd read her brother's letters to a backdrop of gunfire. She felt like she was with him. She couldn't stop imagining the smell of blood, the shells whistling over her head and mortars exploding around her, shaking her bones with their deafening booms. She was constantly exhausted.

In this new apartment, the incessant sound of passing cars jangled her nerves in a different way. She longed for peace and quiet.

One night, she and her roommate had a dinner party and served fresh fish. A few days later, Loraine heard a strange noise in the kitchen and looked into the can where they'd thrown the fish bones to see it crawling with maggots. It was disgusting, but what disturbed her more was her next thought: what was she supposed to *do* with this mess? At home she would have gone out back and dug a hole and buried it, but here—her mind flashed to the sidewalk outside and the streets and more streets, everything for miles around covered in concrete. Where could you even go to put your hands in the earth?

This thought bothered her more for her daughter than for herself. On her days off, she took Amelia all over the city, looking for parks with grass clean enough for the child to play.

Loraine hated that Amelia had to spend this whole, hot summer indoors. A few times the toddler had broken away from her on the sidewalk and charged toward the street, terrifying her. All those cars and busses roaring by, spewing all that black smoke, which was just going to rise up into the air to join the clouds and rain back down as poison. It was like the song said, "Don't drink the water and don't breathe the air." For a few weeks that summer, all anyone could talk about was the river in Cleveland that had caught on fire.

A few weeks later, though, the talk in the cafe had switched to a different topic: the big concert in upstate New York where everyone had spent three euphoric, rain-soaked days dancing. Loraine would have loved to have gone, but she had no way to get there and no one to help her with Amelia, and besides, she wasn't feeling well.

She knew she needed rest, but it was more than that—she needed to get someplace where she could breathe a little better, where her daughter could run barefoot without stepping in dog shit and broken glass and where she wasn't waiting all the time for a catastrophe she couldn't even name. Later when she heard Joni Mitchell sing about Woodstock, the lyrics, written that same summer, could have been channeled straight from Loraine's own mind: "I'm going to camp out on the land/I'm going to try an' get my soul free . . . We've got to get ourselves/Back to the garden."

For Loraine, her next move felt obvious. One day, she left.

She was not alone. "There's a definite panic on the hip scene in Cambridge," wrote student radical Raymond Mungo that year, "people going to uncommonly arduous lengths (debt, sacrifice, the prospect of cold toes and brown rice forever) to get away while there's still time." And it wasn't just Cambridge. All over the nation at the dawn of the 1970s, young people were suddenly feeling an urge to get away, to leave the city behind for a new way of life in the country.

Some, like Mungo, filled an elderly New England farmhouse with a tangle of comrades. Others sought out mountain-side hermitages in New Mexico or remote single-family Edens in Tennessee. Hilltop Maoists traversed their fields with horse-drawn plows. Graduate students who had never before held a hammer overhauled tobacco barns and flipped through the *Whole Earth Catalog* by the light of kerosene lamps. Vietnam vets hand-mixed adobe bricks. Born-and-bred Brooklynites felled cedar in Oregon. Former debutants milked goats in Humboldt County and weeded strawberry beds with their babies strapped to their backs. Famous musicians forked organic compost into upstate gardens. College professors committed themselves to winter commutes that required swapping high heels for cross-country skis. Computer programmers turned the last page of Scott and Helen Nearing's *Living the Good Life* and packed their families into the car the next day.

Most had no farming or carpentry experience, but no matter. To go back to the land, it seemed, all that was necessary was an ardent belief that life in Middle America was corrupt and hollow, that consumer goods were burdensome and unnecessary, that protest was better lived than shouted, and that the best response to a broken culture was to simply reinvent it from scratch.

What felt to each like a deeply personal, unique response to the pressures and opportunities of their own lives, was in fact being made almost simultaneously by thousands of other young people all across the country at the same moment for almost the same reasons.

They were acting, in part, on a characteristically American assumption that if things get bad where we are—too hectic, too dangerous, too messy—we can simply decamp to a new frontier and start again, that all we need to begin a new venture or even create a new society is a new piece of land. But while there have always been individuals, families, or groups who walked away from city life with high hopes, no other moment in American history has seen anything like the shift that happened as the 1960s turned into the 1970s.

In the shadow of the Vietnam War and amidst widespread social upheaval, this ever-present American urge to reinvent ourselves in the wilderness spiked into its largest, most influential and most radical manifestation ever. That decade, as many as a million young Americans uprooted themselves, almost en masse, abandoning their urban and suburban backgrounds in favor of a life in the countryside.

They were almost all white, well-educated, and from middle-class or wealthy backgrounds. This was not a coincidence. For many, the choice to live a life of radical austerity and anachronism was certainly a rebellion against the comfort and prosperity of their Eisenhower-era childhoods, but that same background of comfort also offered a security and safety net that made such radical choices possible. For some, trust funds and allowances actually financed their rural experiments; for most others, family support was more implied than actual—if things really went wrong on the farm, they knew, their parents could bail them out or take them in. But even those who had cut ties with their families altogether were still the recipients of a particular, inherited confidence. Writing in 1968, sociologist Kenneth Keniston noted that the undergraduates he studied were concerned about finding "exciting, honorable and effective ways of using their intelligence," but that in over a decade of interviews, he had not met a single one who was worried about finding work. White parents who had exited the Depression into the middle class had raised their children to take affluence and freedom from want for granted, and to expect that a college education entitled you to a good job, whenever you might choose to pursue it. "The feeling—to be very Superkids!" Tom Wolfe wrote in 1968, "feeling immune, beyond calamity. One's parents remembered the sloughing common order, War & Depression—but Superkids knew only the emotional surge of the great payoff."

But parents who'd lived through the Depression and the Holocaust hadn't shed their own anxieties, and they didn't fully succeed in hiding them from their children. Postwar kids listened to adults assure them that the world was now perfectly safe, but they saw evidence to the contrary everywhere—in their father's penny-pinching and their mother's overstuffed pantry, in photographs of Dachau and of Hiroshima. Parents and teachers who insisted to children that ducking under desks would save them from a nuclear attack succeeded only in pushing the children's fear deeper—not only were they not safe, many concluded, the adults wouldn't even admit it. They'd have to save themselves.

"Our work is guided by the sense that we may be the last generation in the experiment with living," wrote the authors of the Port Huron Statement, the 1962 manifesto that helped kick off a decade of student activism. Young people's Cold War fears were temporarily assuaged by the Atomic Test Ban Treaty of 1963—only to be replaced immediately by another horrifying specter. "The Bomb had receded to the status of an abstract threat," writes historian and former student activist, Todd Gitlin, "but the Vietnam war was actual, nothing potential or abstract about it; napalm was scorching actual flesh, bombs were tearing apart actual bodies, and there, right there, were the traces, smeared across the tube and the daily paper—every day you had to go out of your way to duck them."

The sudden, spontaneous back-to-the-land movement emerged from the collision between this crushing, apocalyptic fear and the generational confidence that convinced its young people they were still entitled to the world as they wanted it. As Keniston put it, "Never before have so many who had so much been so deeply disenchanted with their inheritance." To a privileged generation exhausted by shouting *NO* to every aspect of the American society they were raised to inherit, rural life represented a way to say *yes.*

Especially early on, the decision to begin a new life in the country felt urgent, lifesaving. "When I left the city I felt that one year among green trees and breathable air was all I asked out of life—that if I was going to die soon at least I would grow one flower first," wrote Elaine Sundancer of her 1969 decision to leave San Francisco for a commune in Oregon.

"The move to the country is a doomsday decision," declared journalist Mark Kramer. "It almost always starts out as a retreat, after other alternatives become too unpalatable." Reflecting on his own 1969 move "from city politics to rural subsistence farming," he noted, "It turns out that a farm with friends is a very pleasant street corner to hang out on while waiting for the bomb to fall."

As the decade wore on, back-to-the-landers—both those who chose to live communally and those who did not—were driven by more personal sources of urgency. Some quit good jobs, convinced that no paycheck was worth even a single morning of struggling into neckties or pantyhose. Some yearned for quietude after exhausting years of sit-ins, marches, and the numbing shock of mourning leader after slain leader. Some hoped to sow the seeds of a new society, one whose ideals they and their friends could start living out immediately. Others just wanted a life that would replace TV dinners with organically grown tomatoes, radio jingles with early-morning songbirds, and suburban "boxes made of ticky-tacky" with quirkily unique living spaces they'd build themselves. Whatever their individual reasons, together, their numbers were immense. The 1970s remain the only moment in the nation's history when more people moved to rural areas than into the cities, briefly reversing two hundred years of steady urbanization.

But despite the huge numbers, the decision to go back to the land felt so personal that many had no idea others were doing the same. "Only afterward was it called a movement," wrote Robert Houriet, one of the period's keenest observers. "At the outset, it was the gut reaction of a generation."

While it's hard to identify an exact starting time for a spontaneous, mass "gut reaction," the clearest candidate is the autumn of 1967.

Over the preceding months, one hundred thousand young people had converged on the San Francisco neighborhood of Haight Ashbury. "The Summer of Love" had been invented and publicized by Haight Ashbury's business council (the Haight Independent Proprietors), over the vocal protests of the Diggers, street activists who were already struggling to feed, house, and treat the thousands of runaway teenagers who had been pouring into the city for months. In a broadside titled "Uncle Tim$ Children," activist Chester Anderson wrote, "The HIP Merchants—the cats who have sold our loverly little psychedelic community to the mass media, to the world, to you—. . . don't see hunger, hip brutality, rape, gangbangs, gonorrhea, syphillis [sic], theft, hunger, filth." As Digger and actor Peter Coyote remembered the moment, "a number of older hands realized that the area was poised to become unlivable due to the accelerated influx of new residents. . . . It was obvious that we could not craft an autonomous life on top of the asphalt, and many people planned moves to the country."

That same autumn, the psychedelic newspaper the *San Francisco Oracle* put out its most widely read issue ever. In it was an interview with Timothy Leary in which he explained, in part, what he had meant a few months earlier by his exhortation for young people to "drop out." "The main message," he said, "is to get out of the city and go to the land."

Those leaving San Francisco tended to head north up the California coast or inland to the Southwest, but the trend soon followed to East Coast cities as well. Richard Fairfield, who had started observing and documenting American utopian movements several years earlier, noticed a "mass upsurge of nation-wide interest in rural living in the hippie subculture" in the months following the Summer of Love.

And in fact, a country commune boom was already under way. By one contemporary count, there were twelve rural communes in 1967; just a few years later the numbers had skyrocketed to the thousands—as many as ten thousand by some estimates.

The height of the commune boom was brief but it had a tremendous lasting impact—not, as many assume, simply on American spirituality or communal organizations alone (though both of those are true), but more profoundly: on kicking off the biggest, most widespread urban-to-rural shift in American history. "Not since the fall of Babylon have so many city dwellers wanted to 'return' to the country without ever having been there in the first place," wrote one observer in 1972.

Publications like the *Whole Earth Catalog*, invented by or developed to support early rural communes' efforts at self-sufficient living, and organized structures like co-ops and organic food networks soon became vital resources for the waves of other, noncommunal but still radically self-sufficient back-to-the-landers that continued throughout the decade. In 1970, Schocken Books, capitalizing on the counterculture's sudden interest in instruction manuals for subsistence living, reissued a previously little-read volume with a new foreword by Paul Goodman. Scott and Helen Nearing's *Living the Good Life* immediately sold fifty thousand copies and became a classic, inspiring thousands of eager young people to try their own hand at single-family homesteading.

By the mid-'70s, the commune period had ended but the back-to-the-land movement was still in full swing: radical social experiments in group living had been replaced by individual families' radical experiments in self-sufficiency—including my family's.

CHAPTER 2

It didn't take Loraine long to find others who shared the idea beginning to percolate in her own mind.

In Plainfield, Vermont, a young Goddard College professor had opened her farmhouse to an interested group who wanted to come there to live and work. The professor, Anita Landa, had been inspired by the theories of Herbert Marcuse and Paul Goodman, the same thinkers who had influenced the Berkeley Free Speech Movement several years earlier. In the oppressive, stifling culture of postwar capitalist America, Marcuse wrote, people had been taught to "find their soul in their automobile, hi-fi set, split-level home, kitchen equipment." Landa's group would escape that oppression by living and working cooperatively, with as few modern amenities as possible. In practice, this meant that a score of people, including small children, were crowded into Landa's modest farmhouse or camping nearby while they busily renovated a barn into living quarters.

When Loraine arrived, she offered her newfound expertise in the kitchen, preparing big communal dinners. She bunked up with some others and Amelia slept in the children's room.

Once the urgent barn renovation project was complete, the group turned their attention to the next set of priorities—and immediately ran into trouble deciding what these should be. Only a few months in, serious fissures had formed in their unity. The farmhouse, some felt, while pleasingly simple, was still basically bourgeois—it had conventional plumbing and electricity, for example, which were wasteful and meant eternal dependence on a precarious, corrupted system. And more important, while it was all well and good to share living space, to really do away with oppressive capitalist structures, the property itself should be owned in full by the collective. When some of the group put this demand to Landa, she balked and they splintered.

Among those who felt most strongly that the setup with Landa wasn't working was Craig. Craig, his wife, and their small daughter had come East from California for Woodstock and arrived at Landa's shortly after. Craig was movie-star handsome, with a warm, winning smile. He sometimes wore his long, brown hair in two thick braids to keep it out of the way while he worked.

Part of Craig's frustration was in knowing that the results of his months of construction work on the barn—which had been, everyone agreed, an amazing feat of design, speed, and cooperation—did not in any tangible, legal way belong to him. Landa was incredibly generous and no one actually feared that she would change her mind and kick everyone out, but that was partly the point: for Craig, trusting his future to someone else's continuing generosity was exactly what rankled. For him, the need was clear: the people doing the work and sharing the space should themselves own the fruits of their labor. If Landa couldn't concede to this, he would move on.

Fletcher Oakes agreed. He and his wife, Nancy, were slightly older than many of the others—meaning late instead of early twenties. Neither of them particularly telegraphed their radical politics or commitment to counterculture living through their looks. Nancy had the sweet smile, shoulder-length curls, and big, round glasses of a midwestern kindergarten teacher. Fletcher wore long sideburns but kept his wispy hair clipped short. His buttoned-up plaid shirts and nebbishy, thick-framed glasses made him a dead ringer for Woody Allen, except for his thick Chicago accent.

Fletcher, Nancy, and their two sons had recently come from Colorado, where they'd lived at the pioneering artists' commune Drop City. They'd arrived there at the tail end of a building boom that had dotted the austere desert landscape with ten bright-painted geodesic-inspired domes. Fletcher was a photographer and filmmaker, and Nancy was a painter. They both admired the way Drop City's artists had prioritized simple, barebones living and construction projects in order to free themselves to make art. At Landa's, the autumn's barn renovation had been too rushed to leave time for anything but building, but Fletcher was looking for a community in which life was simplified enough to leave time for creative pursuits.

Nancy, if anything, was even more enthusiastic about the possibility of a new beginning. She had never quite felt at home in Landa's farmhouse, a discomfort she ascribed to not having much say over the systems that were already in place. She had loved being part of Drop City's dome building and admired the innovative experiments so easily undertaken there. The thought irked her, as she washed the dishes in the farmhouse's conventional kitchen, of all that waste water vanishing hardly used into the septic system. Given a chance to develop systems from scratch, surely, she felt, they'd be able to come up with better ideas.

Loraine loved the idea of a little group striking out on its own to start anew. She needed no convincing that freedom and an absence of established rules would lead to a rush of innovation: she was finding this true every day in the kitchen. Having shed her mother's shoulds and should nots, she invented and discovered new things all the time by seeking out her own resources and trusting her own instincts. Why wouldn't the same approach work on the scale of a whole community?

Craig, Fletcher, and Nancy were happy to have her with them. Loraine thought of herself as shy and timid, but the others recognized her as one of the group's most vital leaders. She managed to combine a "universe will provide" faith with a no-nonsense Yankee work ethic in a way everyone found immensely reassuring. She was also the group's only native Vermonter—the only one, in fact, who'd lived in northern New England for more than a few months.

As it happened, Loraine hailed from a very old and esteemed Vermont family—her great-grandfather had returned from the

Civil War a decorated hero and had become the state's fortieth governor.

She grew up in Rutland, Vermont's third-largest city, in a big, white house framed by two huge willows that draped their long tendrils across the lawn. Loraine spent hours swinging on the branches, trusting her weight to the trees.

Loraine's was one of the last houses on a dead-end street that abutted a scrubby wilderness. Within a few years the trees would be cut down to make room for more housing as the city expanded, but as children she and her five siblings and the rest of the neighborhood's kids had the run of the woods. They knew its topography by heart: the best spot to leap across the brook; the best route through the underbrush up to the pond if you wanted to get there unseen; the depressions in the thickly needled forest floor that let you build cozy "cabins" by laying sturdy branches across the swells on either side and covering this roof with hay; the saddle-shaped rock that you could pretend was an Indian pony from which to fire a volley of invisible arrows as your cowboy friends pelted you with pinecones. The boys and girls staked out different places to establish their forts and regularly left off building to raid one another.

Loraine liked to look for teaberry growing low beneath the trees—in season, the berries tasted sweetly dusty like Necco Wafers, but you could chew the plant's wintergreen-flavored leaves all year round and pretend they were Clark's gum.

Once, when Loraine came inside, breathless and pink-cheeked, full of stories about the fairies she'd seen in the woods, her mother had scolded her. "You have an overactive imagination," she said. The fairies became one more thing Loraine learned to keep quiet about, another example of the chasm between herself and the girl her mother expected.

Loraine was a good student, but school took its toll in other ways. The cheerleader popularity her mother wished for her loomed hopelessly out of reach. Her wavy, mouse-brown hair defied all attempts to smooth it fashionably under control. Her optometrist father had prescribed her thick, bottle-lensed glasses that further magnified her large, credulous deep-blue eyes. She

hated the glasses but was helpless without them. She was pain-
fully shy. At eleven, a growth spurt had left her a full head taller
than any of her classmates, even the boys. That same year, her
whole grade had to be bussed across town while their own school
underwent renovations. In the hallway, Loraine overheard some
boys snickering that she was too tall for sixth grade. "She must
have stayed back," one of them said. "She must be stupid." Her
face flashed hot. She spent the rest of her adolescence trying to
slouch herself out of anyone's notice.

By the time she became a teenager, she was already an expert at avoiding conflict. Her mother was a shouter, a woman
of exacting standards and unpredictable rages. Nelly had
grown up working-class in a remote quarry town on the New
York-Pennsylvania border, watching her parents and neighbors
struggle and founder through the Depression. Determined to
escape the dinginess and uncertainty of her own mother's life,
Nelly somehow got herself to college in Philadelphia and earned
a degree in nursing. She thrived in her job as head nurse on
a hospital ward, but when she married Loraine's father, it went
without saying that she'd quit. Stuart was an eye doctor with
a promising career, but Nelly was equally attracted to his blue-
blood heritage. As Loraine put it later, "By the time she realized
what an asshole my father was, she was in too deep."

Loraine was their third child. She and her four sisters were
expected to help with chores—vacuuming rugs and drapes,
dusting the heirlooms and knick-knacks that were the pride of
Nelly's adult home, clearing the supper table once their father
and brother had finished eating. While Loraine chafed at being
forced to iron bedsheets or to scrub garbage cans with bleach
until they gleamed, it was simply easier to obey. But she found
herself smoldering with disgust: all this work for the veneer of
perfection, her mother obsessed with sweeping every domestic
mess out of view, as though a shiny surface meant nothing was
rotten on the inside.

She found small ways to rebel, sneaking into the kitchen after supper to soundlessly extract an extra slice of pie or dish
of pudding for her little sisters. Her brother, a growing boy, was

allowed to openly help himself to the refrigerator, but Loraine's resentment was tempered by the fact that she could see that he was stifling under his own set of pressures and that he too was biding his time until he could escape their mother's frustrated rage and their father's rare, intense attentions.

The summer Loraine turned fourteen, she built herself a cabin—really a lean-to out of sticks covered with tarp—near the family's garden. It was quiet, unlike the house, and her parents didn't object when she began sleeping there. When a thunderstorm left her drenched, she figured out how to improve the waterproofing. The next year she got a job at her beloved Girl Scout camp, which meant that her favorite two weeks of the year now extended to the whole summer.

She came home transformed. Her mother took one look at her eyeshadow and newly blonde hair and sat her down at the kitchen table. "Look at you, you look just like a whore," she announced. But the weeks away from home had permanently released Loraine from the burden of her mother's expectations. Her grades, formerly perfect, began to slip. In advanced bio, in lieu of a term paper, she turned in a long, well-crafted parody; her teacher praised its wit even as he gave her an F.

Loraine spent a good portion of her senior year hunched over, picking out songs on a ukulele. Its simplicity offered her a creative expression she'd never felt playing oboe in the school band. It didn't hurt that she'd also met a musician, a man in his twenties, who loved music as much as she did. Loraine learned to harmonize as Peter strummed along on his guitar. Before long they got good enough to perform together for friends and for the tiny, sympathetic audience at the local psychiatric residence where he had once lived.

She informed her mother that she planned to become a folk singer. "You have delusions of grandeur," her mother spit back. But at other times, Nelly cried out in desperation, "You were supposed to be the first woman president of the United States!" Loraine was surprised to hear that her mother's ambition for her had reached so high, but it didn't matter—no role Nelly might imagine for her would fit the person she was becoming. She simply could not make her mother understand: she was not throwing away her future, she was allowing herself to discover it.

Everyone was changing. Boys who had crewcuts the year before now wore beads and Indian headbands. Girls who'd never even worn dungarees to school were embroidering flowers on their bell-bottoms. Suddenly kids who'd never given you a glance in the hallway would come put their arms around you at a party and speak earnestly about the importance of love. Loraine felt like she was in a boat being swept down a river. She could hardly remember what the shore had been like.

At Landa's, among a group of people at last with whom she had so much in common, Loraine had begun to think about the further possibilities of starting over, entirely from scratch.

Her parents' life offered nothing that she and her friends could not replace with a purer, more thoughtful version though their own hard work and love for one another. When Loraine thought about it this way, Landa's flush toilets and plugged-in appliances became anchors, dragging her back toward a life she'd fought so hard already to escape.

And too, the new group's commitment to total reinvention offered Loraine a source of support she badly needed: a new form of family. Her first attempt to make a new home life for herself had ended badly.

Loraine had graduated from high school, but her academic free fall meant she didn't get into any of the colleges she applied to. She started spending more time with Peter; within a few months, she was pregnant. Later she reflected that she truly hadn't understood how this might happen. Her parents' admonishments to be a "good girl" had centered on scolding her about her hair and clothes and enforcing a generalized sense of shame. Her formal sex education had consisted of an incomprehensible medical pamphlet her mother had handed her without comment and a baffling schoolyard metaphor involving hotdogs and hamburgers. She and Peter got married and moved into an apartment near a rifle range. Loraine was not quite nineteen.

Amelia was still in diapers when Peter began acting oddly. Loraine was used to a certain amount of volatility at home, so she shrugged it aside until the night he chased her around the house with a knife in the full throes of psychosis. She scooped up the screaming toddler and fled. When Peter was institutionalized, she found herself alone, a single mother.

For Loraine, the promise of communal life meant not just badly needed help with childcare but also a chance to reinvent the whole premise of family. Like her, no one in the splinter group could find much to emulate in their parents' relationship with each other or with their children. The more Loraine thought about it, the more it seemed to her that fully escaping the trap that was her mother's life would require her to cast aside the nuclear family itself in favor of a less constraining model, one that allowed its participants some flexibility and left itself better open to love.

All she and the others needed to get started was an untarnished setting, a blank slate to begin the world again, but better.

Then, a few weeks into 1970, Craig got a call. His father was dead. It was a terrible blow, but one with a silver lining in the form of a modest inheritance. Suddenly there was money for a down payment.

Within weeks of spotting the buck deer in the high meadow above the former potato field, the 116 acres officially belonged to them— or anyway, technically, temporarily to Craig. The plan was to get started building right away. But by late April, to Craig's surprise, the three fields remained snow-clogged and sodden.

While Loraine, Fletcher, Nancy, and the others busied themselves with preparations for the big move, Craig decided to make himself useful elsewhere.

Craig's sister Melissa was living in New York. She had introduced him to some guys in a communal loft on Second Avenue. They belonged to a national organization called Earth People's Park, which would soon spawn one of the most innovative—and notorious—open-land experiments in American history.

"You've had this idea too, right?" Stewart Brand wrote in a *Whole Earth Catalog* article explaining the project, "And here it is, underway. The power of the idea is that everyone has had a piece of it by themselves." What America's hip youth most needed, the thinking went, was a kind of permanent Woodstock, a rural space, open for concerts but that would also offer the kind of rustic mutual-aid community that had made those three days feel so special. Most importantly, the land would be ownerless and without restrictions: Free Land for Free People.

In January 1970, organizers announced a meeting called Earth People's Open in San Francisco. In addition to a swarm of members from the Hog Farm and other well-known communes, it attracted a Who's Who of the hip world: David Crosby; Ken Kesey and his Merry Prankster righthand man, Babbs; Paul Krassner, founder of the influential satire magazine, *The Realist*; the *Whole Earth Catalog*'s Stewart Brand; Joan Baez's sister Mimi Fariña; the actor and activist Peter Coyote; and Woodstock's gap-toothed MC, Wavy Gravy (née Hugh Romney). Using funds donated dollar by dollar from people across the country, organizers would purchase a huge chunk of land, maybe in the Southwest, that would serve as a kind of hippie homeland, open to all.

Over the three-day rap session, a healthy debate ensued about what form the open land should take and what would constitute responsibility for it. As Gravy remembered it, "The rap that rang truest came from Peter [Coyote], who spoke of one park as a prison. The idea instantly adjusted itself to a frame of pieces and parcels of earth in all ecological regions. No big rock scene. Just quiet earth warmings and friendly eco-fairs. Always free access and keepin' in touch. A flexible, flowin' and growin' idea in action, with both ends always open, and subject to change."

Within days, the newly formed organization had an office on Grant St. in San Francisco, a bank account opened by Mama Cass, acting treasurer, and a lawyer, Tony Serra (brother of Richard), whom they shared with the Black Panthers. Wavy Gravy, among others, began fundraising in earnest for what they expected would soon be a nationwide movement.

The New York chapter had moved into the Second Avenue loft while its members awaited word from national headquarters about where and when they could move to the new land. In the meantime, they spent weeks preparing a big display for the first

Earth Day celebration on April 22. Craig, never one to miss a big event, had headed down to help.

They were calling their structure "the world's first inflatable geodesic dome," but in fact it was neither first nor geodesic. Nor really even a dome. It was impressive, however: all along the west side of Union Square they erected a huge plastic "bubble," inflated by fans. Visitors could walk inside, to "breathe pure air" and let the space "prove how quiet it can be in a busy city." That night on the evening news, Americans across the country caught a glimpse of the bubble, looking like a giant, larval Quonset hut, "Earth People's Park" emblazoned proudly over the doorway.

Ever resourceful, as soon as they'd helped deflate the Earth Day bubble, Craig and some friends rolled up the hundreds of yards of plastic sheeting and hauled them up north. Craig's nascent commune now had supplies with which to start building.

By May 1, the snow had finally gone and Craig thought for sure the land would have dried out enough to begin work. But when he arrived, eager to enter the tunnel-like bower of branches that led up to their three cozy, enclosed meadows, he found in front of him acres of waterlogged mess. Even at the bottom of the road, his truck's wheels spun helplessly. The long, flat stretch leading in to the lower field had entirely vanished under a muddy lake. Craig enlisted a friend and they set to work with shovels. It took a whole weekend to drain it enough for cars to get through.

The trees had burst into leaf almost overnight, and the fresh new grass turned the fields verdant. The lower field called out as the ideal building site—its eight acres stretched out toward the sunset, cozily enclosed by trees but still euphorically open to the sky. But even now it remained stubbornly squishy. The upper field, where they'd stood near the border of ancient maples and seen the deer, was too steep for structures. Blessedly, the flattish middle field with its old cellar hole had dried better. Craig let the others know it was time to move in.

Nancy got a lift in someone's VW bus, overstuffed with supplies and children. She never forgot the moment she clambered out of the backseat and looked around her future home for the first time. Everywhere she turned, the surroundings exploded with green new spring life. Birds darted past, busy at work. Best of all were the open emerald fields, held close by their lush ring of trees, hiding every hint of the world beyond. It was perfect, the place she'd dreamed of, their own small Eden.

The Earth People's Park guys still hadn't heard about where they might begin their own rural living experiment, so many of them had decided to spend the summer on Craig's land, helping.

One had a big van that he parked near the road. Of all the city guys, he was the most quintessentially New York: tough and smart and raunchily witty. His friends started calling him "Jedidiah." They meant it ironically, like a fat man called Slim, but, he confessed to Craig, "I really like that name." The idea of being a cantankerous mountain man appealed to him—it was so far from his urban childhood.

Jed was wiry, with a shock of curly black hair. He wore glasses and had a thick New York accent and a wild, intellectual curiosity. He was always talking about ideas he got from *Mother Earth News* and *Scientific American*. He was good with his hands and could fix or jerry-rig anything; no matter how crazy a plan sounded at first, when Jed talked through an idea, the others usually found themselves listening.

Unlike everyone else, Jed still had a job in the city, working in his family's small shop, which, he indicated, had been robbed several times. This experience seemed to have colored his world-view somewhat. Friends who visited him in the city reported that his apartment had something like twenty different locks on the door. Even in Vermont, when the evening conversation tipped over into dope-fueled conspiracy theories as it sometimes did, Jed's paranoia ran a little high. Like some of the other city guys, he liked to wear a holstered pistol—against bears, he said, though almost none had been spotted in the area for decades. Later, some of his commune-mates remembered teasing him when they noticed him check his holster before stepping away from the fire and into the dark night—what, was he worried some muggers were going to jump him from behind the spruce trees? He laughed, but he didn't stop wearing his gun.

There were a lot of city- and suburban-bred men in rural communes across the country for whom the freedom to own and wear a gun contributed to the appeal of living in the woods—its romantic swagger one part Davy Crockett, one part Jesse James, and one part Che Guevara. Craig, Fletcher, Nancy, and Loraine didn't see a need for guns, apart from possibly a rifle if they decided game should be part of a self-sufficient diet, but they didn't push the issue. The group's belief in personal freedom made room for this kind of predilection, not so different from that of another New York guy, Chico, an architect who had arrived on the hill and instantly discarded his clothes for the rest of the summer.

Before long, the middle field and surrounding woods were dotted with lean-tos, tipis, and crude structures of eccentric design. The Earth Day bubble's plastic sheeting didn't exactly make for a vision of Mother Earth simplicity, but scrounging and scavenging and figuring out ways to make use of waste materials trumped other aesthetic considerations. Besides, soon the group's bigger, more elaborate building plans would get under way.

Some of the guys put up a big cook tent on a flattish spot near the old cellar hole in the middle field. The tent itself was basically a simple box frame fashioned from saplings and covered in more plastic sheeting, but it was big enough to contain several chairs, a prep table, an Ashley woodstove, and the set of simple wooden shelves that held a collection of wooden bowls, one for each communard. Nearby stood an antique icebox designed to hold the large blocks of ice no longer for sale anywhere, but since all perishable food got consumed immediately, it worked fine even without.

For the fifty-pound bags of soy beans, oats, and brown rice, Loraine had the idea to store them in metal garbage pails with the lids tied down against raccoons. She also oversaw the construction of a big fire pit like the one she'd learned to cook over at Girl Scout camp. A grate over the coals held the big pots in which she would cook the group's simple meals of soups and stir-frys. Almost the moment the kitchen was in place, she set to work.

Craig found a private spot in a small stretch of woods below the middle field for his tipi, canvas with a round door. His wife had opted not to join him on this new adventure, and their marriage had effectively ended. Craig badly missed his daughter, but it was hard not to feel excited about regaining his single-man freedom. He was twenty-three.

Fletcher found a quiet corner for his commercially made canvas tent, but Nancy eagerly built herself a sapling-and-plastic structure of her own design (she and Fletcher had an open marriage and preferred separate quarters). A few dozen yards from Nancy's, within earshot, she and some others set up the children's room—a 5′ × 10′ frame, covered in plastic, over a tarp floor upon which they spread the children's sleeping bags and foam mattresses. Amelia had just turned three and had a hard time at first sleeping without her mother nearby, but Fletcher and Nancy's sons were slightly older; the kids had had their own room at the farmhouse too, so this wasn't much different.

Almost as soon as they arrived, Loraine had walked up the road to the middle field. But instead of following it as it veered right and split the fields, she kept going straight, following the old stone wall under the trees. The row of ancient maples she'd noticed on her first visit had plumped out into their summer finery, a deep, tranquil green. She put her hands on the silver-grey trunks, feeling the grooves of the bark, her fingertips discovering what might have been the smooth, round scars of old tap-holes, long-since healed. These trees had witnessed, she imagined, all the human activity that had passed through this place for more than a century. It comforted her to think of them standing close by, watching over her in silent, unconditional grace.

A few yards into the woods behind them, she found a relatively flat spot framed by four young trees. Using the trees as uprights, she built herself a lean-to cabin like the one she'd lived in for a few weeks as a teenager. She lashed cut saplings to the standing trees as crosspieces. Then she wrapped the whole structure tightly in Earth Day sheeting, leaving walls that could be rolled up to let air in. She dug a trench around the outside so that downward-coursing rainwater would flow around her living space instead of through it. Her few possessions she kept in a small trunk at the foot of the mattress she'd hauled into the woods and placed in the cabin's driest corner; whenever she went out, she made sure to leave her guitar in this spot too. She liked that every time she came and went, she had to pass through the row of old maples, putting out a hand to their trunks to steady herself as she stepped over the old stone wall.

True to his word, Craig immediately began to make plans to sign over ownership of the land to the group. He got in touch with an activist named Bob Swann who was helping to develop an innovative new category for nonprofit, group-owned real estate. Swann's model would soon evolve into Community Land Trusts. Within a few decades there would be hundreds of these in the US, but Craig's group was among the very first.

One gorgeous June afternoon, the group gathered under one of the big maples in the upper field to sign the newly drafted deed that would make all of them—all, without exception—legal owners of the place they now called home. Craig's inheritance had covered a third of the land's $15,000 cost. The plan was to take turns paying the monthly mortgage bill—with no more than one annual payment each to make, they'd own the land outright in no time.

The new commune was now officially known as Myrtle Hill Farm. Though it would soon be borne out by the acquisition of chickens, two milk cows, and a beef calf named Bullneck who they planned to slaughter themselves, at the time they signed the deed, "Farm" was pure optimism.

The days quickly took on a loose rhythm. Some early riser would put on coffee or get a pot of oatmeal started for the children. By the time the sun rose hot above the high hill to the east, most people had rolled out of their tents or lean-tos. When some decision needed to be made—where to dig a hole for the outhouse or what provisions someone needed to bring back from a run into town—everyone dropped what they were doing to circle up for a meeting. The group would have no formal leader, they had agreed, and all decisions would be made by consensus. For big plans like what structures to build first or what they could produce to raise the cash they'd still need until they could become totally self-sufficient, the discussions could take hours. People were patient with each other, but no one had entered this life with a goal of spending their time sitting around and talking. For small decisions, it usually worked better for people to just take initiative themselves. There were innumerable daily tasks that had to be cared for: finding firewood, feeding the chickens, milking the cows, hauling water for cooking and washing. The spring near the corner of the lower field that Craig, Loraine, and Fletcher had noticed on the first day was running clear and full. Some of the guys dug it out a little bit so they could dip in the big five-gallon buckets that they loaded into Craig's truck for the fifty-yard drive up the road to the cook tent. At night, they all gathered back at the middle field for the hot meals Loraine and Nancy had prepared over the open fire.

It was like a weeks-long camping trip, but more romantic because this was not a mere vacation, but, for all of them, their new way of life.

At night, while Loraine washed dishes and Nancy put the children to bed, the men passed joints around the campfire and made plans: wind-powered generators for electricity; a methane-gas entrapment system for the outhouse; a bicycle-powered sauna; a radio station. There were bigger ideas under discussion too: a kibbutz-style school for commune children; the possibility of a coming violent revolution; and the pros and cons of group marriage. Sparks from the fire rose up and winked out. Over the field, the stars hung fat and low, more than any of them remembered ever seeing before.

When the fire finally sank to a red glow, everyone made their way through the dark woods and fields to their own sleeping quarters—or to someone else's.

Loraine, still too shy to perform her songs directly to an audience, wandered among the lean-tos and tents with her guitar, singing everyone softly to sleep: "We came to a new land/ Looking for a new life./ We're going to find a new way/ We're going to make a new day."

Sometimes, when the last notes had faded away, Loraine softly pushed aside the flaps of someone's tent and slipped into his warm bed in the darkness, her heart pounding; sometimes she returned to her own bed to find someone there waiting for her.

Decades later, even after everything that followed, everyone who had been at Myrtle Hill that first summer remembered it the same way: as utterly, perfectly idyllic.

CHAPTER 3

One afternoon, Craig drove down the hill into the village to pick up a few things at the general store. The village was tiny, even by northern Vermont standards. Officially, its population was registered at 649, but that included everyone living up on hill farms and out on back roads, not just in the blink-and-you-miss-it village center. The general store, with a deep porch and two gas pumps out front, along with the bite-sized Busy Bee Diner across the street, represented the village business district. Two doors down from the store stood the compact, white-painted town hall, and a few doors down from that, the modestly spired, white clapboard Congregationalist Church.

It was a hot day. Craig was wearing jean cutoffs and a sleeveless t-shirt, showing off his tan, muscular arms. His long brown hair was loose over his shoulders and he had on the custom-made, steel-toed logging boots he'd splurged on with a tiny bit of his inheritance after seeing the company listed in the *Whole Earth Catalog*. They looked like a combination between combat boots and moccasins, their crisscrossed laces climbing high up his calf. Strapped to his waist, he wore his big hunting knife in its leather sheath.

As he browsed the shelves of canned goods, Craig suddenly sensed someone was watching him. He turned to find another young man, dressed in work clothes with a brown beard and shoulder-length hair looking at him in friendly curiosity. They introduced themselves. Eliot and his wife Peg had just bought an old farm nearby and were in the process of renovating the house. He told Craig how to get there and Craig promised he'd stop by soon.

As the crow flies, Eliot and Peg's farmhouse lay only a scant mile from Myrtle Hill, but a direct path would have had to traverse several steep hills and a swampy valley. Thus, once the roads wound around these obstacles, the actual distance came closer to three miles—a pleasant-enough hour's walk, but Craig decided to drive.

The route took him bumping through his neighbors' farm with its low, white house and tall red barn. On the paved town road, the truck dropped into a smooth quiet for a few hundred yards before another crunching turn back to gravel. This road ran close against the lake, skirting a few vacation cottages packed along the shore. Beyond them, the teeth-rattling ruts forced Craig to slow down. He entered a long stretch of woods where sunlight filtered through the leafy canopy, dappling the road. There was nothing visible anywhere but trees. Then, around a curve, the trees suddenly parted to reveal open fields. A yellow house appeared to the right. Directly across from it, another cheerfully disheveled dirt road broke off in a T. It ambled straight through the fields for a hundred yards before disappearing into a line of maples. Craig noticed the cupola of an elegant, old red barn just visible above the trees. He glanced at it, curious, but continued on ahead.

The next house, another few hundred yards past the yellow one, was Peg and Eliot's. It sat back up off the road, a classic, early-19th-century New England farmhouse, with four windows below and two dormer windows above. The dormers sat flush with the front of the house, their roofs like raised eyebrows, giving the whole house an eager, inquisitive look. Like many local farmhouses, its generations of owners had extended it sideways by adding first a kitchen and then a small attached barn and a shed, each with separate doors and low roofs, so that the house now draped itself languidly over its small rise. Its windows gazed down over the road to bright green fields on the other side. The field's far border was marked by woods and the low bushes that signaled a stream. Rising up behind, at the center of the hilly horizon, was one perfectly rounded hill, as symmetrical as if it had been scooped.

Peg and Eliot had spent the last several weeks enthusiastically fixing up their new home. They wanted to replace its current 50s-era decor with a clean, rustic look: original-wood floors, exposed beams, and whitewashed walls. The first stage of this project had meant tearing out paneling and linoleum. Craig immediately offered to help.

The couple had met at college in California. They'd graduated a few years earlier and had gotten married in an outdoor wedding at Peg's parents' vacation farm. Her mother came from a well-to-do Boston family that had already passed an industrial fortune down through four generations. Her own wedding to Peg's father had been immense and formal, with polished silver and towering floral arrangements—the contrast with Peg and Eliot's hilltop, hippie celebration with its recorder music and square dancing and picnic reception couldn't have been greater, but Peg's parents loved it. Her mother was athletic, a former tomboy who rode horses and had attended progressive schools as a child. Peg's father had followed his own father into the newspaper business; he was a successful journalist and innately interested in the world as it changed.

Peg had wild, dark curls and a dancer's lithe physique. Her hands flew as she talked and fell still as she listened intently. Her full lips and wide green eyes radiated an earnest enthusiasm that was all California, with no trace of uptight New England.

Almost the moment she arrived at college she realized that she'd lucked into a spectacular moment to be young in California. Her parents might read about the youth movement in *Time,* but she was living at its epicenter. Every weekend was something different. A friend would say, "Hey, we're going to this winery— there's gonna be music," and then everyone would pile into the car. A few hours later you'd emerge into a leafy rose-and-lemon paradise to find that thousands of others had somehow found their way there too and that the band was inventing a rambling, ecstatic new sound that perfectly matched the crowd's mood.

She and her friends were obsessed with Zap Comix. As soon as a new one came out, they'd pass around the joint they'd saved for this moment and spend the night flopped on the floor, absorbed in R. Crumb's lusty, psychedelic visual wandering. It seemed to Peg later that the drugs were the catalyst, not only for this euphoric new culture that was bursting alive but also for its lurking horror. You got stoned and flipped on the TV and the next thing you knew US soldiers were pointing rifles at Vietnamese peasants and you were spiraling down, everything you'd been taught about American values flying apart in front of you. The feeling of being high became indistinguishable from the vertiginous sense of rushing headlong into the future.

Peg had spent part of her junior year abroad, living in rural Spain, in a village where people supported themselves by raising cherries and cork. One of the staples of the local diet was goat cheese. The family she lived with had not owned goats, but she had seen them in the community stables. The animals' wily intelligence and bony, bold invincibility appealed to her.

She admired what looked to her like the simplicity of the villagers' lives—days ordered by food preparation and by the rhythms of planting and harvesting and caring for animals. Their concerns didn't appear to extend much beyond meeting their families' daily needs. Even if they had had electricity for televisions and radios, she thought at the time, the outside world with its violence and chaos would still fade to an abstraction behind these immediate, pressing needs of food, clothing, and shelter. It looked so simple: the people fed the goats and the goats fed the people. Peg had wished she could stay forever.

Eliot's family was Canadian. His father had been born in the dirt-floor log cabin of a struggling homestead farm in Saskatchewan and had made it a central aim of his adulthood to raise his own family in a context of comfort and prosperity. The California suburb he chose had satisfied this goal perfectly, but his son was miserable there. Eliot couldn't have said then what it was he was seeking, but he knew for sure it wasn't to be found in immaculate lawns and indistinguishable houses. He'd grown into a tall, rangy, intellectual young man with an intensely penetrating gaze.

At Pomona, his father wanted him to study business or engineering, but he majored in cultural anthropology instead. After commencement, he enrolled in a graduate film program at UCLA. The intensive collaboration of feature films didn't appeal to him, but he was drawn to ethnographic documentary. He liked the fact that, with relatively simple equipment, working almost by himself, he could create something unique and beautiful that would allow its viewers a glimpse into the world of people with lives very different from their own. He and Peg went back to Spain for several months to shoot footage of the villagers she had so admired. It was clear to Eliot that this way of life was coming to an end and it had felt important to bear witness and try to preserve some vital essence before it vanished.

But the contrast between himself and his subjects actually highlighted what irked him about becoming the kind of professional his father expected—when the farmers fed their goats and milked them, or even when they brought their products to the market, all of their work directly benefited themselves and their families. By contrast, he could make the most beautiful documentary in the world, but if he wanted anyone to see it, he would still have to rely on the cooperation of distributers and movie houses. Even in this industry, where the goal was ostensibly to make art, there were still dozens of people, each with their own demands and priorities standing between himself and the realization of his work.

He felt miles from settling on a career, but he and Peg were already fantasizing about retirement. As soon as they turned 65, they'd decided, they'd move to Vermont where her mother's family had summered for generations.

Then one weekend in 1969, Eliot and some friends went hiking in the wilderness of California. On a remote mountaintop, they dropped acid. During his trip, Eliot had a profound epiphany that seemed to identify the nagging dissatisfaction that had plagued him since childhood: what was missing from his life was a connection to Mother Earth, to the land. Not only did he not know the name of a single tree or plant of the hundreds that surrounded him on this California mountainside, he didn't have the first idea about how one coaxed even a simple head of lettuce from the ground. He came home charged with new direction. "Why wait to get old to move to Vermont?" he asked Peg. "Let's do it now."

Peg had agreed immediately. Her trust fund allowed her to buy the first farmhouse she and Eliot saw, plus its surrounding one hundred acres, plus the new, green Ford pickup truck, which was now parked in the driveway, half-filled with torn-out linoleum, and which they readily offered to lend to Craig whenever he needed it.

As they worked, Craig described what Myrtle Hill was trying to achieve, and Peg and Eliot listened closely. Eliot admired the philosophical purity of starting entirely from scratch—he was embarrassed by the fact that the farmhouse had running water and electricity, and he hoped soon to free himself of both—but when Craig explained his group's consensus process, Eliot was less enamored. He couldn't imagine having to wait for a dozen others to agree before doing what he wanted.

The camaraderie of communal living appealed to Peg but not much else did. She had already come to love the kitchen of her new house. Its sink was lavender porcelain, fed by a clever hot-water system that ran from the stove. Even its counter gave her joy, with its perfectly placed window looking out over the sloping back meadow that collected morning sunlight on every dew-dropped blade. Peg had always prided herself at being fashionably ahead of the crowd in her tastes and enthusiasms but when she heard about how they were living over at Myrtle—cooking over campfires and living in lean-tos—she thought, "They're out there, I'm square." But the comparison didn't bother her at all.

In June, Peg and Eliot threw backpacks into the pickup and drove thirty miles north to the Canadian border. They were loath to stop working even for a week, but earlier that spring they had made a plan with some college friends, Chris and Ellen, to go camping in the Maritimes.

Like them, Chris and Ellen had married soon after graduation. Ellen was from suburban Pasadena, a strong, athletic woman with frank, blue eyes, and straight, blonde hair.

Chris was similarly pale, with a burly build and a shaggy, tousled flop of blond hair. He was as gregarious as Ellen was reserved, his natural expression a wry grin.

Like Eliot's father, Chris's parents had both grown up in rural poverty in Saskatchewan. At the turn of the century, his grandfather had left a law career in Toronto to accept the Canadian government's invitation to become a homesteader. With no previous farming experience, he and his wife had worked their 160 acres with a steadily increasing desperation until the Depression finally put them under. Their son, Chris's father, had escaped back East to the city, putting farm life and its attendant poverty and humiliation permanently behind him.

Chris had never given his grandparents' experience much thought. That is, until recently.

Straight out of school, he had landed his dream job as a business reporter for the *Toronto Globe and Mail*, the nation's preeminent paper. He had studied journalism in college and loved almost everything about it—the deadline-fueled adrenaline, the conversations with people he might never otherwise meet, the quickly becoming expert in far-flung subjects, the righteous-feeling pursuit of truth. The first day he entered the newsroom, he was elated. You couldn't ask for a more prestigious job so early in a career. But almost at once, he began to butt heads with his editors, career newsmen whose gruff assurance and unquestioned confidence in their version of the truth he'd once admired and aspired to. Now when he watched them chain-smoking in their green visors, all he could see was their indoor pallor and their soft hands. His admiration slowly curdled into dread.

The question of his future began to plague him. If the route he thought he'd chosen, climbing a newsroom hierarchy, now seemed stifling and untenable, what were the other options? A job like his father's, working for some faceless company and disappearing every morning in grim resignation?

As he contemplated spending the rest of his life behind a desk, Chris found himself wondering about all the skills that his father had grown up resenting and seen as unfit to pass on to his son: when to plant and harvest, how to harness a horse and plow a field, even how to chop firewood. Despite his parents' insistence to the contrary, it was this that began to seem like real work.

The business beat did not help this state of mind. At first, learning about the inner functioning and handshake deals of banks and corporations had felt thrillingly like sneaking into a forbidden club, but more and more he couldn't stop thinking about the flimsiness of the whole operation. The more he learned about the financial systems that kept Western society humming, the more abstract and arbitrary they appeared.

Then they found out Ellen was pregnant. Chris's vague dissatisfaction now veered sharply toward panic. How can you take care—*really* take care—of your family's daily needs? Every answer of the kind that had offered his parents so much security—a good education, a steady office job, a mortgage—seemed terrifyingly dependent on the good word of authorities who were these days proving themselves over and over to be liars. He and Ellen were both strong, smart, full of energy. Why did they feel so entirely powerless?

"If the system broke down," he thought, "you'd just fucking die. You'd just stand there and die."

There had to be another way.

The June camping trip to the Maritimes ran into snarls before it even began. When Peg and Eliot met up with Chris and Ellen, the weather report was showing steady rain in Nova Scotia. No one, least of all Ellen who was hugely, heavily pregnant, wanted to spend a week drenched and miserable. "It's not raining in Vermont," Eliot said. He and Peg were eager to get back since they were still working on the house and figuring out the garden. The learning curve was steep, they told their friends—both of them still bent as many nails as they hammered cleanly—but exhilarating. Chris and Ellen agreed to help.

They arrived into a verdant wonderland. After years in the dusty ochres of California and the urban grayscale of Toronto, Ellen and Chris could not get over sheer volume of green that met their eyes in every direction. The trees were bursting with new leaves, and the emerald expanse of the fields was broken only by swaths of bright yellow dandelions. The air carried a freshness that reenergized them with every breath. Even the faint whiff of cow manure wafting over from a neighbor's fields smelled pleasant, borne by the first soft breezes of summer.

The two couples spent the week working and laughing. Peg and Eliot appreciated how much faster everything went with two more eager, able-bodied adults. It took no time at all to till up the soil and plant the huge garden: carrots, cabbage, squash, beets, tomatoes, peas, broccoli, potatoes. They cleaned out the barn and finished tearing up the flooring. Sitting down at the end of the day with aching muscles and a cold beer, Chris felt a depth of satisfaction he had only hoped existed.

Ellen was rapidly falling in love with the beauty of the place. Her huge belly meant that she couldn't help much with renovations or planting, but she appreciated the directness of the week's work—nothing about it was arbitrary. Her friends planted so that later they could eat. If they'd pulled nails out of scrap lumber, it was so that the wood could be used to build again or to burn for heat in the winter. As a child Ellen had understood instinctively how her father's job was responsible for her family's comfort as well as for his exhausted inability to engage or connect with his children. She had long known that she wanted to do the opposite with her own adulthood, but until now she hadn't had any idea of what that might look like.

And too, she had always suspected herself capable of more demanding physical challenges than her suburban girlhood had offered. She'd always been athletic, but it was one thing to work on your tennis serve in order to help you win more games, and another to swing an axe and split a pile of firewood so that you and your family could stay warm. In a place like this, she'd be able to test her own strength.

When it was time for them to leave, Ellen and Chris packed reluctantly. No one wanted the week to end.

Peg had a solution. "Why don't you come live here?" she asked them.

What could they say but yes?

There was still the small matter of the baby. Chris and Ellen decided to return to Canada, where the hospital stay would be free. Chris would give notice at the newspaper. Then, once the baby was born, they'd come back. In the meantime, Peg and Eliot would work on the house and try to find local jobs—teaching high school Spanish, maybe.

In just a few short weeks, they'd begin their new adventure, together.

Peg grew up outside of Boston in a big, old colonial house not far from Walden Pond. On one visit home, she and Eliot made a pilgrimage to the former home of the pond's most famous resident.

"I went to the woods because . . . I did not wish to live what was not life, living is so dear; nor did I wish to practice resignation, unless it was quite necessary. I wanted to live deep and suck out all the marrow of life," Henry David Thoreau wrote in 1854, explaining his decision to build himself a cabin and spend two years living in it, alone. Like many liberal arts students, Eliot had read *Walden* in college. He had liked it well enough at the time, but now, undertaking his own quest to escape living what was not life, Thoreau's writing began to carry a new kind of weight.

A huge number of his contemporaries felt the same way—the *Whole Earth Catalog* listed a $0.60 *Walden* paperback, calling it "the prime document of America's 3rd revolution, now underway." Young back-to-the-landers reading or rereading Thoreau found a lot to admire. They liked his open, ecstatic worship of nature, of course, but other writers offered that. For the counterculture generation of the '60s and '70s, Thoreau represented the whole package. They liked his penchant for crankily rejecting whatever smacked of the mainstream ("I say, beware of all enterprises that require new clothes and not a new wearer of clothes") and his insistence on the moral benefits of paring down to the bare essentials ("In proportion as a man simplifies his life, the laws of the universe will appear less complex, and solitude will not be solitude, nor poverty poverty, nor weakness weakness"). Best of all, he was an outspoken pacifist and a war resister who had gone to jail for his beliefs. They looked up to him a little like an older brother, as someone who'd forged the way in his own time, making the same bold moves they were trying to make—away from war and injustice and toward nature and simplicity.

It's possible Thoreau might have recognized commonalities with his late-20th-century fans as well. He too was reacting to a time of increased mechanization and an increasingly sophisticated economy that produced more and more abstracted jobs for its educated men. Frustrated with what he saw as his Harvard classmates' increasing emphasis on "securing the greatest degrees of gross comfort and pleasure merely," young Thoreau dedicated himself to finding an alternative. "How to make the getting of our living poetic!" he wondered. "If it is not poetic it is not life but death we get." This meant teaching for a time, until his brother's untimely demise from tetanus ended the school they'd started together. He also worked in his family's pencil factory, helped edit the Transcendental literary magazine, *The Dial*, and lived with his friend Ralph Waldo Emerson's family as general handyman and gardener. When Emerson bought fourteen acres abutting Walden Pond, Thoreau saw an opportunity. He convinced Emerson to let him build a cabin in exchange for clearing some of the land. After borrowing an axe from Bronson Alcott (Louisa May's father), he got to work.

As has been often pointed out, Thoreau's cabin was not a hermitage—it was within walking distance of Concord and Thoreau often went into town to visit friends. Neither was it an attempt at total self-sufficiency since Thoreau made no real gesture toward farming and accepted gladly the meals his mother and sister regularly brought him. As he himself put it, "I went to the woods because I wished to live deliberately, to front only the essential facts of life, and see if I could not learn what it had to teach, and not, when I came to die, discover that I had not lived." For Thoreau, like many philosophers and mystics throughout history, the goal of "fronting only the essential facts of life" could only be realized away from the hustle of society, in close relationship with nature.

Even to his contemporaries Thoreau embodied a particular ideal for an individual's relationship with the natural world. His friend Emerson admired his "simplicity and clear perception," noting that he "gives me in flesh & blood & pertinacious Saxon belief, my own ethics. He is far more real & daily practically obeying them, than I." Better than anyone else before or since, Thoreau articulated a romantic, recurrent, Western longing to find a fully realized expression of selfhood through direct, physical work in a wilderness setting.

If rural communards engaged in "America's third revolution" wondered what Thoreau would have made of their own, communal "experiment with living," they needn't have—the evidence existed. The 1840s saw a huge number of utopian societies spring up across the country as part of the Second Great Awakening. Almost all had a religious orientation of some kind. The small handful that remained secular belonged to the Transcendentalists.

One of these, Brook Farm, was the brainchild of George Ripley, a Unitarian minister and Transcendentalist who had grown frustrated with how little time daily work left for the life of the mind. As he explained his plan in a letter to Emerson, hoping to convince him to join, "Our objects . . . are to ensure a more natural union between intellectual and manual labor than now exists; to combine the thinker and the worker, as far as possible, in the same individual; to guarantee the highest mental freedom, by providing all with labor, adapted to their tastes and talents and securing to them the fruits of their industry . . . I wish to see a society of educated friends, working, thinking and living together, with no strife, except that of each to contribute the most to the benefit of all." The plan called for the men and women living and working at Brook Farm to cooperate in running the small dairy operation, earning them each a share of any profits, and leaving them with enough time to pursue other, more intellectually satisfying work if they chose. "If wisely executed," Ripley wrote Emerson, "it will be a light over this country and this age. If not the sunrise, it will be a morning star."

Ripley bought a small farm in West Roxbury, Massachusetts, in 1841, which quickly became home to several dozen young idealists. Margaret Fuller, pioneering journalist and first editor of

The Dial (and, fifty years later, great-aunt of Buckminster) was a frequent guest at Brook Farm. She donated a cow to the dairy's herd. Thoreau and Emerson both declined invitations to join, each preferring his autonomy. Emerson offered Ripley his moral support but Thoreau, characteristically, was more blunt: "As for these communities, I think I had rather keep bachelor's hall in hell than go to board in heaven."

One of the group's founding members was Nathaniel Hawthorne, who joined hoping that communal living and shared labor would free him, as promised, for more time to write. At first he embraced farmwork with a kind of grumbling irony: "This morning I have done wonders. Before breakfast, I went out to the barn and began to chop hay for the cattle, and with such 'righteous vehemence,' as Mr. Ripley says, did I labor that in the space of ten minutes I broke the machine." But even his tongue-in-cheek enthusiasm ("I have milked a cow!!!" he wrote on his third day, of Margaret Fuller's "transcendental heifer") disappeared after a few weeks of shoveling manure. He quickly became frustrated with farmwork's failure to offer either "the highest mental freedom" or a sense of moral purity: "In the midst of toil or after a hard day's work . . . my soul obstinately refuses to be poured out on paper," he wrote. "It is my opinion that a man's soul may be buried and perish under a dung-heap or in the furrow of the field, just as well as under a pile of money." He left at the end of his first summer and later fictionalized his experiences at Brook Farm in his novel *The Blithedale Romance*.

Many of Brook Farm's other residents, though, seem to have found a comfortable balance. In its first few years, over 150 children and adults called the farm home and a number of them later remembered their time with fondness: "We were happy, contented, well-off and carefree; doing great work in the world, enthusiastic and faithful, we enjoyed every moment of every day," wrote one. Even Hawthorne later admitted that his five months at Brook Farm was "the most romantic episode of my own life." Though the farm never became financially solvent (most of its income one year came from the small fees charged to its huge number of visitors) and in later years struggled to find a united philosophy, the community lasted for eight years before a fire destroyed an uninsured building, leaving an insurmountable debt that forced the group to disband.

Brook Farm was not the only Transcendental commune that both Thoreau and Emerson opted not to join.

Fruitlands was the joint project of an English journalist named Charles Lane and Bronson Alcott, the visionary American education reformer. Lane had been deeply influenced by Alcott's work at his progressive Temple School and invited him to England. Alcott's school had recently folded, due in part to parental protest over Alcott's insistence on asking young children to offer their own interpretations of biblical scripture and on maintaining an interracial student body, and Emerson loaned him the money for the trip to England, hoping that it would boost his friend's spirits.

When Alcott returned four months later, Lane and his ten-year-old son accompanied him, full of plans for the new community that Alcott had proposed and Lane had agreed to bankroll. Like George Ripley, they hoped to offer members the possibility of splitting their time between physical labor and the life of the mind. But Brook Farm, then in its second year, was far too relaxed for their taste. Alcott called it "insufficiently ideal" while the severe and humorless Lane deplored the Brook Farmers' "miserable, joyous, frivolous manner." Fruitlands' day was to begin with a bracing, early-morning dip in the pond and a pre-breakfast music lesson. As Lane and Alcott laid it out, the rest of the day's agenda was split between necessary outdoor labor and "interesting and deep-searching conversation."

At Fruitlands, the goal was total purity—of mind, body, and morality. Their ideal of self-sufficiency was as much a critique of capitalism as it was a practical solution to daily needs. Like other political progressives of the time, they eschewed products of slave labor including cotton, sugar, rum, and indigo clothing dye, but they didn't stop there. "Neither coffee, tea, molasses, nor rice tempts us beyond the bounds of indigenous production," wrote Lane. "No animal substances neither flesh, butter, cheese, eggs, nor milk pollute our tables, nor corrupt our bodies." Even salt was suspect. The group's diet was to consist of water, nuts, whole grains, and, from their orchards, their namesake fruits.

Right away, the project attracted several enthusiastic, if eccentric, adherents. Among others, there was an English nudist who believed strongly in the benefits of moonbathing; a young man who had famously subsisted only on crackers for a year and who exercised his own brand of personal freedom by greeting everyone he met with a torrent of obscenities; and a man who, in defiance of current fashion, sported an enormous beard and who had been jailed for fighting with a group of men who had tried to forcibly shave him (he refused to post bail in protest). Aside from Alcott's wife Abigail and their four daughters, including 11-year-old Louisa May, the only other woman was a poet named Anna Page, who was soon kicked out by Lane for eating part of a fish while dining with neighbors. As Louisa May recounts the scene in her lightly fictionalized satire, "Transcendental Wild Oats," Page defended herself to Lane: "'I only took a little bit of the tail,' sobbed the penitent poetess. 'Yes, but the whole fish had to be tortured and slain that you might tempt your carnal appetite with that one taste of the tail,'" Lane admonished her.

Ever supportive of his friend Alcott, Emerson visited Fruitlands. "They look well in July," he reported in his journal. "We shall see them in December." Even a less astute observer than Emerson could predict that the experiment was destined for trouble. The group's strictures against beeswax and wool meant that they were headed into a long New England winter without candles and wearing only hand-spun linen. (Abigail Alcott, generally amenable to her husband's dictates, had rebelled against the total ban on animal products and refused to give up the whale-oil lamp that allowed her to read and mend everyone's clothes at night.)

More urgently, the orchards that were crucial to their food supply were not yet well-established and they hadn't come up with a viable substitute. Progress on their other crops had been hampered by an original goal of doing without animal labor. This rule was amended to allow oxen after the men spent several days attempting to till fields with shovels, but one of the animals they acquired to draw the plow was probably a dairy cow; none of them apparently had enough farm experience to tell the difference. Other obstacles to a robust harvest included the founders' philosophical objection to using animal manure as fertilizer, and Alcott's ban on planting root vegetables on the grounds that they disturbed the life of worms.

Very rapidly, the founders' planned daily schedule devolved into less and less time spent in farm labor and more and more time in "deep-searching conversation"—at least for everyone but Abigail Alcott. As Louisa May put it, the men "were so busy discussing and defining great duties that they forgot to perform the small ones." For the two short seasons Fruitlands lasted, Abigail took care of the communal household more or less single-handedly, caring for five children, cooking meals from an eccentric and rapidly diminishing larder, and once, when an approaching storm threatened to decimate their only successful crop while the men were all away lecturing, harvesting an entire field of wheat alone, aided only by the children.

According to Louisa May's account, someone once asked Abigail, "Are there any beasts of burden on the place?" She answered, "with a face that told its own tale, 'Only one woman!'" (According to Louisa May, Anna Page did not contribute much domestic help during her stay at Fruitlands; perhaps resenting this, Louisa May bluntly reported her feelings about Page: "I hate her.")

After his visit, Emerson wrote in his journal that Fruitlands' founders "are always feeling of their shoulders to find if their wings are sprouting," instead of holding up their half of the domestic bargain. In her own journal, Abigail noted the gender double standard: "Miss Page made a good remark, and as true as good, that a woman may live a whole life of sacrifice and at her death meekly says, 'I die a woman.' But a man passes a few years in experiments of self-denial and simple life, and he says, 'Behold, I am a God.'"

Emerson's skepticism proved prescient. As Louisa May put it, "With the first frosts, the butterflies, who had sunned themselves in the new light through the summer, took flight, leaving the few bees to see what honey they had stored for winter use." By December, everyone at Fruitlands had left except for Lane, his son, and the Alcott family, who were deeply in debt and otherwise homeless. Lane tried to convince Bronson to come away with him but failing this, he and his son left to join the Shakers. Bronson Alcott was so distraught he climbed into bed and refused to eat for three days in an apparent suicide attempt. Abigail eventually prevailed on him to get up. The family returned to Concord and tried to put their life back together.

Louisa May's account of Fruitlands' short life is perhaps the best and most biting satire of any countercultural communal experiment in any era. While she spares nothing in her critique of its founders' hypocrisy and narcissism, she ends on a sympathetic note: "To live for one's principles, at all costs, is a dangerous speculation; and the failure of an ideal, no matter how humane and noble, is harder for the world to forgive and forget than bank robbery or the grand swindles of corrupt politicians."

As planned, Chris and Ellen returned to Peg and Eliot's just as the nights were starting to get chilly. Peg had fixed up the bedroom on the first floor for them and moved herself and Eliot into the other, smaller bedroom directly above it, under the peaked roof. Peg and Eliot had made good progress on the garden over the past few weeks but had run into unforeseen trouble with some of the renovations. These were not the most pressing updates they needed to give their friends, however. As soon as Peg helped get everything settled in, Eliot broke the news: there'd been a major change of plans.

For one thing, Peg and Eliot had made no headway with finding jobs. In truth, they hadn't really tried very hard. They'd been thinking again about the Spanish villagers, with their self-sufficient farming and their diet of goat cheese.

What did this new household really need in order to live? Nothing, once you thought about it, that wasn't already here. There was plenty of groundwater, along with the stream cutting through the bottom of the field across the road. For food, they would have the garden, and it would be easy enough to get chickens and a cow—and goats, of course. To support the animals, they had ample land for pasture, as well as hayfields for winter fodder—the same resources that had supported the residents of this farm for more than a century. As distant as the Spanish peasants' way of life had seemed from the perspective of the suburbs, it wasn't so long ago that people around here had farmed in much the same way—tractors had only really become common here during the 1950s, and electricity and telephone service were still novelties on some back roads. What was stopping them from going back to that now?

Self-sufficiency, Eliot had come to realize, was freedom.

But it had to be total. They'd never be truly free of the industrial, capitalist systems that corrupted the earth and appeared anyway to be on the brink of collapse as long as they were stuck relying on tractors or trucks or anything else that used imported gasoline. Horses, on the other hand—their fuel supply could be grown, baled, and stored on one's own land, conveniently aided by the horses themselves. Eliot had already begun scouting horse-drawn farming equipment.

For Peg, this new plan was the next best thing to running away to Spain and becoming a peasant herself, as she'd often dreamed of doing. She would make her own cheese, using the techniques she'd been learning from a friend. She'd also found an antique, crank butter churn, gorgeous in its simplicity. Forty years later, it would still be one of Peg's favorite possessions.

To Chris, Eliot's argument appealed tremendously: milk from your own cow, firewood from your own forest, vegetables from your own garden, tended and harvested using tools simple enough to fix by yourself. In other words, exactly what he'd been looking for. He was in.

Over the next few weeks, Peg, Chris, and Eliot entered into a thrill of preparation. There were animals and equipment to source and purchase, and stalls and pastures to be made ready. If there was an element of added satisfaction for Chris and Eliot imagining how disgusted this return to preindustrial farming would make their Depression-escapee fathers, it went unmentioned.

One night, giggly with exhaustion, one of them hit upon the perfect name for the new farm. What started as a joke, an apt description of the many projects under way (and their varying degrees of success) quickly picked up shades of the discussions that had motivated and fueled this project in the first place, the sense that everything seemed to be spinning out of control, in the nation, in the world, and, until now, in their own lives.

This farmhouse and its surrounding land would henceforth and forever be known as Entropy Acres.

And, of course, the household's barely contained chaos had another source. Peg and Eliot hadn't been the only ones to contribute a major twist to the plans they'd all made in June.

A few weeks before returning to the States, Ellen had gone into labor. She and Chris had headed to the hospital but as it turned out, this was the last of their arrangements that went as expected.

The baby, to the total shock of Chris, Ellen, and their doctors, had in fact turned out to be twins.

Chris was an attentive father, and it was a tremendous boon to have two other adults on hand to help soothe and entertain the babies, but there was no question that the twins' primary care fell to Ellen. When the others sat up late at night eagerly discussing the season's plans, she was either nursing, shushing one of the boys back to sleep, or asleep herself.

The ideal of a self-sufficient way of life appealed as much to her as it did to the others, but in her case, there was an added irony: the reason she couldn't participate more in the ideologically driven work and planning was that she was already, herself, a complete source of nutrition and protection for two small lives. And it was utterly exhausting.

CHAPTER 4

O ver at Myrtle Hill, the summer had slipped by in a haze. For Loraine, the romantic camp-out thrill had not faded at all—sleeping out under the stars, meals eaten together around the fire, and joyful impromptu parties whenever someone showed up with a portable radio or enough booze, grass, or acid to share.

They had managed to get quite a bit work done, though. For a garden, they'd turned up a large, sunny section of the upper field and planted lettuce, carrots, potatoes, and rutabagas. At one end of the middle field, they'd spent a few days digging a deep hole for an outhouse—a doorless two-seater that looked across the road to the garden. The cook tent's flat, Earth Day-sheeting roof pooled full and collapsed in the first big rainstorm, but they'd rebuilt it again the next day, this time properly sloped; they still had trouble on windy days keeping the sheeting from blowing in and melting against the hot Ashley stove. For the five dozen chickens, they'd put up a shed of scrap wood near the top of the lower field, once it dried out. Jed and some of the other men had also spent a few days running a barbed-wire fence around the field's perimeter to pasture the two Jersey cows, Gypsy and Alice. The planned barn had yet to materialize, though—to milk the cows, you just carried a bucket and stool right down to the field and let them keep grazing while you worked.

Thanks in part to the enthusiasm of their Earth People's Park comrades, there were usually plenty of able bodies to help with whatever seemed most pressing. Within a few weeks, Myrtle

Hill's stable population had risen to twenty, but the stream of visitors meant the constant presence of many more. Some weekends as many as eighty might appear for dinner, lining up for a bowl full of the beans and rice that Loraine and Nancy had cooked in huge batches over the campfire. Before eating, they gathered in a circle. Sometimes they sang a song Loraine had taught them, the words slightly altered from her Girl Scout days: "Oh, the Earth is good to me / And so I thank the Earth / For giving me the things I need / The sun and the rain and the apple seed / The Earth is good to me / Hallelujah!"

One of the new permanent residents was a friend that Fletcher and Nancy had met at Drop City. Jim the Bear's thick brown mustache couldn't quite hide his wide, toothy grin, joyful and hesitant at once. He was slight but strong—beautifully built, as Loraine put it, "like a carnival huckster." Everyone liked him. More important, he was also one of the only people at Myrtle Hill who had any real construction skills. And his were not just any skills. He was a bona fide genius at inventing whatever contraption or system they suddenly needed. He reminded Craig of Gyro Gearloose, Donald Duck's friend, the crazy inventor with a thinking-cap powered by three black birds. Craig watched Jim work with frank admiration.

It was Jim who pushed for what would become the summer's most ambitious project: a geodesic dome.

Like Fletcher and Nancy, Jim had been very influenced by his time at Drop City and had fallen in love with the geodesic form. The three of them were eager to re-create some elements of that experience in their new community. Craig and the others needed no convincing. Building the dome would be easy, Jim assured them.

He was right, and wrong.

Though in the summer of 1970 geodesic domes were at the cusp of becoming ubiquitous at rural communes, even just a few years earlier, the idea of building one would probably not have occurred to anyone at Myrtle Hill.

In the spring of 1965, a young artist named Clark Richert attended a lecture by Buckminster Fuller at the World Affairs

Conference in Boulder, Colorado. Like many other young people who thronged to hear Fuller on his tours of college campuses, Richert left the conference enthralled with Fuller's vision and eager to try his own hand at building a geodesic dome. As it happened, he had recently been offered the perfect opportunity: two friends, Gene and Jo Ann Bernofsky, had bought a few acres of land near Trinidad, Colorado, with the idea of starting a new society—or at least, establishing an out-of-the-way place where they and their friends could make art and live as simply as possible. They had invited Richert and another friend, Richard Kallweit, to join them.

They named the new community Drop City after an earlier art project in which Gene Bernofsky and Richert had painted rocks and dropped them off of buildings into the path of unsuspecting pedestrians, a practice they called "drop art," liking its rhyme with "Op Art." (Though the residents of Drop City were in no way averse to psychedelics, Timothy Leary's famous, LSD-flavored "turn on, tune in, drop out" was still a year in the future.) Their philosophy was that it was possible, amid the extravagant excess of American society, to live richly and well on others' refuse. Within a few years there would be dozens, then hundreds, then thousands of similar experiments under way all across America, but in 1965, Drop City was sui generis. It is now widely recognized as the first hippie commune.

The Bernofskys were just as taken with the idea of building domes as Richert had been. The problem was figuring out how. Fuller had patented his design in 1954 and there were thousands of domes in existence all over the globe, but the plans were not easy to come by; it wasn't until the following summer that Fuller would make the formula for a simple "sun dome" available through *Popular Science,* which recommended it enthusiastically as a swimming-pool cover. Undaunted, the Droppers set about recreating the formula for themselves. One day, while driving through rural Colorado, Richert and Gene Bernofsky passed a farm with a geodesic greenhouse. They screeched to a halt and clambered over a fence to take measurements. Following these figures, Richert built a model from drinking straws. With the confidence and improvisation that would characterize all of Drop City's projects, they decided just to start building.

Using whatever materials they could find, buy on the cheap or abscond with undetected (including lumber from a disused railroad bridge and, at least once, planks from a barn that turned out not to be abandoned after all), they put together their first dome. They had asked some neighbors what materials locals usually used for their houses: tarpaper, covered with chicken wire and stucco. It immediately became clear that the dome's unusual planes made this arrangement impossible. Jo Ann Bernofsky had the idea to tack the sagging tarpaper to the dome's surface with hundreds of bottle caps. Local bars were bemused but more than happy to offer the Droppers all the bottle caps they needed. The result was a cozy ice-cream scoop of a house, with pentagonal windows facing the sky and smaller, rectangular ones near the floor. As Jo Ann recalled, "It was extremely exciting to have pulled it off. And it was wonderful and magical to be in this space that was totally unlike any space I'd ever been in before."

Encouraged by this success, Richert decided to start on a more ambitious project the following spring: a forty-foot "Theater Dome" the group could use to stage some of the light- and projection-based art they were working on. This included their collaborative, psychedelic masterwork, "The Ultimate Painting," a huge, round disk from which images emerged and retreated as it spun on its motorized base.

Their building efforts attracted the attention of a young, Fuller-obsessed inventor living in nearby New Mexico. Steve Baer's first visit to Drop City turned out to be a major turning point, not only in the lives of Baer and the Droppers but also in the history of American architecture.

Almost the moment he hopped out of the car, Baer became Drop City's most important collaborator. Richert had finished the frame of the Theater Dome but was still casting around for ideas about what to cover it with. Baer suggested steel, cut from the tops of junked cars. This instantly appealed to the Droppers. They found that junkyard owners would often willingly negotiate, either letting them take tops for free or, at most, charging 25 cents each. One owner suggested a barter: car tops for a dozen freshly hatched chickens.

The process of removing the tops was extremely labor intensive but very satisfying in its combination of hard work, low cost, environmentalism, and outlaw daring. Standing on the top of a rusted-out Chevy or Studebaker, you had to chop through the roof with an axe and then swing the blade in a steady motion to slice around its edge. As Dropper Peter Rabbit described it, "It was dangerous; razor-sharp axes skittering off the steel, slicing at legs. When you hit one of the roof supports an incredible jolt travels up the axe handle and paralyzes your wrists and hands. Jagged steel edges catching clothing, tearing flesh, hands stiff, clenching, clenching. After chopping for an hour if you try to open your hands the fingers insist on closing themselves into fists again. Blisters, blisters on top of blisters, bone weary."

But the work paid off: the resulting sheets of steel could be folded around plywood templates to form the needed shapes; once joined over a dome's frame, the seams could then be sealed with tar. The variety of car paint made for a visually appealing patchwork effect—industrial and homey at once. As an additional bonus, other refuse from the cars could be repurposed in the building process: windshields became skylights or picture windows, and, in one case, a few dozen rearview mirrors became a gorgeous, functional solar collector.

Baer left his first visit to Drop City inspired both by the group's energetic resourcefulness and by their fearlessness about undertaking geodesic building projects that he had previously thought of as requiring acute mathematical precision. He soon returned to Drop City with plans for his own designs, based in Fuller's formulation, but tweaked according to Baer's own interests: in soap bubbles and the shapes they formed when clustered together, and in the potential for enthusiastic novices to undertake complex building projects with no previous experience. The first Baer-designed "zome" that Drop City built was made entirely from car tops bent to shape and bolted together with no underlying structure. It cost $14, half of which went to the cost of screws.

The collaboration between Baer and Drop City would eventually lead to a quickly spreading collection of ten gorgeous, bright-painted space-age shapes rising from the austere landscape. As visitor William Hedgepeth described the scene: "Angular, unearthly, demented, like gawky igloos in a kaleidoscope . . . Yellow blue green red pink purple: brazen things just lying up there, coldly geodesic, looming on the little rise way out here in southern Colorado wasteland . . . like some Buck Rodgers Indian village, like some half-forbidding netherworld where idealistic troglodytes lurk and live in fields of candy-colored toadstools."

In 1966, Fuller awarded Drop City the first-ever "Dymaxion Award" for "poetically economical structural achievement." The Droppers were justly proud—and grateful for the $500 prize, since supporting themselves financially remained their greatest challenge.

Or maybe second-greatest. Drop City and its psychedelic dome-scape rapidly became famous just at the moment that young people began pouring out of the Haight after the Summer of Love, looking for the next hippie utopia. In 1967, the year that marked the very start of the nationwide surge of rural communes, Drop City was already so inundated with transient visitors who severely taxed their already-scant resources, that the daily work of the commune had ground to a halt.

By the time Fletcher, Nancy, and Jim arrived, the overcrowding had become intolerable to the group's founding members. As Gene put it later, the Bernofskys had left "broken-hearted."

But Drop City's influence was already permanently assured. Steve Baer turned his zome and dome formulas and trippily-eccentric construction advice into the oversized, hand-lettered *Dome Cookbook*. It was the first readily accessible source of dome-building instructions and one of the first items offered in the new *Whole Earth Catalog*. Now, for the first time, interested counterculture dome builders had a resource.

"Seeing Drop City, especially the mistakes and weak materials, gave me great confidence," wrote Baer. He passed that confidence on to a whole generation of eager builders.

Myrtle Hill's dome builders started off enthusiastically, but it wasn't long before they ran into trouble.

The dome's wooden frame went up as easily and satisfyingly as the Droppers' had, but that's when the problems started. Jim, Fletcher, and Craig had decided to stick with Baer's car-top design. Later it would become clear that tar and steel made much better building materials in the Southwest desert than in a climate where winter temperatures sometimes drop to thirty below, but at first they had an even more pressing problem: sourcing the car tops.

The few salvage yards Myrtle Hill's builders could find proved unreceptive to working with them. Undaunted, Craig and Fletcher took to driving around back roads, looking for farms with junked cars in their yards. When they spotted one, they'd hop out and knock on the door to introduce themselves and explain their project, asking politely, "Can we take your car tops?" Craig's charm went a long way, but they got a lot of no's. The people who said yes would come out to stand on the lawn and watch in open amusement as the men sweated and hacked through the thick steel. Some even invited their friends over, not to miss the show. But the yesses were rare. As much as Craig and Fletcher relished the long aimless drives over back roads, they at last had to admit defeat.

More than a month after the dome's frame went up, its base wore only a single row of multicolor steel triangles.

Nancy had looked forward as much as Fletcher and Jim to this new round of dome building, but other obligations had absorbed her time. She and Loraine were Myrtle Hill's only permanent female residents and, as they put it, the group's "chief cooks and bottle washers." While they worked, their young children played in the woods nearby, amusing themselves with games of their own invention. When other women came to visit, they often offered to help as best they could, though Loraine found that explaining how to stoke a campfire hot enough to bring a five-gallon pot to boil or showing someone accustomed to an automatic dishwasher how not to waste painstakingly hauled and heated rinse water usually took longer than just doing the task herself.

Then one day, a visitor arrived who changed Loraine's life. From the crowd of skinny young men who made up the usual new faces at dinner, this woman stood out. She was at least twenty years older than anyone else, for one thing, and large and British. She introduced herself as Herb Mary.

Herb Mary seemed to know everything. She took Loraine on long walks through the woods, pointing out edible and medicinal plants and explaining, in her strong, poshly accented voice, their use and preparation. She showed Loraine how to safely collect and prepare nettles (high in vitamins A and C); how to treat a bee sting with broad-leaf plantain (the best method: chew the leaves until bitter, then apply to the wound) and turn the long-leaf variety into cough syrup (chop it into a jar of honey and then let it cure for several months by burying it deep underground to keep it at a steady forty degrees). Loraine absorbed it all, fascinated.

Then, after a few days, Herb Mary vanished. Loraine never saw her again. By then she'd learned enough to think of herself, with rare confidence, as an herbalist. The woods and meadows, beloved to Loraine from childhood, now revealed themselves as not just a destination for escape but also as a source of nurturing and healing. For the rest of her life she would continue to read everything she could find on the subject, but she never again had another teacher.

Someone had introduced Loraine to a set of eye exercises that would supposedly allow her to conquer her lifelong myopia. She had stopped wearing her glasses but the exercises weren't working yet. She'd never shaken her adolescent habit of stooping to hide her height, and now, unconsciously, she also started leaning intimately close to people as she spoke. This, plus her huge, intensely blue eyes, her long skirts, and curtain of hair added to the witchy, herb-woman vibe she had begun to actively cultivate.

Loraine's blurred vision and weeks with Herb Mary contributed to her sense of dream-walking through that summer. For years afterward, when she asked her commune-mates if they remembered an older British woman called Mary, they just looked at her blankly. She never stopped wondering where Herb Mary had gone.

But things like that happened a lot at Myrtle. No one believed in coincidence, and so the smallest occurrence could flash with a kind of thrilling magic. Examples came everywhere: just as you poured out the last amber threads of honey, some visitors would arrive bearing another tin as a gift. Or you'd take a midnight stroll to a high meadow with someone you wanted to get to know better and just when he grabbed your hand, you'd look up to see a bright streak shoot through the breathtaking sky. This mood—what one commune scholar termed the "blissful state of positive paranoia . . . The belief that the universe is a conspiracy for one's benefit"— stemmed partly from smoking so much pot, of course, but it was more than that. No one could get over how lucky they were to get to live this way, so purely and close to the earth and all together.

Then one morning, Loraine climbed out of her sapling-and-plastic cabin to notice that her beloved line of maples had begun to blush scarlet. Once the hills reached their full glory of color, she knew, the snow wouldn't be far behind.

She had watched the dome's slow progress with increasing trepidation. The men overflowed with beautiful, daring ideas, but to her, the amount of planning and talking about work didn't seem at all proportionate to the actual amount of work that got done in any given day. When she tried to mention a few things they might do in preparation for winter—get in a supply of hay for the cows, for example—sometimes the men didn't even seem to register that she'd spoken. Maybe if she had a more forceful personality, Loraine thought, she might have more success, but her growing confidence as a cook and herbalist had not altered her lifelong aversion to conflict.

Nancy didn't fare much better. Her eagerness to start developing a water-recycling system had slowly faded when she got no response from the guys. She and Loraine listened to each other and the two of them did what they could, but the connection between their ideas and the priorities of the group faced a huge obstacle: at the nighttime, pot-inspired planning sessions around the campfire, the two women were not actually present. They were still cleaning up from dinner or were out in the darkness with flashlights, putting the children to bed.

In fact, the children's tent was one of the things that made urgent the question of what would happen at the end of summer. The children were supposed to clean their sleeping quarters themselves, but Amelia was three and Bryn, the oldest, was only seven, and Loraine and Nancy had been too busy to enforce this chore very often. Plus, Myrtle's kids had had to share the tent for days or weeks with visiting children whose own parents might or might not see it as their responsibility to help keep things clean. The tent had devolved into a muddy, reeking tangle of sodden sleeping bags. Something buried in the mess had started to stink like a dead animal.

Before long, everyone was rolling out of bed in the morning cold and stiff. Even for the heartiest, the thrill of successfully living outdoors in hand-built shelters was fading fast. Fewer and fewer visitors camped out on the weekends now, which put a dent in the commune's supply of fresh faces and welcome consumables.

The Earth People's Park guys had at last gotten word from the national organization about land of their own, only fifty miles from Myrtle Hill. Six hundred acres abutting the Canadian border was now officially "Free Land for Free People." A number of the New Yorkers had headed there immediately, but some had decided to stay and formally join Myrtle Hill. Jed, in particular, threw himself into helping figure out the problem of the group's winter quarters.

Finally Craig hit upon a plan to which the others agreed. They'd put up a quick barn for the animals to live in through the winter, and the commune's human residents would find a house nearby to rent until spring, when they could figure out a more permanent shelter of their own. As far as caring for their new animals through the winter, someone would just have to commute back up to the hill every day for milking and feeding.

On later reflection, this plan had several levels of folly, a few of which rapidly became apparent. For one thing, unlike in the city, there were hardly any rentals available in a region where most families owned the house they lived in. Craig and Fletcher resumed their back-country drives, now refocused on seeking out every available farmhouse in a two-hour radius from Myrtle Hill.

But even the few they found that might prove big enough became a lost cause the moment the owners took one look at their prospective tenants' long hair and eccentric, filthy work clothes.

After their fifth rejection, Craig finally admitted defeat. "Who the hell's going to rent to twenty-three hippies?" he thought, climbing back in the truck. Though the group technically had no formal leader, Craig felt personally responsible for making sure that his comrades and this fragile new organism they'd invented together survived through the winter. The others were counting on him too, he knew. For the very first time, he started to panic.

All around them, as he and Fletcher drove on the long, winding dirt roads toward home, the high, rolling hills exploded in red and orange. The Day-Glo profusion stood bright against the emerald fields below, their green now deeper and more vibrant than at any other time of year. It was the green of last-ditch glory before the snow.

CHAPTER 5

O f the many important turning points in Craig's life, one of the most significant, as he reflected on it later, was the long, hot afternoon of May 15, 1969, which he had spent lying with his face pressed into the blazing pavement of the Santa Rita prison yard.

In high school in New Jersey, Craig had been a football jock. The kids on one side of Cranford's tracks, whose fathers headed into the city every morning in suits, called themselves "JCs" for "Joe College." The kids from the other side had parents who worked nearby, in the Merck warehouse or on the line at the General Motors plant. Those kids called themselves "the Americans."

Craig was a JC. He was an indifferent student with the kind of good looks and easy charisma that made him appear to be rolling through life without a worry. In truth, his home life was strained, and he was restless and bored.

Then, the summer before his senior year, a girl he liked had invited him to come with her to a civil rights rally her temple was joining. The event was in Washington, D.C., which meant a five-hour bus ride sharing a seat with a pretty cheerleader—reason enough to go, even if he hadn't also been curious about what the day would entail. Craig put on a tie and climbed aboard. It was August 28, 1963.

Craig came home from the March on Washington forever changed. Eager for a better view, he had worked his way through the crowd and had found himself only a few hundred yards from the steps of the Lincoln Memorial when King delivered his "I Have a Dream" speech. In some ways, Craig's exhilaration at having been present at such an obviously historic moment never wore off. He was now determined to remain at the center of the action.

Within a few months, his thick brown hair had started to creep past his collar, and he was heading into Manhattan every weekend. In low, dark, West Village coffee shops he saw Dylan and Zappa and Phil Ochs. A few days after his high school graduation, he heard Ken Kesey, author of *One Flew Over the Cuckoo's Nest,* being interviewed on the radio. Kesey had arrived in New York after a cross-country trip to the 1964 World's Fair in an insane school bus driven by Neal Cassady from *On the Road* and was inviting listeners to find him in Central Park the next afternoon. The few hours Craig spent talking with Kesey's busload of Merry Pranksters left him more determined than ever to follow their larger-than-life example.

He spent only one semester at the sleepy Connecticut college that had offered him a full football scholarship before he transferred to drama school in Manhattan. He was going to become an actor.

This plan hit a hitch when his girlfriend Lorrie, a dancer and Barbazon model, got pregnant. They hated the thought of settling down, but it seemed like the only option—and they could not ignore the benefits: Craig's becoming a family man would help protect him from the draft.

Newly married, Craig and Lorrie moved back to the suburbs, where they immediately began to go crazy with boredom. Craig covered the inside walls of their apartment and the sides of his Renault with an explosion of psychedelic, painted flowers. All anyone could talk about was what was happening in San Francisco and they were dying to see what they were missing. As soon as their daughter Zoe was born, they took off for California—Lorrie and the baby by plane, Craig on a meandering cross-country road trip.

In addition to adventure, Craig's journey had a grimmer purpose: his best friend had protested the draft by mailing his draft card to LBJ, and now he was in trouble. He'd enlisted Craig to help him get over the border into Canada.

This task complete, Craig met up with Lorrie in San Francisco. They were a few months late for the Summer of Love. The Haight-Ashbury scene had already begun to dissipate, so Craig and his family spent the next year bouncing back and forth between Berkeley and the hills of Mendocino.

Then, in April of 1969, when a group of Berkeley activists decided to reclaim a disused university-owned lot and turn it into a People's Park, Craig found himself once again at the heart of the action.

People's Park (namesake of the later "Earth People's Park") would soon become an explosive turning point in the late 1960s and an important catalyst for the urban counterculture's sudden surge toward the countryside, but the project itself started off innocuously enough.

In early 1969, some Berkeley activists took note of an empty lot near the university campus. The lot had been cleared of houses a few years earlier and earmarked for sports fields but had since languished, gathering junk. The activists decided it would make the perfect place for a badly needed public park. When their formal requests to the university went ignored, they decided they didn't need the administration's permission after all. They simply began building.

In a proclamation titled "Who Owns the Park?" printed over an image of Geronimo holding a gun, activists defended their claim to the site as a protest against historic, colonial land ownership of all kinds. "Your people ripped off the land from the Indians a long time ago," its last line read. "If you want it back now, you will have to fight for it again." The manifesto's author, Frank Bardacke, later expressed their justification more simply: "We're using the land better than you used it. And it's ours."

Each morning that spring, Craig met with a few dozen other organizers at the Mediterranean Coffee House on Telegraph to discuss the day's action. In just a few weeks, he and hundreds of other volunteers tore up three acres of asphalt with pickaxes and replaced it with rolls of grass donated by sod farmers in Sonoma. Very quickly, the garbage-strewn lot became a green oasis with bushes, flowers, and lawns and a *Yellow Submarine*-inspired playground that included climbable seven-foot high letters spelling K-N-O-W. As historian-participant Todd Gitlin described it, "Work on the Park was joy, not a job. Local longhairs tamped down sod next to students, housewives, neighbors, parents. Fraternity boys mixed with freaks; professors shopped for shrubs . . . Beneath all the divisions of straight versus hip and student versus nonstudent, People's Park . . . touched some deep hunger for a common life."

Berkeley was then in its fifth year of more-or-less nonstop student protest. The size of antiwar marches around the country would continue to grow for several more years, but by 1969 many veteran organizers had become exhausted and dispirited. The teargas and clubbings with which police had responded to protesters at the Democratic National Convention in Chicago the summer before had illustrated to many how little provocation authorities needed before responding with violence. As a site for radical change, cities had come to feel not just frustratingly futile but also—as would be proven again very soon—inescapably dangerous.

The act of transforming even a modestly sized piece of pavement into a living square of grass and trees was a potent symbol. At a moment when the political left was beginning to splinter, hippies, revolutionaries, Black Panthers, middle-class academics, street activists, and neighborhood families could find common ground, literally. In the words of poet Denise Levertov, then a Berkeley professor, "The Park was a little island of Peace and hope in a world made filthy by war and injustice."

"Building the Park was a way of saying, 'If we had control over our lives, this is what it would look like,'" explained student activist and historian Ruth Rosen. Following in the protest style of the Civil Rights Movement's sit-ins, the People's Park activists had decided to, simply and without asking permission, make real the world they wanted to live in. And increasingly by 1969, that world was green.

As Bardacke put it years later, "In a down-to-earth way, we were showing in our very activity the image of a new society. We were saying: Our job is to form a counter culture, a more rural culture." In the rhetoric of the largely urban protestors, "rural" meant peaceful, anticorporate, clean, safe, and free—the opposite, in short, of every quality the city had come to represent.

Craig and the other People's Park's builders imagined these few acres of newly planted grass and flowers as a tiny square of Mother Earth, inherently imbued with a purity and freedom not possible in a man-made setting. By creating a space as green and as open as they could manage, they lodged a protest—not just against the idea of private land ownership but also against the urban setting itself.

"The Park has brought the concept of the Whole Earth, the Mother Earth, into the vocabulary of revolutionary politics," wrote Berkeley poet John Oliver Simon. These concepts would expand and extend even further a year later with the first Earth Day, but a movement-within-the-movement was now under way. The environmental movement of the 1970s was characterized by its dual emphasis on both the protection and conservation of wild places and its focus on green technology. Its signature activism became the direct action—most famously practiced by Greenpeace (founded in 1971). Working on the Park, wrote Simon, "has given the dispossessed children of the tract homes and the cities a feeling of involvement with the planet, an involvement proved through our sweat and blood."

But to many, even sympathetic observers, the Park's greenery was a thin cover for a much more cynical dare to the university. "The park issue is not the issue," one city councilman told the press. "The protesters were out of confrontation issues. And as soon as you give them a park, they'll dream up another confrontation." Though the university's administration bristled at the activists' blatant land-grab, they agreed not to take any action at the park without prior notice to organizers.

Governor Ronald Reagan felt differently, however. He had won just over a year earlier on a platform that promised a harder line against civil unrest. Frustrated with the university's reluctance to quash student protest ("[D]on't you simply explain to these students? . . . [W]hat do you mean 'negotiate'?" he scolded faculty), he decided it was time to take a stand against the "communist sympathizers, protesters and sex deviants" he'd promised his electorate he would subdue.

Just before dawn on Thursday, May 15, police poured into Berkeley. They sealed off a large portion of the neighborhood and quickly erected a chain-link fence around the Park. A bulldozer began tearing up the newly planted lawns and knocking over swing sets. News traveled fast. By noon that day, several thousand protesters had gathered at the barricades, chanting, "We want the park!"

Tensions rose rapidly. Someone opened a hydrant. Some others toppled a bread truck. By the time Craig arrived, it was mayhem. The police fired tear gas; protestors began throwing rocks. In one image caught on video, a police officer and a protestor face each other, both gripping the officer's baton; in each trying to wrest it away, they pull each other into a strange, circling dance.

Then police backup arrived: the Alameda County Sheriff's Deputies, called in by Reagan's chief of staff, Edwin Meese III, and known to the protestors as the "Blue Meanies" for the way their riot gear helmets, jumpsuits, gas masks, and general demeanor recalled the villains of the Beatles' *The Yellow Submarine.* In Gitlin's words, "Amid rampant disbelief the deputies lifted shotguns to their shoulders and opened fire." At least a hundred protestors and a score of officers were injured in the melee, though both sides claimed many more. Police fired at a group of people standing on the roof of a movie theater nearby. One man was permanently blinded by shotgun pellets; another, James Rector, was killed.

With four hundred other protestors, Craig was rounded up and bussed thirty miles away to Santa Rita, where he remained for three days. For Craig, the swagger he'd felt when discussing the possibility of prison with fellow activists dropped away almost the moment he found himself actually locked up. The deputies stripped him down and treated him for lice with chemical blasts from a high-pressure hose. In the overcrowded holding pen where male protestors were mixed in with all the other men who'd been recently arrested, Craig witnessed a stabbing and a rape. He was terrified.

Eventually the guards separated the protestors and led them outside to the prison's yard. Alongside hundreds of others, Craig was forced to lie nose-to-pavement in the sun for hours while guards came by periodically to step on his head. "Commie pinko faggot" had long since lost its sting, but when one guard said, with real hatred in his voice, "You're a bunch of rich college kids. You don't know what a day's work is like," it stuck with him.

Even seasoned protesters were shaken by the use of shotguns by the police and by the death of James Rector. In the weeks following what quickly became known as Black Thursday, the Berkeley neighborhood around the Park became a militarized zone, its streets barricaded with razor wire and curfews enforced by the three thousand National Guardsmen called in by Reagan. For three weeks, protesters and soldiers faced each other across the Guardsmen's drawn rifles, into the barrels of which protesters sometimes slipped single flowers. Some protesters attempted to tease and provoke the Guardsmen into anger, but for weeks the standoff remained peaceful.

Which made what happened next especially shocking. One afternoon, protesters who'd gathered for a peaceful rally on the Berkeley campus began to hear a loud thudding. They looked up to see military helicopters flying low overhead. With almost no warning, the copters suddenly began to drop smoking canisters of tear gas onto the panicked crowd. It was impossible not to see the visual parallels between this and television images of the same helicopters dropping napalm on Vietnamese villages. As Ruth Rosen ran frantically, only to find police barring the plaza's escape routes, she thought in terror, "We're going to be shot at. We're the Viet Cong."

It wasn't as hyperbolic as it sounded—many of the law-enforcement agents were Vietnam vets and used the same military metaphors themselves. Years later, reports revealed that Reagan had accused organizers of having buried sharpened bamboo poles in the sod to booby-trap the Park. The wind off the

Bay picked up the tear gas and schoolchildren miles away had to be hospitalized.

For many, the weeks of People's Park protest became a turning point. As Yippie and antiwar activist Stew Albert reflected, "People's Park ended the movement, really. The repression was so brutal." A full year before Kent State would bring the same horror to a larger American public, many young, white activists suddenly felt shocked to realize that they could be killed by agents of their own government.

For some, the decision to leave was obvious—anywhere would beat staying to be mowed down by gunfire in a crowd. Others welcomed the invitation to expand the ideas that had inspired People's Park. A symbolic green space could never be free if population centers could be so thoroughly controlled by counterrevolutionary forces. "We're not going to change the status quo by living in the cities and fighting the cops, they're way too strong," Craig reasoned. "We're going to have to go up into the country and start new."

The center of the action had become, not just potentially or romantically, but actually dangerous. Craig also had the well-being of his wife and daughter to consider. Like most of the other arrested Black Thursday protestors, he had decided to take the offered plea bargain: the charge knocked down to a misdemeanor with one to two years' unsupervised parole on the condition that he leave California. His experience at Santa Rita had convinced him anyway that it was time to go.

The guard's accusation haunted him. Political activism had certainly felt like real work, but Craig knew what the man had meant, and what's more, he knew it was true. Part of what had made him walk away from his Joe College trajectory was that college forced you to spend your youth indoors, soaking up the abstract ideas that older generations had decided would best prepare you for an adulthood doing the same abstract indoor jobs they'd invented for themselves. And that was if you were even lucky enough to escape being sent to your death in an immoral war.

As he reflected on it, he realized that his deepest satisfaction in recent years had come from his time in Mendocino. There, a group of city kids had gathered around an old-timer named Hank who had opened his land to concerts and taken it upon himself to teach the newcomers whatever skills they wanted to learn— the less relevant to suburban life, the better. Under Hank's tutelage, Craig had learned how to change a truck's transmission, set a salmon weir, plant a garden, and shoot a rifle.

It was as he prepared to leave California for good, hoping to make it back East in time for a big concert in upstate New York, that he had started to think seriously about what it would be like to continue the education he'd begun at Hank's. What he wanted was a way to remain on the cutting edge of new ideas but with the threat of violence replaced by music and friends and getting his hands dirty every day with the work of shelter, food, and survival.

At Woodstock, Craig made straight for the Freak Out tent and volunteered to help talk down the kids churning through bad acid trips. The idea and staffing for the tents came from Wavy Gravy's rural New Mexico commune, the Hog Farm, who had also been invited by the festival's organizers to help serve as the security team—or, as Wavy Gravy dubbed them, the "Please Force." Gravy's wife Bonnie Jean (later Jahanara) had overseen the setup of a field kitchen. As the rain fell, turning the hillsides to mud and stranding concert-goers in their tents, Gravy announced over the festival's loudspeakers, "What we have in mind is breakfast in bed for 400,000"—Dixie cups of muesli delivered across the campgrounds by hundreds of volunteers. Over the course of the weekend, the Hog Farmers and others working in the Free Kitchens ended up serving thousands of simple, macrobiotic meals of beans, rice, and vegetables. Many people later credited the commune's unharried production and cheerful assurance that there was plenty to go around—seconds, even— with setting the peaceful tone of cooperation and unity for which Woodstock is often remembered. "We're feeding each other," Romney declared from the stage with his famous gap-toothed grin. "We must be in heaven, man!"

The Hog Farm's efficiency, generosity, and loaves-and-fishes ingenuity impressed Craig deeply. He wanted his own group, once he started one, to devote itself similarly to this essential, radical act of feeding good food to hungry people.

Now, just a year later, if Craig couldn't find a housing solution, it was his own beloved group who risked going hungry—or worse, drifting apart so soon after they'd come together.

Every evening now at Myrtle Hill, fewer and fewer faces appeared around the evening's fire. The nights had gone from refreshing to chilly to truly, bitterly cold. It was a genuine struggle for everyone to get out of their sleeping bags in the morning. If your clothes got wet for some reason, the sun no longer got hot enough during the day to get them fully dry, and it was too cold to go without. Even Chico, the New York architect who had spent all summer hammering together the dome's frame wearing nothing but a tool belt, had finally conceded to pants. Everyone had started spending what could have been good work time huddled around the cook tent's small Ashley stove, trying to get warm.

If Craig and the others didn't find a solution immediately, it was clear—Myrtle Hill, the forward-thinking, world-changing social experiment, would be over almost the moment it had begun.

Even though their own fate remained in limbo, should they still go ahead with the plan to build a barn for the animals, someone wondered? They had already begun gathering a pile of old boards and beams for this purpose. And that's when Craig and the others realized what needed to happen. No, they would not build a barn. Instead, they'd use the barn's materials to build a house for themselves. If they started immediately and worked fast, Craig was sure, they just might get it done before winter.

Loraine remained slightly skeptical—her Vermont childhood had meant occasionally trick-or-treating in snow boots—but she didn't have a better idea. She busied herself with putting away what she could of the garden's meager harvest and collecting the herbs she wanted for winter, hanging them in bunches from the cook tent's support poles to dry.

But she had to admit—it was like the men had suddenly flipped a switch and were now working at double speed, like a filmstrip racing in fast-forward.

The barn materials could not quite stretch for a whole house, Chico determined. They had no shortage of lumber on the land, of course, and they did cut some trees down to use as beams, but the walls required milled planks. A local sawmill sold them a truckload of slats for almost nothing, but they still fell short.

Five miles up the road, a huge construction project was about to get under way as the new interstate slowly worked its way north from Boston, headed toward Montreal. Two houses that stood in its path were slated for removal.

Politically, the commune opposed the new highway's trail of destruction as it sliced through hills and carved up communities, but in this case it offered them an opportunity they couldn't afford to pass up. Just hours before the houses' demolition, Craig, Fletcher, and a few others got permission to go in and scavenge any materials they could find. One New York member was a filmmaker who had a trove of movie lights, which he quickly set up to let them keep working through the night. The men went in with chainsaws and pulled out every salvageable piece of wood they could manage—flooring joists, doors, windows, beams—loading it all into the brand-new pickup truck they'd borrowed from Peg and Eliot at Entropy Acres. In the morning, the houses looked like they'd been chewed, and the pickup's shock absorbers never recovered, but Myrtle Hill had all the lumber it needed.

One problem still remained, though: manpower. With every frosty morning, the ranks of willing workers thinned as previously devoted communards took advantage of Myrtle's do-your-own-thing ethos and took off in search of someplace warmer in which to do it. Craig, Loraine, Fletcher, Nancy, Jim the Bear, the three children, and the others for whom Myrtle Hill was now, truly, their only home, needed help. Luckily, they knew where to find it.

CHAPTER 6

As enclosed and private as Myrtle Hill's land felt to its residents, the sudden presence of dozens of eccentric newcomers in a town of only a few hundred residents hardly constituted a secret. Many locals had spent Myrtle Hill's first season hovering uncertainly between curiosity and trepidation.

Early that spring, when news about who exactly had bought Freeman Brooks' back acres reached the village's governing body, the selectmen looked at each other in concern. The youngest of the three men, Charlie Barrows, was also the chair that year. No one said so explicitly, but Charlie knew his youth somehow made the commune's arrival his problem to tackle.

Charlie and his wife, Lois, had met at the state university a decade earlier. They were each among the tiny handful of their high school classmates to go to college—and, to their own surprise, almost completely alone in returning home after graduation instead of seeking out a more lucrative professional economy elsewhere. Charlie and Lois didn't have any friends their own age in town who shared their love of opera or with whom they could talk about books. It was a little lonely.

The town's elders embraced them immediately, however. They both got jobs at the local bank, and Lois threw herself into meticulously restoring their beautiful, 19th-century, ten-room brick house, right next door to the town hall. Lois had grown up working class in a southern Vermont town that had emptied out during the Depression, the farms bought up over the next few decades by vacationing city people. Her childhood home had lacked running water and electricity, and her new, well-appointed house remained her pride and joy for the rest of her life. While she and Charlie caused a minor scandal by applying a coat of vivid paint to their front door ("We don't have purple doors, we have white doors," a neighbor scolded them), they were not particularly rebellious. Charlie came from one of the town's most prestigious families. His parents owned a sizable portion of local storefront real estate, but Charlie's thoughtful, scholarly temperament left him disinclined to follow his father into business. Still, when his boss at the bank informed him it was his turn to serve on the select board, Charlie obeyed without complaint.

And now he'd found himself tasked with averting the strangest potential crisis to face the village in decades.

The problem wasn't an influx of city people per se—the local economy counted on summer residents from Boston, and everyone knew farmers who had cashed out by selling their land to wealthy retirees. Just recently, Charlie had helped put together a mortgage for three newcomers going in together on a parcel of land. The friends planned to build their own homes after they returned from working abroad—Charlie had listened, fascinated, as they'd described their time living in the Himalayas. But this new group felt different. The word "commune" had spooked Charlie. *Time* and *Newsweek* offered mixed portrayals—rosy for a while, but then, after the Manson murders, much more sinister. He didn't know what to think. The sea change that seemed to be sweeping through the whole nation had arrived with shocking speed in his tiny, slow-moving community. Somehow it had fallen to Charlie to navigate his town's sudden collision between past and future.

All summer, rumors had circulated in town about what was going on up on those old potato fields, behind the trees. No one could actually hear or see anything, not even a rising tendril of wood smoke, but long-haired hitchhikers suddenly popped up everywhere; it seemed like you couldn't use the pay phone in front of the diner without having to wait for young girls in dirty skirts to wipe their eyes and hang up.

The commune struck a lot of people as a bad idea. And Charlie, as he put it later, "tried to kibosh it."

He had started by going to Freeman Brooks in hopes of talking him out of the sale. He got there too late, but even if he hadn't, Brooks had no interest in this hysteria. The young buyer had struck him as earnest and hardworking—and besides, what a man chose to do on the privacy of his own land concerned no one but himself. Brooks had sent Charlie away. The family whose farm lay between the commune's land and the main road heard Charlie out, but even if they denied the hippies road access, as Charlie proposed, another route existed and they could just go around. The bad blood wasn't worth it. None of Charlie's other ideas had worked out any better. The commune moved in and spent the summer blissfully unaware of their opposition.

But Charlie still felt the expectation of the village elders weighing on him. One night, after an evening of drinking, he decided to take matters into his own hands.

Charlie's wasn't the only rural community nervously monitoring a commune's arrival. As it turned out for many localities, they had not misjudged the moment—1970 *did* become a watershed year in the personal, cultural, and political life of many rural regions.

In Vermont, the population rose by 15 percent in the 1970s. In the same decade, Oregon's population rose by 25 percent and New Mexico's by 28 percent. A 1975 *New York Times* article reported that rural populations had increased "perhaps for the first time in the history of the Republic."

While the number of exurban, rural newcomers continued through the decade, the back-to-the-land movement's first rush was, often startlingly to locals, also its most socially radical.

A perfect count is now, as it was then, impossible, but the most reliable scholarship indicates that at the height of the communal period, between 1970 and 1973, communal groups across America probably numbered in the tens of thousands.

"Communal societies have long been an American cultural fixture," notes the period's most prominent scholar, Timothy Miller.

Several of the European religious groups who arrived in America to escape persecution held communal living among their central tenets. While many eventually blended in with the mainstream, some groups with intensely held standards for lifestyle and piety continued to live apart, most famously and lastingly the Shakers, Mennonites, and Amish, all of whom arrived in America before the Revolution. In 1732, one group called the Dunkards established a monastic-like community near Germantown, Pennsylvania, called Ephrata; their communal living and self-sufficient economy lasted over fifty years. A century later, Bronson Alcott's Fruitlands had plenty of company: the Second Great Awakening saw huge numbers of utopian communal groups spring up across the Northeast—as many as eighty in the 1840s alone.

What makes the late-20th-century communal explosion so significant, Miller argues, is not that it is unique, but that it is by any measure, the largest and most widespread.

"In a period of just a few years, a communal fever gripped the alienated youth of the United States," Miller writes. To some degree, groups that might have existed at other times under other labels—artists' or political collectives, economically interdependent housemates, group marriages, cooperative religious societies, cults—came, starting in the late 1960s, to fall under the label "commune." But even restricting that term's definition to groups of unrelated adults living in close proximity, centered around a shared household economy and a self-conscious "sense of common purpose and of separation from the dominant society," this period boasts extraordinary numbers. At least twice as many communal living experiments existed in 1970 alone than in all the rest of American history combined.

Some observers have argued that the impulse toward communal living among hip young people followed naturally from their experience living in Freedom Houses during the Civil Rights Movement. Others point to this generation as kicking off the now-commonplace practice among middle-class young people of going to college far from home and living in peer-only dorms. Others see a clear continuity between the urban "crash pads" and collectives of the early hip scene and the rural communal retreats that followed. And a number of scholars give credit to the "widespread use of psychedelic drugs" as an important contributing factor. Certainly two of the most influential proto-communes—Timothy Leary's Hudson Valley mansion, Millbrook, and Ken Kesey's Merry Prankster–filled ranch in La Honda, California—both explicitly organized themselves around group LSD experimentation, undertaken in a context of privacy and freedom made possible by their nonurban settings.

While urban communes numbered in the thousands during this period as well, for a huge number of young people in the late '60s and early '70s, the impulse to live communally went hand in hand with the urge to leave the city.

In the fall of 1970 there were as many as fifty communes in Vermont, a state with fewer than half a million people. Two years later, one scholar would count two hundred.

Many groups kept entirely to themselves or limited their connection with other communes to those where friends, relatives, and former members had settled or those within borrowing-a-cup-of-buckwheat distance. In a lot of cases, as impossible as it sounds, "Hippy groups a few country miles apart were unaware of each other's existence," Robert Houriet reported. Some learned of a neighboring group only after a local at the post office or hardware store made the reasonable assumption that all the long-haired newcomers who had suddenly appeared around town must know each other. Most rural communards spent most of their time truly isolated in the backwoods worlds of their own making.

For some groups, though, particularly those with an overt political interest in the revolutionary power of collectives, developing formal networks and coalitions became a priority. In the fall of 1970, some of Vermont's more political groups began to spread the word about an event planned for "harvest time," a kind of hippie convention its organizers dubbed, "A Gathering of the Tribes."

Craig had gotten involved. Myrtle's urgent housing crisis still loomed, but in this social revolution now under way, the bigger picture was a priority too. Craig had always seen part of his role at Myrtle Hill as keeping in close contact with other like-minded groups. His connection with the New York communal scene had already proved an invaluable source of supplies and support. And so, though it meant more time away from the hill, he had volunteered to help spread the word about the Gathering. He and a friend called Cro drove to every commune they knew of or had heard about, passing along information and invitation.

This included the two couples at Entropy Acres, but they were overwhelmed—Peg and Eliot with a new barn-full of animals, and Chris and Ellen with caring for their newborn twins; none of them felt particularly drawn to communal collaboration anyway.

Cro's commune, where the Gathering was to be held, was a politically radical working farm on Vermont's far-northern border. The group's formal name was Earthworks (or sometimes Earth Air Fire and Water), but, like many other Vermont communes, it most commonly went by the name of its closest town: Franklin. The commune had been founded after a radical young UC Berkeley academic named Jim Nolfi had impressed a wealthy, progressive older couple with his Marcuse-inspired ideas about communal self-sufficiency as an antidote to oppression of all kinds. The couple had agreed to fund a commune where these ideas could be lived out in a practical experiment. Nolfi and his wife Barbara, together with a few other equally radical couples, including Cro and his wife Mary Pat, soon moved into a farmhouse and began farming with horses.

Like a lot of similar groups, Franklin held a dynamic tension between future and past. They saw themselves as working toward a revolutionary, ecological, feminist, postcapitalist, postnuclear-family future, for which they prepared by adopting the technologies of the past. They built themselves a horse-drawn wagon by cutting off the top of a VW bus and fitting it with stays. A visitor to Franklin recalled watching the scholar-radicals harvesting a crop of wheat, the women in their long dresses and the men in straw hats, like an image straight out of Millet.

On the weekend of the Gathering, several hundred communards from around the state arrived at Franklin to camp in the fields and converge for meetings and conversations on various topics of interest: solar heating, maple sugaring as a cash crop, the question of whether to stockpile arms for the revolution.

The group from Myrtle Hill eagerly embraced Craig's idea to take on the same role the Hog Farm had played at Woodstock: feeding the multitudes. Loraine oversaw the endless chopping of onions, potatoes, and whatever other donated vegetables appeared: the stone-soup model of meal planning. Some others set up a fire pit like the one at home, but with a grate big enough to hold the cleaned-out fifty-five-gallon drums that would serve as pots. Loraine filled these with rice or vegetables and water, monitoring the fires carefully to keep the food from scorching, as best she could. The meals were simple but massive, hot, and gratefully received. One night, as they gathered around a bonfire for the evening's meeting, the whole group linked arms and danced in a circle, singing, "Wearing my long wing feathers as I fly / I circle around / The boundaries of the earth." All weekend, the air hummed with a palpable excitement.

On the Gathering's last evening, Ravi Shankar performed, sitting on the front porch of Franklin's farmhouse. The frosty October air made it hard to tune his sitar, so he'd wrapped it in down sleeping bags. When he began to play, the hundreds of people sitting on the lawn sat in such rapt silence that even those in back could hear every note as it bounced off the surrounding hills and came back in an orchestra of echoes.

By the end of the weekend, the communards had discussed plans for a communal school, a newsletter, an ongoing system to barter and trade labor, a traveling medical clinic, a car-share program, and a people's bank, among other ideas.

And crucially for Myrtle Hill: the Gathering also elicited a life-saving response to their pleas for help. A new crop of workers would soon join them to construct what they were already calling the Big House. They had no time to waste.

One of the new recruits was a sixteen-year-old runaway named Amy. Amy had met Craig during his Gathering publicity tour when he'd stopped by the southern Vermont commune where she was living. The connection they made turned out to be the start of a lifelong friendship. When she came looking for Craig at Myrtle Hill's kitchen site at the Gathering, Loraine immediately put her to work chopping vegetables. Amy loved the experience of helping prepare the massive meals and, even more, of being part of such a vital and ambitious project. She quickly made herself indispensable. She had a bouncy, endearing charm, enhanced by her huge mane of frizzy, brown curls. She combined a teenager's open, fresh-faced enthusiasm with the physical and intellectual maturity of someone much older. Everyone she worked with immediately appreciated her quickness and good cheer. When the Gathering drew to a close, it went without saying that Amy would return with Craig, Loraine, and the others to Myrtle Hill.

It was time for her to move on in any case. Amy had left her home near San Francisco a few months earlier, shortly before her sixteenth birthday. For over a decade, starting from the age of three, she had been the victim of sexual abuse at the hands of her stepfather. When he finally went to jail (an extreme rarity in the 1960s and a testament to the egregiousness of the case), she felt like a jack-in-the-box that had popped free. No authority figure—certainly not her mother or anyone else who'd failed to protect her for all those years—had a prayer of telling her what to do. The streets were full of kids her age who had taken off on their own, and Amy found friends everywhere she went. She also couldn't shake the fear that her stepfather would somehow escape from San Quentin and return to kill her, as he'd threatened to do. Every night she woke rigid with terror from nightmares in which he broke out and knew exactly where to find her. Finally she thought, "Fuck this, I'm leaving." Just before Christmas, with the help of some friends, she left home for good.

A series of adventures took her across the country and deposited her a few weeks later at Johnson's Pasture. Among its cluster of sister communes, it was known as the Baby Farm—either because so many of its residents were teenaged runaways or because so many of them were pregnant. The group was spending the winter in a simple, two-story house they'd built out of re-claimed lumber covered in tarpaper with a big sleeping loft un-der its sloped shed roof.

One early spring day—just around the same time Craig, Fletcher, and Loraine saw the buck deer at Myrtle Hill—some visitors on motorcycles stopped by Johnson's Pasture bearing jugs of red wine to share. It was the first gorgeous sunny day of the year. Snow still lay heaped in the fields, but there was no question now that winter was in retreat. The day's warmth and thaw had charged the air with a contagious energy. In celebra-tion of this, plus the rare treat of having enough booze to go around, the young communards decided to spend the afternoon and evening having a party. Their youth, plus the fact that this was the first alcohol many of them had tasted for months, meant that by the time night fell, some people had already gotten ex-tremely drunk.

Amy had what she later guessed was a glass or two of wine, but alcohol always made her sleepy, so she left the group stand-ing in the snowy field and went inside to lie down. Others, sim-ilarly tired or drunk or making love, were crashing in the loft's other beds. At some point, Amy was joined by the boy who'd been her lover that winter.

Amy's bed was at the back of the house, where the slanted roof met the wall at its low end. That night, she had a dream so vivid she never forgot it: a devil with an evil leer and lurid, bright-red skin was flicking a whip at her face. Each time it touched her, she felt its sting on her cheek. The devil was screaming some-thing that it took her a moment to comprehend: "Get up!" the devil was shouting. "Get the fuck out of here!" She opened her eyes to a scene of chaos.

While everyone was asleep, someone had kicked over a can-dle. Now the whole house was ablaze. People were screaming and running in the smoke-filled dark as flames licked over the roof.

As Amy groggily came to, she heard the dream-devil say, "And get him out of here too!" She hauled the boy sleeping next to her upright. He was heavy and naked and passed out cold but she screamed and pulled. Somehow they both made it the full length of the loft, burning chunks of roof raining down around them, to the single window on the far side. Then they jumped.

The moment his bare feet hit the snow, the boy, Mark, came to and took off, stark naked. He ran a mile and a half over frozen fields to pound on the door of the nearest neighbor who had a phone. After delivering his message, Mark collapsed in shock. He had third-degree burns all over his face and body from the melted tar that had dripped on him as he slept under the sloped roof. Amy had similar, though smaller, drops scattered across her face—the whip flicks she had felt in her dream.

The neighbors immediately called the fire department. "The hippie commune is on fire," they told the dispatcher before hastening to take care of the naked, badly burned boy in their living room. This message turned out not to be specific enough. There were two communes on the same back road. When the firefighters mistakenly arrived at Total Loss Farm, its alarmed residents quickly joined them in heading back out toward Johnson's Pasture. The dirt road there was so steep and rutted that, in mud season, there was zero chance of a fire truck getting through. The firefighters, aided by the Total Loss communards, had to hop out and push their four-wheel-drive Jeep, containing a portable hose pump, through the thick mud in the darkness.

By the time they arrived, it was too late. There was nothing they could do but hose down the cinders and attend to the group who had been standing on the hill for over an hour, watching in horror as the house, with some of their friends still inside, burned to the ground. Several people had attempted to get back in, but the flames were too intense. A pregnant girl could not find her husband. "Where is he? Where is he?" she kept screaming.

Four people died that night, the pregnant girl's husband among them. The other three were teenagers, two boys and a girl who had arrived at the commune only the week before. The fire at Johnson's Pasture was the deadliest recorded accident at any American commune during the period.

Mark was rushed to the hospital in Brattleboro. Eventually, three others with less serious injuries joined him. One girl injured her back and ankle jumping out the second-story window;

another burned her hand. The third was Amy. Her arm and back were red with burns—she realized later that on her dash across the loft she had run, not just through smoke, but through the fire itself, something she never would have been able to do if she had been fully conscious.

At first, she didn't want to go to the hospital. She had already packed snow onto her arm and, in her shock, the burns didn't feel painful enough to risk interacting with authorities who might somehow discover that the name she'd given was fake and send her back to California. And too, she, like the others, couldn't bear to turn away as the firemen went about their grim work.

Their friends at Total Loss Farm tried to offer help. "Would they come home with us to beds and coffee and a real brick chimney?" Raymond Mungo wrote later, "No they would stand and stare at the ruins, rooted rooted rooted to the earth until morning. And then?"

In the months following the fire, the survivors tried to rebuild and to keep the commune together. But, understandably, it was never the same. For Amy, the invitation to live at Myrtle Hill came perfectly timed. It was also, more importantly, the beginning of several vital, lifelong friendships that would carry her into adulthood.

The afternoon she drove to Myrtle Hill for the first time was a perfect, Indian-summer day, the sky intensely blue over the fiery, scarlet hillsides. Crowded in the back of the pickup truck, everyone sang as they bumped along. Fletcher belted Irish brogues in a beautiful, rich baritone. For the rest of her life, Amy would remember that afternoon as the day she came home.

The commune's newest residents found spaces for themselves and settled in. Amy stayed in Craig's tipi. Another couple, calling themselves Pancake and Hershe ("like the syrup"), arrived from Franklin a few days later and claimed an old Chevy station wagon that had permanently come to rest at the edge of the lower field, near the spring. They all got to work immediately.

The urgency of the situation infused every day with a focused intensity, with sheer adrenaline insulating them somewhat against the bitterness of the wind. Everyone contributed, according to his means: Jim the Bear and Chico had the most construction expertise; Craig excelled at getting people motivated; Loraine, aided by Amy, kept everyone fed; Nancy minded the children; Hershe helped build and took over care of the animals; and everyone else pitched in wherever they were needed. But it was Jed, the New York City mountain man, who emerged as the true hero that fall.

All summer he had bounced between Myrtle Hill, the newly founded Earth People's Park, and his family's shop in the city. But there was no questioning Jed's commitment to Myrtle Hill or his central status as a group heavy. When he drove up after a time away, everyone was glad to see him. He had never failed to hop down from his truck at the top of the road without unloading a cache of thoughtful, vital offerings—lumber a friend had "liberated" from a construction site or a fifty-pound bag of oats or a bike for the kids.

And now that they were in crisis, his contributions became literally lifesaving, none more so than a gas-powered generator and accompanying power tools, without which this whole construction project would have been impossible instead of merely insane.

One day, just as Loraine began to truly worry whether her lean-to's roof would give in and soak her under the first, wet snow, Jed appeared with another godsend: a giant Army tent.

They set it up immediately and moved the Ashley woodstove in, cutting a hole in the canvas for the stovepipe. Someone built a triple-high row of bunks along one end. It was better than being outside, but the nights remained frigid. Hershe quickly learned to be careful when sleeping in one of the top bunks: they were so close to the roof that in the morning, if you sat up too quickly, you could poke yourself in the eye with the icicles that had formed in the night from the frozen condensation of your own breath.

A few weeks later, when the first snows came, the communards made room at the far end of the tent for the cows. Their pleasant body heat and soft animal noises in the night mitigated somewhat the intense smell of manure.

Under the circumstances, the house went up with surprising speed. Following instructions in the copy of *The Owner-Built Home* Craig had ordered after seeing it listed in the *Whole Earth Catalog,* they put up a two-story, 24' × 32' structure next to the dome in the lower field. On the front, its two rows of windows faced the short way across the field, collecting the southern light; the rear north side had no windows, the better to block the wind.

The layout of the house was starkly simple: upstairs, a sleeping loft, reachable by ladder. Downstairs, an open common room finished with floorboards pulled from the condemned houses. A wood-burning cookstove, a sink, and shelves for food demarked one end as the kitchen; the other end held the Ashley and a big table, crowded with chairs. The house's only interior door closed off the builders' most ingenious coup: the privy. The tiny extension off the main room had ferro-cement walls and contained only a simple seat. Hidden beneath it was a fifty-five-gallon drum that, when full, could be accessed from the outside, sealed with a lid, and replaced. Its original design, conceived and planned around the summer's campfire, called for collecting and using the methane gas; in the absence of a workable system for this collection, though, the barrels were ultimately dragged out to a field and spread as fertilizer. The tiny shitter was chilly but nowhere near as cold as trekking to the outhouse. Most amazingly of all, it didn't stink.

The Big House had no phone, electricity, or functioning place to bathe, but it did have a kitchen sink with running water. Earlier in the fall, they'd succeeded in putting in a well (an attempt to dig one by hand hadn't worked, so a professional had finished the job for them). Someone had found an old pump for the sink, sparing everyone the backbreaking task of hauling their water from the spring.

As soon as she got the go-ahead from the builders, Loraine set up the Big House kitchen and surveyed their stores: a few big bags of rice, soybeans, and various flours; a huge tin of honey; and the few pounds of rutabagas and turnips that were all she'd managed to put away from the summer's haphazard garden. It wasn't much, but they wouldn't starve.

One early December afternoon, everyone finally moved out of the tent and into the finished house. The sleeping loft had some vicious drafts, but just having a layer thicker than plastic or canvas between themselves and the wind was a huge relief. Craig had been right: they'd managed to build an entire house, big enough for all of them, all by themselves in under two months.

The very next day, it snowed three feet. The Army tent collapsed, suffocating one of the cows.

The winter days were astonishingly short, but they began to take on a rhythm. In the morning, whoever woke up first would come down and stoke the fire in the cookstove to heat up the kettle of water carefully left out the night before. This water was specifically reserved for pouring over the sink's pump to thaw it. Once that was done, you could pump another kettle of water to boil for coffee.

In the evenings, when the dishes were done and the kids were in bed in their corner of the upstairs loft, the adults pulled chairs around the Ashley stove. After passing a joint from their carefully rationed supply, everyone would take turns reading aloud from *God Bless You, Mr. Rosewater* by the light of a kerosene lamp, warming their hands around mugs of tea from the wild mint and chamomile Loraine had gathered and dried that fall. For Amy especially, these evenings would remain among her most-cherished memories.

So few remained that everyone now had enough space to carve their own bedrooms out of the open loft by hanging blankets and tapestries for walls. These didn't achieve privacy, exactly, since they didn't block the sound at all, but they let you avoid bothering others if you wanted to stay up late, reading by candlelight.

During the day, there was no time to rest. The minute they finished the Big House, a new, urgent round of work presented itself: the focus on building first the dome and then the house meant that no one had figured out how to obtain a winter's supply of firewood.

Bundled as best they could against the cold, Fletcher, Amy, and the others headed out again into the snow, with saws and a wooden toboggan to collect branches and haul them home. The Ashley and the cookstove gobbled up everything as fast as it was cut, but not even Loraine could coax anything more robust than a smoky, miserly fire. Finally a neighbor who'd been watching them toil like ants in the woods, waist-deep in snow told them this was because they were burning freshly cut, green wood—for good, hot fires, they should have cut, split, and stacked the wood months ago to give it time to dry. But what could they do? Even if they'd had any money to buy some, the local supply of dry cordwood had been long since snapped up. As Fletcher reflected with typical irony, the daily work of cutting and hauling trees warmed them up, at least.

For Amy and Hershe, cutting wood provided the added satisfaction of working alongside the men, of lifting and hauling and feeling themselves grow strong, of spending the ever-shorter daylight hours outdoors, and—though they didn't think of it in these terms yet—of participating in what was clearly understood as the "real" work of the commune, in contrast to Loraine's endless hours in the kitchen and Nancy's efforts to keep the children from going stir-crazy.

One night, after thick flakes of snow had fallen past the windows for hours, Loraine decided it was time to reveal an amazing surprise: in the first few weeks of the summer, she'd managed to make and bottle a batch of dandelion wine. When she poured it into empty mason jars for them to drink, it looked, in the flickering lantern light, like liquid sunshine. There was plenty to go around. It tasted like rusty, bitter cough syrup and was surprisingly strong. Everyone got giggly. Then someone suggested they take some sleds down to the end of the commune road and over to the neighbor's high, sloping hayfield. They all bundled up and headed out. For the next few hours they whooped and shrieked across the fields, racing and rolling through the thick, cold powder before collapsing on their backs, the fat white flakes dropping into their eyelashes from the dark sky, the whole earth tipping softly beneath them.

Nights like this made them remember why they had chosen this life together, but they also had to admit—everyone was completely exhausted.

The frantic push to get the house up had been complicated further by a mysterious illness that had run through the group that fall, hastening the commune's already-steep attrition rate. Finally, someone had returned from a Thanksgiving visit home to their parents' with a diagnosis for what ailed them all: meningitis. A local doctor confirmed the diagnosis and told Craig it was a miracle no one had died. Others weren't so lucky: several groups battled outbreaks of the hepatitis that had killed a southern Vermont communard a year earlier, and the members of at least one group contracted tuberculosis.

Craig had been laid up alone in his leaky, drafty tipi for two full weeks, feverish and shivering, too weak to do anything but sip the herbal infusions Loraine brought him. Craig missed his daughter intensely, but when he thought about his ex-wife's decision not to join him and raise their baby at Myrtle Hill, he fluctuated between sadness and relief, particularly as the optimistic glow of summer wore off and the life-and-death stakes of what he'd undertaken began to sink in.

Craig's illness, combined with the endless press of urgent projects—and the fact that no amount of discussion about leaderless groups and consensus decision-making stopped him from wanting to be in on every element of planning or the others from coming to him with every new problem—had left Craig utterly depleted. What he needed was a period of rest and recuperation. Despite his pride at having gotten the house up in time for winter, he dreaded the thought of spending the next few months cooped up there. He decided it was a good time to expand the tour of communes he'd begun leading up to the Gathering of the Tribes. Only this time, the tour would be nationwide.

Just before the new year, Craig and his friend Cro, joined by Fletcher and Fletcher's five-year-old son Jason, embarked on a cross-country road trip, waving goodbye as they headed down the road in Craig's truck—the commune's last working vehicle.

From a summer high of nearly one hundred, Myrtle Hill's residents had shrunk to a handful: Loraine and four-year-old Amelia; Nancy and eight-year-old Bryn; Amy, almost seventeen; and Hershe and Pancake. Years later, Craig would refer to this group as "the homebodies," but Hershe put it more succinctly. The people who stayed through that first winter, she said, were the ones with no place else to go.

CHAPTER 7

Craig's truck was too slow and elderly to make it across the country, so he arranged to leave it with a friend in favor of picking up a Driveaway car, a souped-up Chevy Z27 Camaro, small but fast. The car's owner needed it in Oakland, but not for a few weeks. Craig, Cro, Fletcher, and five-year-old Jason hit the road.

The men had a loose wish list of groups they wanted to visit as they made their meandering way across the country. Fletcher wanted to go back to Drop City. Cro was interested in the cluster of communes around Taos. Craig's destination was California. His best friend had gotten restless in Canada and come back to the US, his draft board issues still unresolved. Craig had heard he'd gotten involved with a small, direct-action street theater group whose politics were turning more and more radical. Craig wanted to check up on him.

But even en route this trip had a mission that went beyond adventure. The four of them were emissaries, connecting their northeastern network of communes to the nationwide communal explosion that was just about to reach its peak. Craig and Fletcher wanted to learn from other groups' experiences, to bring some of the best ideas back to Myrtle Hill—and, hopefully, to avoid others' catastrophes.

The first stop was in Tennessee.

The Farm was seventeen hundred acres of hilly farmland, seventy miles south of Nashville. By Myrtle Hill standards it was immense: several hundred people were living in tents and school busses spread out over the commune land. Eventually, the group would establish several cottage industries, including a variety of soy products (including what some consider the first soy ice cream), a solar panel manufactory, a robust printing operation, and—most famously—a world-leading midwifery practice. But at the start, the group survived on cash crops of organic soybeans and sugarcane, members' savings, and donations from supporters of The Farm's charismatic leader, Stephen Gaskin.

A few years earlier, Gaskin, a Korean War vet, had begun delivering spiritually themed lectures on Monday nights at San Francisco's Free University. His lectures incorporated a wide range of traditions and theologies into mesmerizing, free-form sermons that soon began drawing crowds in the thousands. When the mood in the Haight started to sour, he and a group of followers bought a tract of land in rural Tennessee and decided to start a new community. The whole group—two hundred people—drove across the country in a caravan of remodeled school busses and converted bread trucks.

Craig admired The Farm's collective yet entrepreneurial economy. They had more rules than Myrtle Hill—members had to take vows of poverty and eschew all animal products, including honey and leather; ashram-like, they also had to accept Gaskin as their spiritual leader—but there was still plenty of personal freedom and an open embrace of psychedelic drugs as part of a healthy spirituality.

One hundred miles to the east was another Tennessee county with a long future ahead of it as a center of rural communal living—in particular, for the LGBTQ community. Today, the area around Short Mountain is home to as many as a dozen different groups—what one writer called "a kind of sexually nonconforming Amish country." In the late 1970s, activist Harry Hay founded the Radical Faeries, drawing explicit connections between gay manhood and a spiritual embrace of nature. But long before the Faeries adopted Short Mountain as their most important homeland, rural enclaves across the country held a particular appeal for those forced to live in the closet. For many, the backwoods offered a measure of privacy and freedom that would have been impossible in the city, and a utopian chance at inventing a less-oppressive society. For lesbians, the confluence of the feminist, gay rights, and back-to-the-land movements led to a huge number of women's land communities, many of which are still flourishing—one scholar recently counted ten in southern Oregon alone.

From Tennessee, Craig, Cro, Fletcher, and Jason headed west. In Missouri they spent a few nights with a group that was supporting itself by selling homemade natural peanut butter; elsewhere they stayed at an abandoned resort in the middle of the desert. Once, when they saw an eagle that had been killed by a car, they stopped to gather its feathers.

At night, driving through the Midwest while the others slept, Craig opened up the Camaro on the long, straight flat roads, the gas stations and small towns of America shooting by outside the windows in the otherwise empty darkness.

Some of the communes Craig would have most liked to visit were not on the itinerary. Already, even though the national movement was only just reaching its height, a few of the period's most influential and important communes had already come and gone.

Morningstar and Wheeler's Ranch

In 1962, a gregarious bass player named Lou Gottlieb decided to invest the profits from his career with the popular group the Limeliters into some northern California real estate. He bought a thirty-two-acre ranch in Sonoma with a plan to subdivide the property and sell it in lots. It wasn't until 1966—after he'd quit the band and discovered LSD—that it occurred to him to make the ranch his home. Gottlieb, forty-two, had recently met Stewart Brand, who had brought up the idea of a rural retreat. As Gottlieb remembered it, "Stewart was talking about having a 'back-forty' in the country and I told him, 'Well, I have one. Let's go take a look at it.'"

He was joined by some friends, including Ramon Sender. Sender was an avant-garde composer who'd escaped the Spanish

Civil War as a child, after his mother was killed by the fascists. Sender had a lifelong affinity for communitarian experiments of the past, and he brought this perspective, crucially and influentially, to the forward-looking experiments of this new era.

Before he became friends with Gottlieb, Sender had been married to a great-granddaughter of John Humphrey Noyes, the founder of the Oneida Community. That group, started in 1848, had three hundred members at its peak and lasted for almost forty years. The Oneida Community supported itself with a variety of cottage industries, including most famously the silverware and cutlery company that still exists today. The community's members lived and worked together, practiced a form of free love called complex marriage that actively discouraged monogamy, and brought up the children as a group. The community ultimately couldn't survive Noyes' attempts to hand over control to his son and it folded toward the end of the 19th century.

In the late 1950s, Sender and his wife traveled to Oneida, New York, to visit her grandparents, who were still living in an apartment in the mansion that had formerly been the group's communal house; her grandfather had been born there, a product of Oneida's experiment in planned breeding. Inspired by what they saw, the young couple soon joined a group called the Bruderhof (formerly, the Society of Brothers), a pacifist Christian community that had recently arrived in America from Germany. That group still exists, supporting itself in part by making wooden toys and children's furniture.

Though Sender quickly left that group, disliking its then-practice of self-flagellation (his wife remained), the communal elements of that experience had appealed to him deeply. He wanted to try something similar but without the extreme practices. Sender had also spent some time with Ken Kesey and the Merry Pranksters and had witnessed the way that a group of artists living in close quarters gave rise to an endless variety of collaborative innovations. And so it was Sender who first suggested to Lou Gottlieb that he use his Sonoma ranch for a purpose beyond personal retirement.

At first it was just a few couples, pooling resources, sharing meals, roaming amid the orchards and redwoods, and basking in the near-paradisical splendor of Northern California. One perfect afternoon, the group dropped acid under the redwoods and shared a collective vision of the Virgin Mary, "the manifestation of all mother-love." Around the same time, someone discovered that the ranch's original name had been Morningstar, a symbol of the Virgin. This confluence further united the group in their growing conviction that their little living experiment had some important destiny.

Then, in March of 1967, one of the Diggers called Lou Gottlieb with a request.

That spring, as the coming Summer of Love began to gain national attention, the street-activist Diggers—alone, it seemed to them—were doggedly preparing for a mass influx of homeless, penniless teenage runaways. The Diggers had set up a Free Medical Clinic as well as a Free Kitchen in the Panhandle of Golden Gate Park, where they served simple, hot, daily meals that included miniature loaves of bread baked ingeniously in coffee cans.

Ever-resourceful in their gathering of supplies, the Diggers had heard about the orchard at Gottlieb's ranch and were calling with a proposal: "Could we send a detachment up to take care of the orchard in return for the apples?" they asked. "Don't call me, I'll call you," Gottlieb told them. But it didn't take him long to make up his mind. "Okay, it sounds right," he said.

And like that, Morningstar became "The Digger Farm." The Communication Company, a duo who had obtained a Gestetner printing machine and made it their mission to blanket the Haight with Digger missives, immediately began publicizing. "The Diggers are starting up a farm. They need help," read one handbill. Another consisted of a two-column, handwritten wish list of farm supplies—trowels, rabbits, a spike tooth harrow, sleeping bags—titled "Digger Farm Needs." Within weeks, Morningstar began receiving waves of visitors, arriving by the vanload or hitchhiking the fifty miles north from San Francisco.

At first, the visitors came out of curiosity and to offer help, as requested. They helped put in a huge garden and brought tools, supplies, and necessary staples (often including "the sacrament," marijuana, which was not yet a viable crop at Morningstar). The ranch's two houses quickly filled up. Tipis and tents began to dot the woods and meadows, soon followed by lean-tos, tree houses, and other simply built shelters.

A dazzled *Time* magazine reporter wrote, "The new-found trip of work and responsibility reflected in the Morning Star experiment is perhaps the most hopeful development in the hippie philosophy to date." The communards put an ad in the local paper, inviting collaboration with locals: "Morning Star Diggers will swap work and organic vegetables for what have you. Diggers are determined to find a way of living that's human, person-to-person. Money makes life impersonal. It's our hope at Morning Star to establish a system of barter with our neighbors." When local law enforcement stopped by to check up on the commune after a sixteen-year-old resident showed up in the local hospital with a yeast infection, even the county sheriff wasn't immune to the magic of the place: "I was charmed," he said later. "I came back to the office and kidded the guys that I wasn't going to be around much longer—I was going to defect."

The commune's residents marveled at the land's seemingly endless ability to absorb the newcomers. Visitors also noted what was then a new phenomenon: huge numbers of young people who had been raised in a comfort that still awaited them if they chose to return to it, now living by choice in intensely austere conditions. To describe it, Ramon Sender coined the phrase "voluntary primitivism."

As many contemporary scholars pointed out, a disproportionate number of those living in states of voluntary primitivism hailed from backgrounds of affluence and privilege of many kinds. One sociologist found that 70 percent of those he interviewed came from families that earned well above the median income. A key motivation, he surmised, was that the "primitivism" was in fact entirely voluntary.

While family background doesn't automatically reveal itself in a glance around the fire circle, many observers noted the overwhelming whiteness of most rural communes. The year before

Morningstar became the Digger Farm, Gottlieb invited his friend the singer Nina Simone for a visit. As he proudly showed her around, she turned to him. "Lou, there aren't any black people here," she said. "Well, what can I do?" he answered. "I want them to come, but we don't invite people. They just show up."

Yes, they did. As the Summer of Love approached and the scene in Haight-Ashbury became ever more chaotic, Morningstar soon became a sought-after retreat for the strung out and exhausted. The resident communards, with their spiritual sensibility and vision of the farm as a kind of ashram, made it their mission to minister to new arrivals. Gottlieb, Sender, and the commune's other founders were still awed by the peace that rural living had brought to their own lives—it would be selfish to deny others the same.

"Morningstar is remedy," someone said, and the motto stuck. As many rural communes saw it, visitors often arrived "suffering from various degrees of urban sickness," as one observer put it. "Some will leave again after a few weeks; others will stay and possibly be cured. In this sense, communes are therapeutic." Newly established country communards were not so different from many other exurbanites before and since, for whom urging the transformative joys of country living on those still suffering city ills became a central mission.

Many groups, including Myrtle Hill, explicitly saw themselves as demonstrating the possibilities of a new society. Their mission was to provide both an alternative and a corrective to American culture. Because part of what they were protesting was the closed-in nature of mainstream society, a central emphasis of the antidote was openness—to experience, to the earth, and to each other. For many communards, any discussion of restricting membership felt uncomfortably, immorally, like reproducing some of the worst elements of the society they'd left. As Sender put it later, "Society's problems were coming to Morningstar to be healed, and no one was willing to stand in the way of whatever it was that was happening."

But as almost every group quickly found out, not everyone who arrived was interested in—or capable of—being healed.

As Morningstar's acres began to fill up with those escaping the Haight, Lou Gottlieb's commitment to serving his fellow seekers and the land itself took on increasing urgency. A particularly drunken group of semipermanent residents had been raising hell for several weeks, partying with motorcycle gangs, and shaking down newcomers for cash to buy alcohol. When one of them pulled a knife in the local grocery store, Gottlieb felt he had no choice but to ask them to leave.

Afterwards, Gottlieb suffered from an excruciating headache accompanied by cold sweats and intense bouts of weeping that left him shaken and chastened. It was clear to him that his illness was a message from the Divine. He had made a terrible mistake. He would never kick anyone out again.

Over the next few months, his resolution evolved into a philosophy: "Land Access to Which Is Denied No One." As he explained it, "Open land means simply that God is the sole owner of the land and that we, as His children, are not meant to fight, quarrel, and kill over the land, but rather to share this natural resource—to each according to his needs." Gottlieb's own evolving spirituality convinced him that embracing Morningstar's chaos and relinquishing all control was important form of ego-reduction.

"Relinquishing control" could also be seen as a practical response to events on the ground, given that control had rapidly become impossible. By early summer of 1967, it had become clear that the experiment under way at Morningstar had taken on a momentum of its own.

The most momentous issue was sewage. Even the relatively modest early influx of visitors had immediately overwhelmed Morningstar's four toilets and left the plumbing permanently incapacitated. The commune's members had taken this development in stride and embraced the practice of *al fresco* elimination. ("Shitting in the garden . . . is a spiritual act, as well as a constitutional right," Gottlieb liked to tell visitors.) The encouraged practice was to dig a hole and leave everything well buried, but the sheer number of people passing through, along with Gottlieb's philosophical resistance to instituting any formal repercussions, made this hard to enforce. Gottlieb, following advice from a sympathetic ecologist, started construction on a bathhouse. The communards enthusiastically began digging a sewage trench and leach lines by hand. They hadn't adequately calculated what would happen when they hit the old lines, though, and soon they were digging knee deep in untreated sewage. That summer, the whole commune was stricken with a hepatitis epidemic. In the Haight, the Diggers posted warning signs: "Please don't come up to Morning Star!" Three hundred visitors arrived that same weekend, undeterred.

It wasn't long before neighbors started to complain about the smell. It was just one item on a litany of complaints: there was the endless noise from chanting and late-night parties; the increased traffic; the free-roaming dogs that menaced local sheep; the wandering hippie girl who had felt sorry for a pastured show horse with its forelock in its eyes and given it a career-destroying haircut. Then there was all the nudity. And the couples fornicating in broad daylight in easy view of neighbors. And the small items that constantly went missing from local homes and stores. And the carelessly tended campfires in a region recently devastated by wildfire.

In the late summer of 1967, a petition was circulated in the community by Morningstar's closest neighbor. At a public meeting called to address community concerns, he complained aloud, "Grow your hair long and don't take a bath. Then you don't have to obey the health laws and you can set a fire anywhere you want." A few minutes later, another woman stood up to announce that her husband's coat had disappeared from her clothesline earlier that day and that one of the communards present was currently wearing it.

Lou Gottlieb was formally served with a cease and desist order until he could get the facilities at his "organized camp" up to code. On hearing this charge, Gottlieb reportedly replied, "If you can find any traces of 'organization' here, let me know and I'll destroy them immediately."

"We're not here to discuss your philosophy," the judge responded. "We're here to discuss toilets."

The county officials were patient at first with Gottlieb's good-faith efforts to improve Morningstar's sanitation facilities (the bathhouse was eventually completed at five times the originally estimated cost and broke down immediately). But it was clear that he had no control, and no interest in controlling, the endless influx of homeless young people now pouring out of San Francisco. Under pressure from Morningstar's neighbors, the county cracked down.

Gottlieb spent the next year in and out of court, arguing for more time to make changes while his detractors argued that every minute the Morningstar chaos continued was a minute too long. At a moment when the commune's future looked particularly dire, the group decided to throw a huge party. The Allman Joys and the Steve Miller Band played and hundreds of visitors poured in. The party was a grand success, but it destroyed what little support remained in the community.

The county started fining Gottlieb $500 every day that anyone but he and his immediate family was found to be living on the property. Frequent law-enforcement spot-checks encouraged the most hassle-averse residents to move on, but many remained. Soon, the communards and the police entered into an almost ritualized cat-and-mouse game: the cops would show up and the commune's residents would scatter—sometimes caught, sometimes not. Eventually, Gottlieb racked up fines reaching to the six figures.

After months of meditation and reflection, Gottlieb struck upon a new solution: if open land was an attempt to restore property to its rightful Owner, why not make it official? In May 1969, he legally signed the deed to his ranch over to God.

Perhaps not surprisingly, this made national news. County officials were still rolling their eyes at this latest twist in the saga when an Arizona woman filed a suit claiming that, since the lightning that had burned down her house had been an act of God, He owed her for damages. The Sonoma ranch He had recently acquired would fit the bill nicely. When a prisoner at San Quentin claimed that he himself was God and thus a competing claimant for the property, the joke was over as far as the

California court system was concerned. "Whatever the nature of the Divine, God is neither a person, natural or artificial, in existence at a time of conveyance and capable of taking title," ruled the judge. Regardless of philosophy, Gottlieb was still legally accountable for Morningstar's fate.

Two months later, the county moved decisively against Morningstar: it sent in bulldozers and reduced every structure but Gottlieb's house to rubble.

But Morningstar's influence and notoriety had already spread beyond its physical presence. In March 1968, a year after the start of the "Digger Farm," recently elected Governor Ronald Reagan had given a speech in which he promised, "There will be no more Morningstars."

That same week, some Morningstar residents were eating dinner at the home of a neighbor. Bill Wheeler, heir to a sewing machine fortune, had retired from his father's real estate business at twenty to become an artist. He had been living in an old farmhouse near Morningstar off and on since 1963, but he and his wife Gwen had recently moved into the studio they'd built on a remote and otherwise uninhabited parcel of land. As the Morningstar residents recounted their latest troubles to the Wheelers over dinner, a woman named Near-Vana boldly challenged him: "Why don't you open your land?"

It was not the first time Wheeler had thought about it. He admired Gottlieb's philosophical steadfastness and had visited the commune often enough to understand its underlying ideal of community and cooperation. And, he admitted later, "I wanted a place in history." Before being asked point-blank if he would open his land, he hadn't realized (or discussed with his wife) that he had an answer ready: "I never closed it," he said.

Morningstar's residents didn't need any further encouragement. Several dozen made their way over and immediately disappeared into the canyons. The idea of Land Access to Which Is Denied No One had found a new home in Sonoma County.

Wheeler's Ranch, as it was soon known, had a lot to recommend it. For one thing, it was over ten times the size of Morningstar.

Wheeler's 360 acres encompassed high, open meadows and deep canyons sheltered by redwood trees. At Morningstar, anyone walking around nude was almost certain to be spotted by a neighbor; here, even someone trying to spy would have difficulty most of the time. Wheeler's access road was steep and awkward, which would prove a helpful deterrent to police cars and motorcycle gangs. Rather than dissuading residents, the difficult terrain encouraged people to construct more permanent living quarters than the tipis and lean-tos of Morningstar. One family built a treehouse; others built tiny cabins out of reclaimed lumber and split cedar. The group established gardens and a shared bread oven. Before long, minicommunities had sprung up in the canyons, as distinct and insular as neighborhoods. Fifteen babies were born at Wheeler's over the years, to healthy mothers. At its peak, the permanent residents numbered over two hundred.

But despite the quieter circumstances offered by the land, Wheeler's Ranch could not escape the same problems that Morningstar had experienced.

For one thing, the only drivable road onto the land crossed the property of a neighbor. Jack O'Brien had emigrated from Ireland as a boy. He had spent his Depression-era adolescence plucking chickens in Petaluma before entering the mortgage business and becoming a self-made millionaire. Not only did he hate to see the hard-won rural idyll of his retirement years despoiled, there was something that irked him personally about what he saw as the flagrant do-nothingness of his hippie neighbors and their silver-spoon landlord. As at Morningstar, what started as a tense but civil relationship between neighbors soon escalated to open animosity.

Though they couldn't see or hear as much as Morningstar's neighbors, locals near Wheeler's Ranch still complained of the roaming hippie dogs that menaced and sometimes killed their sheep. When Bill Wheeler agreed to limit the number of dogs allowed at the commune (his own were grandfathered in), he met resistance from the group. What exactly did open land mean? Was it even Bill Wheeler's place to tell anyone there what to do? Amid the tremendous spirit of community and cooperation, there were once again deep disagreements over what it meant to be perfectly free.

It's possible that, given time, the community at Wheeler's might have resolved these issues for themselves. But four years after county bulldozers razed Morningstar, the treehouses and hobbit holes of Wheeler's Ranch met the same fate. One afternoon Bill Wheeler and his second wife returned from a trip to town to the sound of engines and the sight of all their possessions piled under an oak tree. The studio that had been their home was a now a pile of rubble. When the bulldozers left that night intending to come back the next day and finish the job, the communards decided to take things into their own hands. One by one, they burned every structure on the ridge to the ground—all fifty of them. The next day, they greeted the county workers with the news that they'd beaten them to their task; following orders, the bulldozer operators insisted on removing every last scrap.

Morningstar East/Reality Construction Company

Bill Wheeler was not the only young, wealthy landowner to be influenced by Lou Gottlieb. Michael Duncan, heir to an industrial fortune, purchased a high, remote mesa near Taos, New Mexico. In the summer of 1969, he turned the 750 acres over to the use of two communes. Both groups were offshoots of earlier experiments, but that was just about the only thing they had in common.

On the northern side of the mesa was Morningstar East, started by a group of fifteen or so "refugees" from Lou Gottlieb's open-land experiment. The group spent the first summer industriously building a large adobe pueblo, but its "do what you feel" ethic meant there were not many further communal efforts. There were no outhouses or formal kitchens, though big meals were prepared on an outside stove several times a day.

Before long, almost one hundred people were living at Morningstar East in a collection of tipis, buses, small houses, and hogans. Countless hundreds of others passed through. True to Gottlieb's philosophy, the land remained open to whoever wanted to make it their home. It quickly attracted the original group's same motley crew of "mystics, winos, runaways, and hermits."

A few months after the people from Morningstar arrived, Duncan's mesa became home to another, very different experimental group. Reality Construction Company was the brainchild of Max Finstein, one of the founders of another early southwestern commune, New Buffalo. Finstein had left that group after only a few months, in frustration over what he saw as the insufficient work ethic and spiritual frivolity of some of the other members.

He had spent the winter of 1968 recruiting young radicals from New York and San Francisco to his new project. Reality Construction Company had an explicit mission: to prepare for the coming revolution and to protect themselves against imminent attack by fascist forces. The group spent the summer furiously molding eighty-five tons of earth into adobe bricks and constructing a long, ten-room residence with a communal kitchen and dining room and a nearby outhouse. The group had strict work requirements and a closed membership policy. Visitors were strongly discouraged—occasionally at gunpoint— partly to protect any members sought by the feds for draft dodging or other offenses and partly to protect themselves against the ceaseless wave of freeloaders that were taxing the resources of other groups like Drop City, New Buffalo—and, just a few hundred yards away, Morningstar East.

"Nowhere had I found such diametrically different communes so close together," wrote Robert Houriet. "The two communes represented the extremes with which the movement had begun: the political revolutionaries . . . and the children of faith and fantasy."

But the contrast reveals another split as well, between what each group hoped rural living would offer them. For Reality's urban revolutionaries, living far from society in a remote location promised a sense of security not possible in the city. They could literally create and police a perimeter, controlling access by outsiders. They built a checkpoint across the only road; it was impossible to sneak up on them. In addition, self-sufficient farming and building was for them, as for many, less-revolutionary others, an attempt to relieve anxiety about "the system's" impending demise.

For Morningstar East too, building and farming, at least in theory, were part of the appeal of an alternative rural life. But the intention of Land Access to Which Is Denied No One was a promise of total freedom, a place that imposed no restrictions whatsoever. In Sonoma, the external forces that had shut down Gottlieb's experiment had come from county authorities, spurred by the disgust and frustration of local "straights." Trying again, in an even more remote location and with hipper neighbors, was a renewed attempt at perfect freedom.

However, the diametrically opposed emphases of the two groups on Duncan's mesa brought them into conflict almost immediately. Water, always a source of tension between neighbors in the arid region, brought Reality's near-paranoid obsession with preparation running smack into Morningstar's resistance to planning even a moment into the future. Reality also made it a point to gather firewood only in the national forest. Though this meant relying on trucks to make the twenty-mile journey, it preserved the mesa's scarce piñon trees for a moment of greater need in the revolutionary near future—as one member explained it to a visitor, "When we don't have any gas to get out, that's when we'll need the piñon to stay alive." Morningstar's members shared neither the politically driven sense of doom nor the emphasis on planning and foresight. Their survival strategy, if one could even be articulated, centered around the belief that whatever was needed would manifest itself: they got cold, and turned to find firewood growing right there, a gift from the universe.

In the beginning, the notion had been for the two groups to share fields between their camps. But by the end of the summer, only one group had managed to put in any crops. When hungry Morningstar residents started to filch corn from Reality's fields, the revolutionaries responded with bullets.

No one was injured, but by the time Craig and Fletcher's road trip brought them to the area, any idea of collaboration had officially ended. The next year, Michael Duncan kicked both groups off his property and built a fence across the road.

New Buffalo

Max Finstein's original commune, New Buffalo, remained together, however.

In the spring of 1967, Finstein and eleven friends acquired a
piece of land near Arroyo Hondo, New Mexico, bought for them
by Rick Klein, another wealthy young heir who was systemati-
cally giving away his inheritance to groups he found deserving.
New Buffalo was one of the earliest rural communes founded
with an explicit goal of premodern self-sufficiency. Their original
hope was to live as much as possible like the region's native people. The commune's name referred to the Plains Indians' practice of using every part of the buffalo—the American bison might
be close to extinction, but now communal living could serve the
same life-sustaining function.

Romanticizing Native Americans was nothing new—as Fred-
erick Jackson Turner famously pointed out, Anglo admiration of
and nostalgia for Indians' way of life began almost the moment
that Anglo cultural domination in North America became permanently assured. The heroic mystique of the Wild West had sat-
urated childhood culture in the 1950s—now older, some of those
children chose to proclaim their rebellion by identifying with the
Indians instead of the cowboys.

"How can you get any further from white middle-class America
than trying to live like an Indian?" one New Buffalo resident explained to a visitor. At New Buffalo, "living like an Indian" meant
a mélange of practices drawn from or inspired by the Navajo,
Hopi, and Plains Indians. Like many of their peers, the communards wanted a new way of life that would allow them to both
critique the material excess of the dominant culture and replace
it with a spiritually grounded, ecologically friendly version. "Indian" life represented a satisfying protest and solution in one.

While some communards, including at New Buffalo, did seek
out Native American neighbors as friends and mentors, for many
others, declaring one's "Indian-ness" meant wearing moccasins,
buckskin, and headbands, living in tipis or adobe houses, eating squash and beans, and partaking in peyote rituals—acts,
however reverently intended, that did not necessarily require

interaction with actual Indians themselves. Historian Philip J. Deloria notes that the 1960s–1970s represents just one chapter in a long history of white Americans "playing Indian" as a way of constructing and defining an oppositional identity of their own— New Buffalo's communards were closer, in this way, to the rebellious, red-face-donning protestors of the Boston Tea Party than to their own, village-dwelling Pueblo neighbors.

Dennis Hopper spent a few days at New Buffalo during the cross-country motorcycle tour that served as research for *Easy Rider*. Just as in the film, he picked up a hitchhiking Buffalo who brought him back to the commune. When Hopper later asked permission to shoot on-site at New Buffalo, the group gave it careful consideration but rejected the idea, worried about opening themselves up, both to publicity and to Hollywood's crude understanding of their vision. As it turned out, they were right to be suspicious—in the movie, the protagonists stop by a commune (re-created in the Hollywood hills) where a group of beautiful but filthy, spaced-out young people crowd together in a dark, low-ceilinged kitchen where goats roam freely. Later, the Peter Fonda character, "Captain America," watches as blond, bearded men shuffle through dry fields, scattering dust. "They're city kids," explains Fonda's guide. Hopper's character is skeptical: "They ain't gonna make it."

"They're gonna make it," Fonda says, with prophetic assurance.

In a way, he was right.

New Buffalo went through years of tumultuous changes, including the abandonment of almost all the "Indian" practices, an experimental stint as a dairy farm, and a tense period in the 1980s during which one family drove all the other residents away until eventually being evicted themselves. New Buffalo continues to exist as a privately owned but still cooperative, ecologically oriented community.

But all this was still in the future when Craig, Cro, Fletcher, and Jason stopped by on their way west. They found the group living in the commune's long, multiroomed adobe house to be welcoming and open, not yet visitor-weary. They stayed a short time before pushing on. Drop City was only a few hours away.

*

Their host in Colorado was a friend of Fletcher's named John Curl. Curl had been one of the very earliest Droppers, but he had recently moved out. He explained the reasons to Fletcher.

After Drop City's sudden rush to fame, the original group had never recovered its equilibrium. As Peter Rabbit wrote, "Drop City was continually overcrowded. The level of consciousness decreased—too many people—the energies were hopelessly dispersed. The kitchen was filthy, the food tasted shitty, disease continuously ran through the commune . . . Nobody knew anybody else. People would stay a month or so, get themselves a little straight and travel on. The Droppers were going on the same trip over and over again: coolin' out the runaways, speed freaks and smeck [sic] heads, cleaning up after them, scroungin' food for them, playing shrink and priest confessor—round and round and round." By 1969, several years before the nationwide commune movement would reach its apex, all of Drop City's founding members had left.

A few Droppers, including Peter Rabbit, resettled nearby in a new community designed with the lessons of Drop City in mind. Residents of Libre would live cooperatively and share vehicles and other resources, but this would not be an experiment in group living. New members had to be accepted by the whole community. Everyone could build whatever kind of house they chose—as long as no neighbors could see it. Before long, the road winding up Libre's Greenhorn Mountain led past a gorgeous collection of domes, zomes, and other eccentric designs, including one house whose steeply peaked roofs were modeled on the crystal structure of garnet. Peter Rabbit lived in a zome that he proudly told visitors was a Steve Baer–designed "four-fused exploded rhombic dodecahedron."

Libre's emphasis on interdependence and community, rather than communal group living, turned out to work for its members. The collection of beautiful, unique houses remains intact, with several of its now-elderly founders still in residence.

Drop City, though, was another story. As in all things, it was ahead of its time.

Craig and Cro were ready to press on, but Fletcher wanted to stay in Colorado a little longer. The men said goodbye, promising to meet back up in Vermont in the spring. Eager to show his son the first hippie commune, the place that had changed his life, Fletcher stopped by Drop City one afternoon. He was horrified at what he found.

After the founders' generation left, no subsequent arrivals managed to restore any lasting stability. The gorgeous, bright-painted dome city had been more or less abandoned to the use of biker gangs, drug addicts, and whoever else might pass through looking for a free place to stay. Even as the commune movement continued to spread like wildfire across the country, Drop City was already a "dome ghost town," its otherworldly structures dis-integrating into the landscape almost as fast as they'd appeared.

CHAPTER 8

A t Myrtle Hill, the winter population had dropped to three. Shortly after the New Year, Nancy had left, taking Bryn and Amelia with her.

Somehow it hadn't been totally clear during the summer's whirl of visitors and friends how much the commune's basic economics relied on the generosity of those physically present. Myrtle Hill, the nonprofit entity, owned the land in common but the group had no other formal, shared finances. When the commune's population evaporated, its resources vanished too.

Cars, for example. If Loraine needed to mail a letter or make a phone call, she had to walk three miles down into the village. Even if she'd had any money to buy groceries at the general store, carrying them home meant slogging uphill along the road's shoulder through waist-high snowdrifts. She'd made this trek once, in a snowstorm, hiking up one side of each drift and down the other. It had taken three hours and left her shredded with exhaustion.

A few times, though, she caught a ride home from someone who would have once seemed her most unlikely ally: Charlie Barrows.

The previous summer, after weeks of trying without luck to stop the commune, Charlie had finally decided to go see for himself what was going on up on the old Brooks lot.

One evening, after fortifying themselves with drink, he and two friends drove up the hill from town and turned slowly onto

Myrtle's rutted dirt road. When they arrived at the lower field where the dome stood half-finished, Craig came out to greet them. Charlie couldn't say later exactly how he'd imagined the leader of a hippie commune would behave, but Craig's clear, warm gaze and firm handshake shattered whatever sinister image he'd had in mind. Charlie offered Craig the six-pack he'd brought along and the men sat down to talk.

It turned out that the questions each had about the other—"Who are you and what do you want?"—could be asked and answered straightforwardly. Craig explained his group's ideal of solving the world's ills by undertaking a life of cooperation and simplicity. He described his experiences in California and at Woodstock. Charlie, ever curious about all the places he read about but did not dare to travel, listened intently. He understood now: this group that had sounded so dangerous under the label "commune" was just a bunch of ex-college kids, not so much younger than himself, trying to invent a new way of living. He recognized the frustration Craig described, of feeling herded into an airless future chosen for you by an older generation, and, though he knew he would never choose this particular escape route for himself, he admired their bravery. When he drove back down the hill a few beers later, he felt not only a new appreciation for Myrtle Hill's experiment but also the excitement of having made new friends.

Over the next few months, he and Lois had begun to keep an eye out for the newcomers, but in sympathy now, especially as the snows fell and the men departed. Whenever they could, they offered rides. Loraine spent more than one night in a spare bedroom in the Barrows's big house, too tired for the long, cold walk up to Myrtle Hill. Lois had no desire to emulate the communards' extreme style of life—as she put it, "I've been there, I've done that, I grew up with that—no plumbing, no electricity. I was happy to come out of that chapter of my life. If you folks want to do it, enjoy. I did not enjoy it." But she found they had lots of other things in common—books they'd read and recipes they wanted to try. All of them were politely curious about one another and eager to share.

It took years for anyone to fully realize how crucial an alliance this was for the hippie newcomers. Charlie and Lois's embrace of the communards seemed to tip the town's wariness away from alarm and toward a watchful tolerance. But even more directly, the Barrows's openness to both their fellow townspeople and the commune placed everyone in the tiny community into a friend-of-a-friend relationship and offered both sides a reliable source of information about the other. Now when locals raised concerns about the commune or its residents (though, Lois acknowledged, they did so less and less in her presence), she and Charlie could assure them that Myrtle Hill's experiments did not pose a danger—at least, not to anyone but themselves.

As Loraine spent the short winter days in the Big House focused on inventing scarcity-driven recipes from the dwindling food supply and keeping warm drinking mug after mug of raspberry-leaf tea, she could at least be grateful that Amelia was not there.

After the Gathering of the Tribes, Nancy had gotten involved with some of the other, more radical communes that had begun discussing a kibbutz-style school for commune children. Unlike some of the other big ideas floating around, this one had found organizers, a source of funding, a dedicated teacher, and, at the last minute, a space. The commune school, to everyone's excitement, had rapidly become a reality.

The question of what to do with school-age children faced many parents at remote, rural communes across the country. Lots of groups sent their kids to local public schools, though reliable transportation could sometimes be a problem if the district didn't offer bussing and if the group shared Myrtle Hill's ad hoc relationship with working vehicles. Just by going to school and coming home again, commune kids could find themselves navigating major cultural and philosophical differences and distrust running in both directions between radical groups and their more conservative districts. For communal groups who mostly kept to themselves, the presence of one or two children in public schools might be their only interaction with the community. For a second-grader, it could be overwhelming to find yourself the focus of an entire town's curiosity.

Homeschooling had its pros and cons as well. Even in midsized communal groups, the children's social circle often included only a few others; if you didn't luck into age-mates, you could find yourself playing alone. A houseful of idealistic young adults, though, could become an amazing educational resource, with an exciting range of teaching styles and expertise. Many children raised on communes agree that one clear advantage of having so many adults around is that you could almost always find someone to read to you or to help with a project. But as with many other communal undertakings, consistency and follow-through often remained more elusive than creativity and enthusiasm. For college-educated parents who assumed a similar trajectory for their offspring, a creeping worry that their kids might fall behind on basic skills often led them to seek out more stable educational arrangements.

Formally starting a cooperative alternative school appealed to lots of communal groups as a solution to these problems, but for other reasons too. Orienting themselves around education became, for some groups, a way of further turning their philosophies into action and fulfilling a mission to influence the wider culture. More practically, establishing a school could nicely explain, socially and legally, the reason a group of unrelated adults and children were living together.

The school Nancy was helping start was called Red Paint. A sympathetic back-to-the-land couple had offered the temporary use of their comfortable, durable farmhouse (later, the school would move to an old, country inn with a big ballroom where the kids could ride their bikes all winter). Loosely following a kibbutz model, participating communes could send their children to stay at the school for weeks or months at a time. The children would benefit from a thoughtful, politically progressive education, and a richer social life, leaving their parents free for the all-consuming work of self-sufficient farming and revolution (at places like Franklin where the adults were actively engaged in "smashing monogamy," it was particularly helpful to have children occupied elsewhere). In addition to the permanent full-time teacher, each commune would assign one adult to work on the staff and to provide a familiar face for the children who would be living far from their parents. Nancy had volunteered to be Myrtle Hill's representative.

Shortly after Christmas, she, along with Bryn (eight), and Amelia (four) caught a ride two hours away to Red Paint. At the last minute, Amy decided to join them. She was curious about the school. It was not entirely clear even to her whether she, as a teenager, fell more into the category of child-student or adult-staff member, but it ended up not mattering. She loved the kids and they loved her. Plus, the school's building was warm.

The promise of warmth and a more varied diet than she could provide was also what prompted Loraine to send Amelia away for the whole winter with no regrets. With Nancy, Amy, and the children gone, by the start of 1971, the winter residents of the Big House had shrunk to just herself and the new couple, Hershe and Pancake.

Forty years later, Loraine and Hershe would still talk to each other almost every day, but at first they didn't always get along. Loraine cultivated an earthy witchiness—with her herbs and elixirs and her big, owlish eyes behind curtains of brown hair—that contrasted sharply with Hershe's blonde, brassy, Earth Mother glamour. Hershe had a hippie girl's long, straight hair, but her blue eyes were flinty and clear. Where Loraine was soft and tended toward a romantic dreaminess that elided any conflict, Hershe was hard and practical and never, ever backed down from a fight.

Hershe's autobiography would start, "My grandfather wanted me to believe in God and my father wanted me to believe in country. But I wanted to believe in myself."

In California this had meant surfing—pooling babysitting money with a girlfriend to buy a giant longboard, sweet-talking bus drivers into letting her wedge it between the seats on the ride to Ocean Beach, and spending every possible moment in the water, testing herself over and over against the waves.

When the war escalated in '65, her father got transferred to yet another base—this time, to Pearl Harbor. Hawaii was a revelation. On the first day of her senior year at yet another Catholic military school, she was surprised to find herself amidst a crowd of Filipinos, Japanese, and Koreans, one among a tiny *haole* minority. The pleasure of this discovery was only enhanced by her elders' displeasure with it—the grandmother who refused to stay in anything but whites-only hotels remained convinced there'd been some terrible mistake. When Hershe accepted a date with a Japanese boy, her father told her that the only conceivable reason she'd have done such a thing must be that she was suffering from low self-esteem. When he offered her a cure—$20 to buy herself a new dress—she ripped up the money in his face.

Everything about Hawaii heightened Hershe's already burgeoning sense that the army-base world of her childhood had no bearing on the world she actually longed to live in. More than anything else, it invited her to reconsider what it meant to be American. Hawaii had only been a state for six years when Hershe arrived. When she learned the story of how the islands came to be annexed by the US and of Queen Lili'oukalini's forced abdication, it was almost impossible not to make a connection between that act of colonization and the country's current conflict, the one that kept her father coming and going on overseas trips and brought him home late at night with document bags under his arm, stamped TOP SECRET in angry red letters.

Hershe began to absorb everything she could about what was happening in Vietnam, every leaflet and protest banner further crumbling her trust in her parents' version of the truth. As a final project in a high school class, Hershe challenged her father to a debate over the correctness of the US presence in Southeast Asia. The next fall, a semester at the University of Hawaii gave her even more ammunition for their fights. Her seven brothers and sisters watched with cautious, sympathetic curiosity, but none of the rest of them could muster the bravery it took to tangle with the Colonel—in her courage and ferocity, Hershe was alone.

The summer before college, Hershe worked outside Honolulu at the Dole cannery, which suffused the surrounding neighborhood with the scent of pineapples. At the end of a long day sorting fruit on a conveyor belt alongside three thousand other women, Hershe dashed into the locker room and tugged off her hairnet, smock, and the gloves and mask that protected her skin against a daylong barrage of pineapple acid. From her locker, she pulled an evening gown and prepared for her second shift of the night. As soon as the mirror assured her that everything was in place—dress, hose, heels, false eyelashes, full makeup, hairpiece, and gloves (satin this time)—she hopped on a bus to Diamondhead base. Here, her job as hostess at the officer's lounge was demanding in a different way: smiling until her face hurt, pretending to be flattered by the lewd ogling of men her grandfather's age, giggling at the crude jokes of soldiers whose jobs she associated with the murder of Vietnamese children.

The war kept her father constantly traveling, and in his absences, Hershe took to disappearing too. Once, she hiked with five boys in the Kalalau Valley—a wilderness of steep, waterfall-embroidered hillsides. They picked their way through thick brush, on paths made by the cattle that the *paniolo*, the Hawaiian cowboys, had let loose on beaches only approachable by boat. It was her first experience of wilderness, of leaving behind every comfort and convenience and relying only on her own strength to draw her forward. With every rock she scrambled over and every branch she shoved back with bramble-torn arms, the heavily enforced *musts* and *must-nots* of her girlhood dropped away with the same ease and clarity she'd felt while surfing. Amidst the exuberant green of the hillsides, she began to feel like herself.

A few weeks later, she convinced a friend to drive her up the Pali Road to a mountain overlooking Waikiki and to leave her there with only a liter of water and a loaf of Wonder Bread. She walked, fasted, and meditated for several days, looking down at the world she'd come from, now reduced to a smallness she could at last contemplate.

She hiked down changed. The next time her father left for the war, she left home too, for good.

In San Diego, she immediately scandalized her grandparents by sunbathing in the backyard of their retirement condo in a bikini. When they asked her to leave, she realized that she had no further sources of support but no obligations either. She was entirely on her own, her whole life hers for the making. It was 1967 and she was eighteen. She headed for San Francisco, straight into the Summer of Love.

Within a few days she was living with an ever-shifting group of kids in a second-floor apartment in the Haight. Downstairs lived a knot of speed dealers and junkies whose fights sometimes spilled into the street; the people on the top floor did yoga and meditated all day and never ate meat or did drugs not found in nature. Everyone on Hershe's floor was into the music scene. One of her new roommates was a Brit who limped from childhood polio and worked as an MC at the Avalon Ballroom. He could get Hershe in for free on Wednesdays when the bands rehearsed. She saw every show she could: Grace Slick, Janis Joplin, the Dead, Steve Miller, Country Joe and the Fish. To support herself, she rented a sewing machine for $25 a month and made clothes for bands like Big Brother and the Holding Company: loose shirts and bellbottoms sewn from the batiks and Indian prints she bought cheap from the neighborhood's import stores.

For a while the Haight was heaven. But pretty soon it began to seem like everyone had crabs or the clap or was miserably pregnant. The teenyboppers crashing in Hershe's apartment were getting ever younger and more helplessly stoned.

After a truck driver who'd picked her up hitchhiking propositioned her aggressively, forcing her to leap out at a traffic light, abandoning her purse with her wallet and ID, she decided she'd had enough. "I've got to get out of here," Hershe thought. She couldn't stop thinking about redwoods. She wanted to sleep under ancient trees as tall as the sky.

In Santa Cruz, she stayed at a commune called Holiday where residents hewed chunks of sandstone from the riverbank and sold carvings to try and support themselves. When she got tired of that scene, she caught a ride to the next place on the counterculture network. All of her belongings fit in one backpack. Moving between crash pads and communes every few months wasn't that different, she found, from moving between army bases. The difference was, every move now was her own decision, made for her own reasons. She had never been shy, never worried about talking to new people, about making or keeping friends. Some man or other was always offering her a ride or a place to stay— she chose as she pleased whose invitation to accept and on what terms. Her boldness carried her into whatever room she felt like entering and carried her out again if she didn't like what she found there.

One day, she ran into a friend who was headed east, to Maine, to join a new commune that was starting up. There was space in the van. Without thinking twice, Hershe climbed in. The trip itself turned out to be a drag—the driver was a crazy man who would only stop for gas, ignoring even the most urgent requests for bathroom breaks. By the time they hit the East Coast, Hershe never wanted to see him again, never mind join a community with him. When they made a short detour into Vermont, to a music festival on the campus of Goddard College, she hopped out and did not look back. Though she would never have believed it at the time, she had arrived in the state she would call home for the rest of her adult life.

She met Pancake that afternoon. Wandering around the campus, she saw a tall, skinny boy sitting on the grass, playing an unplugged electric guitar. He had long, dark hair and an appealing, shaggy, Frank Zappa look. The brim of his fedora was covered in peanut butter.

"Why do you have peanut butter on your hat?" she asked. He looked up at her standing above him—tall and strong with high cheekbones and a waterfall of blonde hair, like a hippie version of an all-American cheerleader. He met her direct gaze with a warm, goofy grin. "It's in case I get hungry," he said. "I have a very strange stomach and I have to be prepared for starving." She laughed and sat down. He had been kicked out of college in Boston for a midnight caper that involved traversing a rooftop to the girls' dorm and now he and some friends were spending the summer traveling between music festivals in a VW bus with "Free Timothy Leary" painted on the flank. Hershe thought he was the funniest, smartest person she'd ever met. A few days later when his bus headed off for the next adventure, Hershe was aboard.

When their travels deposited them at Franklin, they made room for themselves by sleeping in the barn. She volunteered to take care of the horses and to teach the commune's kids to ride. In fact, it was the kids, ever curious, who came up with her new name. Nothing goes better with Pancake than syrup, they decided. And what better syrup than Hershey's? She shrugged, but it became the name she answered to for the next several decades.

And Franklin was also the place she'd finally found a way to settle down. She'd always loved animals, but the satisfaction she found living amid the smells of horse sweat and hay and manure went much deeper than nostalgia. She had taken riding lessons at Camp Pendleton, but there, the soldiers had done all the grooming. In Franklin, she quickly learned how to hoist a hoof between her knees to clean it, to cinch a saddle firmly into place, and to push her fingers into a horse's mouth to slip a bit behind its teeth. The experience of quickly mastering skills she'd been raised to consider beyond or below her abilities gave her a new focus. The boldness that had led her through years of restless adventures now coalesced into a new kind of confidence: independence could mean not just coming and going at whim but also providing completely for herself, with her own hands.

At Myrtle Hill, that meant milking and cutting firewood and mucking out the chicken shed in the snow. As unpleasant as these jobs sometimes were, Hershe preferred them to staying inside all day and going crazy with cabin fever. This was lucky for all of them, particularly the animals, because neither Loraine nor Pancake particularly embraced the winter's outdoor work.

Loraine was getting out of bed later and later these days, but she was still doing most of the cooking and baking. Pancake had no problem spending the short daylight hours indoors meditating or curled in a sleeping bag reading, without getting restless as Hershe did. When she needed his help with something he was amiable about it, but his mind was always elsewhere. He liked the outdoors in a going-for-a-walk kind of way, but the endless physical challenges presented by farming in the woods with no electricity did not appeal to him.

Despite the fact that all three of them were sick to death of undersoaked beans and were never fully warm, it was nice, in a way, to have the commune's usual bustle and chaos reduced to a contemplative stillness. In fact, Hershe had taken to spending whole days in silent meditation. To let Loraine and Pancake know she wasn't just ignoring them, she wore a sign around her neck: *In Silence.*

One late-winter afternoon, she was upstairs when she heard voices outside and the sound of the front door pushing open.

A few weeks earlier, Loraine had hitchhiked one hundred miles south to her hometown to pick up new glasses from her father's optometry shop (eye-strengthening exercises aside, she couldn't read without them). On the way back north, she had stopped at the large, rambling farmhouse in Barnet that had recently become Tail of the Tiger, the American headquarters for the Buddhist teacher Chögyam Trungpa Rinpoche.

Trungpa was the author of the best-selling *Born in Tibet*, which detailed the monk's escape to India. From there, still in his early twenties, he moved to England and later Scotland, where he took over the first Tibetan Buddhist monastery in the West and taught meditation to many Westerners, including David Bowie and later Allen Ginsberg.

Shortly before moving to the United States in 1970, a car accident left Trungpa badly injured. Partly due to this experience and partly to startle his Western students out of empty reverence for "exotic" teachers, Trungpa gave up his monastic vows. He smoked, drank, and had affairs with his students, but he also led rigorous meditation practices and excelled at explaining complex Buddhist teachings to his Western listeners. Tail of the Tiger (now Karmê Chöling) was Trungpa's first teaching center in America and one of the first Tibetan Buddhist mediation centers in the US.

When Loraine stopped by, the center had only been open for a few months and she was curious about the famous ex-monk and his house full of devotees. Except for the Buddhist knots painted on the farmhouse door, the house itself was not so different from other communes she had visited—a cluttered kitchen smelling of wheat germ and tamari, long-haired white people in shabby work clothes milling around.

When Loraine tried to imagine a Buddhist monk in this setting, she expected someone distant, robed, and otherworldly. But when she finally saw Trungpa enter the farmhouse's shrine room, she was shocked. When he walked out to lead everyone in morning meditation, he had an air of calm authority, but he was dressed only in a flannel shirt and long johns. This easy informality made Loraine bold. After everyone had stood up and started wandering out of the room, she approached Trungpa and told him about Myrtle Hill. Before she left, she gave him directions and invited him to stop by sometime.

And now he had.

Visitors that winter had been rare (and therefore welcome), but this was more like a visitation. After weeks of near-silence, suddenly the kitchen was filled with voices.

A snowstorm had recently dropped a foot of fresh powder over the already-buried driveway, so Trungpa and the dozen or so acolytes he'd brought with him had been forced to hike the half mile from the main road, sinking in snow up to their thighs. Trungpa was limping by the time he reached the Big House. Loraine greeted him at the door and offered him the seat closest to the Ashley stove. Then she set about conjuring from their meager stores a meal worthy of this occasion.

By the time Hershe climbed down the ladder that connected the upper floor to the kitchen, a party was under way. Pancake was telling stories and keeping the guests laughing. Loraine was chatting brightly as she stoked the cookstove's fire under a huge pot of rice. Before coming down, Hershe had been of two minds about whether to break her silence for the party, but she decided to keep her sign on as she moved through the crowd, helping Loraine with the cooking and relishing her role as observer.

Trungpa seemed thoroughly comfortable, laughing with Pancake and warming his hands over the Ashley. Some of his entourage, though, seemed less enthusiastic. They were mostly women, tall and blonde—to Hershe's eye, Scandinavian and with a faint but unmistakable aura of money about them. A few wandered over to help Loraine in the kitchen. Others arrayed themselves around Trungpa's feet and made a show of hanging on his every word. He ignored them completely. Bottles appeared from somewhere and Trungpa accepted one and took a deep swig. One of the men lit up a joint.

It took three hours, but finally the cooking smells signaled that the meal was ready. Loraine had called on every ounce of her considerable talent to pull together a feast. The ingredients were simple, but each dish was well-seasoned with Loraine's store of dried herbs.

Hershe carefully filled the first plate and carried it over to Trungpa. Holding it in both hands as she offered it to him, she bowed slightly and laughed. He looked up at her, meeting the laugh but dismissing her gesture of deference. "No," he said. "You're my teacher today." He pulled a piece of nori seaweed from his pocket. "This is what I will eat tonight."

Years later it occurred to Hershe that he might have been politely demurring—Loraine had worked wonders but when it came down to it, this was still a plate of beans and rutabagas. But then Trungpa said something she never forgot. Indicating her "In Silence" sign, he said, "You have far surpassed me in meaningful mediation." It was the greatest compliment of her life. She imagined the eyes of the Scandinavians boring into her back as she turned away, smiling.

The dried fruit Loraine had served for dessert had come from a stash she'd discretely put aside where no one else would find it. Hoarding ran against almost every important communal principle—an ominous symptom, some observers noted, of impending collapse. But Loraine had her reasons.

At Christmas, just before everyone left, she and Fletcher had walked down to the village general store to pick up a crate of oranges someone had sent as a gift. The box was too heavy for them to carry, so they stuffed the oranges into every available pocket and sleeve for the long, snowy, uphill walk home.

As soon as the others saw the fresh fruit tumble onto the table, the rinds absurdly bright with the intoxicating promise of juice and sugar, they fell on the oranges and devoured them immediately. Loraine kept a number aside for herself. When someone protested, she explained. This wasn't hoarding, she told them, she needed the vitamins.

She was pregnant. Of all the philosophy-in-action plans that had swirled around the campfire that summer, the one she had personally undertaken had the highest stakes. The baby, she told everyone, was the whole commune's. She had embraced the spirit of the collective and deliberately ensured that no one could know for certain who was the father.

CHAPTER 9

As far as everyone over at Entropy Acres was concerned, spring could not arrive fast enough.

A few times, Loraine or Hershe and Pancake made the three-mile trek over to the farmhouse for the rare bliss of a hot shower, but the dirt road past the boarded-up lake houses didn't see much traffic in winter, so there was no hope of hitching a ride. They would have gone more often if it weren't such a slog to walk—instead of improving as the days turned warm, the road moved straight from ice into boot-sucking ooze.

The two couples at Entropy had encountered some winter obstacles of their own. It quickly became clear that a good portion of what Peg and Eliot had pulled out of the farmhouse the summer before in their enthusiasm to renovate had actually been insulating material carefully layered by generations of previous owners in response to the house's vicious and particular drafts. All of them had shivered through the winter, bundled in thick wool hats and sweaters. Chris, Ellen, and the babies had a little Ashley woodstove in their bedroom, but it was still cold.

Peg and Eliot's room sat directly above Chris and Ellen's. Removing materials to expose the upper bedroom's pine floor and the lower bedroom's lovely old beams had left them with a single layer of rough, gappy planks between the two rooms. It's possible this helped with heat a little bit, but it didn't help at all with sound. It seemed to Peg that the babies had cried more or less nonstop all winter—though it might have only felt nonstop because there were twice as many babies.

The insulation problem was exacerbated by the fact that they, like Myrtle Hill, had neglected to stock firewood during the summer. At the last minute they'd bought the only available supply without thinking to ask whether or not it was dry and thus had spent the last few months trying to warm the leaky house with puny, greedy green-wood fires.

The clothesline over the living room's woodstove held an endless number of perpetually damp cloth diapers. Entropy's farmhouse kitchen had running hot and cold water but no washing machine, let alone dryer. The double loads of dirty diapers would soak outside in a tub until someone, usually Ellen, got a chance to run them through the wooden, hand-cranked washing machine they'd moved from the lawn into a shed when it started snowing. After you loaded the laundry and the powdered soap into the washer's tub, you poured in hot water hauled in buckets from the sink and turned the crank to run the agitator. Then, after you dumped the dirty suds and repeated the whole process with a fresh round of rinse water, you fed the laundry one item at a time through the wringer—two close-set parallel cylinders that turned on another crank and squeezed out every last drop, hastening the drying time. On a hot day on an outdoor clothesline, a whole load of laundry could dry in a scant hour. In winter, Entropy's best option was the clothesline strung across the living room, over the stove, though the strings of diapers had a way of slapping you wetly in the face if you didn't duck in time.

But it wasn't just the promise of getting outside and into warmer weather that had all four of them excited about spring. The new season would mean that the plans they'd been making for months could finally get under way. Peg, Eliot, and Chris had spent the winter evenings leafing through Eliot's growing library, much of which he had sent away for after seeing the books listed in the *Whole Earth Catalog*. The most invaluable resource for finding the noncombustion, horse-drawn equipment Eliot prized, however, turned out to be the local agricultural advertising circular, which ran announcements of used items for sale. Peg and

Eliot drove their new pickup truck all over the state collecting old-fashioned (though still-working) farm equipment, most of which had languished for two or three decades in the back of someone's storage barn.

By the time patches of matted grass began to appear through the snow in the field across the road from the house, they had gathered a horse-drawn mower, a hay-rake, a thresher, and a hay loader, plus a plow and a harrow to break up the soil for planting. Along the way, they'd picked up a number of useful antique tools to join Peg's butter churn—the hand-cranked washing machine, a two-man saw, and gorgeous collection of hand tools.

Having all grown up with televisions, telephones, and dishwashers, everyone at Entropy found the visible mechanics and closed systems of 19th-century technologies beautifully satisfying. When you looked over a machine made of steel and wood, its springs and levers revealed their workings to you directly. Expertise came by examining and using and tinkering—by you yourself and your own hands and strength and ingenuity—not handed down from above by experts who expected you to trust them blindly. There was something about sanding and oiling a rusted tool into working order that made Chris finally feel like he had both feet on the ground.

The barn was now growing full not just of equipment but also of animals. In addition to several of Peg's beloved Nubian dairy goats with their long, silky ears, they had chickens, a pair of Scotch Highland sheep, a Jersey cow named Flash, and, most excitingly, horses. Maryann and Bettyann (named by their former owners) were a pair of beautiful, grade Belgian draft horses, both of them an unusual, luminous dapple-gray with black legs—sisters whose cream-colored tails flicked in unison as they stood side by side.

Peg's trust fund had made possible this outlay of capital, but in every other way they lived frugally on beans and brown rice. There was an irony, half-acknowledged, in investing so much money into the tools they hoped would ultimately set them free from the capitalist system responsible for begetting that money in the first place. But unless they wanted to go all the way back to truly Stone Age techniques, there didn't seem to be much alternative. Besides, this way they could get started immediately.

As Eliot planned it, the ultimate goal was to someday self-produce 100 percent of what Entropy's humans and animals needed to survive—from organic grains and vegetables to toiletries and medicines. In the meantime, he and the others counted themselves superbly lucky to live a forty-five-minute drive from one of New England's most extraordinary stores: Hatch's Natural Foods.

Though Hatch's has been called the earliest natural food store in Vermont, the word "store" conjures a somewhat misleading image. When Peg went there the first time, she was surprised to find, not a storefront shop or grocery, but a large, slightly dingy house on the outskirts of a midsize town. It felt very odd to walk in the front door without knocking. She'd been expecting a regular health-food store but this felt more like someone's home. In fact, it was.

Ira and Mildred Hatch moved to Vermont in the mid-1950s after returning from India where Ira had been teaching at an agricultural college. Around that time, Mildred became a passionate natural foods convert after reading a book by Gayelord Hauser, nutritionist-to-the-stars (and, possibly, bisexual lover of Greta Garbo). Hauser urged the consumption of "whole foods" and called for ingredients like brewer's yeast, molasses, wheat germ, and yogurt—difficult ingredients to locate anywhere during the Eisenhower era, never mind in rural Vermont. As the Hatches began to seek out wholesale sources of ingredients for their own diet, they realized they could save others the same trouble by sharing what they found. As demand increased, they added dried nuts and fruits, whole grains, beans, cheese, and fertile eggs. Their offerings soon took over the entire downstairs of their house. Thanks to the combination of a robust mail order service and the Hatches' own family money, the store managed to stay afloat long enough for the 1970s' counterculture influx to sweep in and discover it.

By the time Peg ducked through the door, proprietorship of the store had shifted from Ira and Mildred to their son David and his wife Terry, who had added a huge number of products in response to demand from the new shoppers (kelp powder, organic rye flakes, 27 types of cheese). They had also installed a commercial pizza oven in a small side room and begun producing 1.5 tons of granola a month. A message board covering one whole wall of the living room served as a communications center for the wider community of natural foods shoppers—including, as one visitor described it, "long hairs, dry looks, young, old, blue collars, white collars, city dwellers, farm dwellers, and not a few who live in rural communes and rude homestead structures far back in the woods."

David Hatch was half a generation older than most of the young communards he encountered, but he was an "open-throated free spirit," according to one who had known him well. He fully embraced the hippie vibe and was happy to put his family's store at the center of the budding counterculture society, even hosting an annual Christmas party for local communes.

David also had strong connections to the wider, national counterculture. Ram Dass (formerly Richard Alpert, colleague and friend of Timothy Leary) was a friend and occasional visitor. Mildred and Ira had equally well-known friends: Scott and Helen Nearing. Before its 1970 reissue made them world famous, Hatch's was one of the few places to offer copies of the Nearings' original 1954 self-published edition of *Living the Good Life*.

The Nearings' books were just some of the hundreds of titles on offer at Hatch's. One room's floor-to-ceiling shelves held row after row of resources on subjects ranging from organic gardening to the Lamaze method. Mildred Hatch had a strong personal interest not just in nutrition but also in natural childbirth. She invested most of the inheritance she received from her well-to-do (and deeply scandalized) family into collecting every book she could find on the subject and making them available as a lending library. Mildred died in 1964, but her son continued her work of providing access to information by advertising her library in the *Whole Earth Catalog*.

Though Mildred didn't live to see the ideas she'd championed for years become central to a whole new generation of adherents (generations plural, some might argue), Ira was well known to Hatch's regulars. He had a reputation for eccentricity—running errands in town by pushing a wheelbarrow up steep hills well into his eighties, for example—and for his gardens, fertilized with exceptional organic compost.

This was not accidental. As an agriculture professor in India, he had a front-row seat to one of the key turning points in organic farming as it came to be practiced in the West.

In the 1940s, a British agriculturist named Sir Albert Howard studied the way Indian farmers returned nutrients to the soil by allowing plant and animal wastes to decompose naturally. Drawing from these observations, Howard developed what he called the "Indore" method for building "biologic" compost to be used as natural fertilizer. Howard intended his methods to stand as both a scientific and moral contrast to the chemical fertilizers derived from weapons manufacturing that were fast becoming ubiquitous in Western agriculture.

Howard's work ultimately led to today's $39 billion market for organic products. But this might never have happened if not for one ardent fan. J. I. Rodale (née Jerome Cohen) was a Lower East Side-born publisher and health-food enthusiast known mostly for publishing magazines with titles like *You Can't Eat That* and *You're Wrong About That* (the more successful *Prevention* and *Men's Health* and *Women's Health* came later). Recalling his discovery of Howard's work Rodale wrote, "The impact on me was terrific! I decided we must get a farm at once and raise as much of our family's food by the organic method as possible." Rodale's own experience using Howard's methods gave rise in 1942 to *Organic Gardening and Farming*. In its first year, he sold only a dozen subscriptions. While readership rose enough to justify the magazine's continued production, its numbers languished until 1968 when the *Whole Earth Catalog* helped Rodale's *Encyclopedia of Organic Gardening* become one of the most ubiquitous books of the back-to-the-land period.

The publishers, with their roots in the midcentury organic movement, consciously acted as a bridge to the new generation of organic farmers and gardeners. Robert Rodale, who had taken over for his elderly father a few years earlier, soothed his older readers in 1969: "They are the hippies, the student rebels, the new wave of far-out young people. Like it or not, we are finding them riding along with us on the roads out to the wide open spaces. . . . You may object to them marching around in the nude and living in one big communal family, but they are at least trying to do that in semi-privacy. Hippie farm life is better than burning the flag or locking up the dean. Let's keep our eyes on what they are doing. Maybe, by chance, they will figure out some new way to live on the land." By 1972, the circulation of *Organic Gardening and Farming* had risen to 750,000 readers each month; by 1981, it reached over one million.

J. I. Rodale did not live to see this huge surge, however. He had embraced his new, late-life popularity with a series of high-spirited media appearances. At a 1971 taping of the *Dick Cavett Show*, the 72-year-old brought along a pile of vegetables to use as props and declared loudly that he would live for another thirty years "unless he was run down by a sugar-crazed cab driver on the streets of New York." A few minutes later, when Cavett began interviewing his next guest, Pete Hamill, they suddenly realized that Rodale, sitting on the other couch, had stopped breathing. Before he reached the hospital, he was dead of a massive heart attack.

For the young people at Entropy Acres, whose model of adult work had always been 9-to-5 professions, the rhythm of a farm's work day had taken some getting used to. The goats and Flash the cow needed to be fed and milked twice a day, every day. Peg couldn't say how she felt about milking—it was simply the work the day required, so she got up and did it. Once your hands got strong and lost their awkwardness, the rhythms of milking became meditative and soothing. On a cold morning, it was an exquisite pleasure to lean against the soft, warm flank of a fellow creature as you steadily pulled streams of foamy, fragrant milk from her udder. Still, on days when the thermometer's needle hovered well below zero, it would have been even nicer not to get out of bed at all. It took some adjusting to realize that being late to work in the context of a farm did not mean inconveniencing a coworker or getting in trouble with a boss, but causing physical distress in an animal wholly reliant on you to relieve hunger or the ache of a swollen udder. A cow, after all, has no concept of Sunday morning, no matter how badly needed her owner's day of rest.

For Peg all this milking led to another revelation: the world's vast variety of dairy products, especially those that used sour or cultured milk, suddenly made perfect sense—fresh milk doesn't last long without refrigeration, and owning a cow wasn't like going to the store for a neatly pasteurized carton whenever you needed it. Flash produced four gallons of milk a day, far more than the household could drink, even once the two fast-growing babies started helping out. The goats' additional gallons had a strong, stinky flavor that was hard to drink by the glassful with so much sweet Jersey milk available instead.

Operating under the same combination of curiosity and necessity that drove almost all the farm's endeavors, Peg began experimenting with the endless dairy supply that soon collected in every available vessel around the kitchen. The soft cheeses of both cow and goat milk came out the best. The goat cheese was delicious spread on crackers, but a single batch was often more than just the four of them could eat. It wasn't easy to find others who wanted to try it. In 1971, goat cheese was still relatively unfamiliar to the general American palate—the person who would later be widely credited with popularizing it as an ingredient was Alice Waters whose Chez Panisse chevre salads counted on the products of Berkeley-area back-to-the-land goat farmers undertaking cheese-making experiments simultaneous to and almost exactly like Peg's.

Not all of Peg's forays worked. Producing hard cheeses proved extremely challenging. For these, Peg heated a pan of milk and stirred in rennet. While she waited for the curds to form, she set up the molds she'd brought home from Spain. Each one consisted of a woven band of dried *esparto* grass, three inches wide, which she coiled into a circle and secured before placing it on a board and covering it with a cheese cloth. Once the curds had formed in her pan of milk, she scooped them onto the cloth, packing them tightly against the walls formed by the woven loop. Then, she folded the excess cheesecloth over the top and weighted it with a brick to act as a press.

But when she set the cheeses out to cure, something always seemed to go wrong. Sometimes they looked okay but tasted terrible; sometimes they crumbled into inedible shards. Even when a batch came out perfectly dense and creamy, she could never replicate it. For better results, she realized, she would need a much more precise system—a way of controlling temperature and humidity, for example, never mind a level of hygiene that would help prevent unwanted bacteria from affecting the flavor. One time, Peg carefully unwrapped the cloth from a particularly promising cheese only to discover a pulsing swarm of maggots.

The successes, though, made the failures worth it. A friend taught her how to make yogurt—another product most American supermarkets still relegated to the ethnic foods section if they carried it at all. The method required you to heat a pan of milk on the stove to hot-but-not-boiling (the friend explained that you could test this by sticking your finger into the pan—if it was uncomfortable but not impossible to hold it there to the count of three, it was the right heat). Then you stirred in a few tablespoons of already-made yogurt, whatever you had as long as it had been produced using a live culture. This mixture needed to be kept at a steady warmth—not too hot, not too cold—for the several hours it took the yogurt culture to reproduce and convert the rest of the milk to its own thick, tangy consistency.

The original recipe called for pouring the milk/yogurt mixture into jars and placing them in a warm oven to set. But keeping the heat perfectly low and steady for hours in the oven of a woodstove was beyond Peg's fire-banking abilities; she also didn't want to rely on electric yogurt-makers as many others were doing. Instead, she employed an alternative method of packing the jars into a Styrofoam cooler, which she then filled up with warm water, being careful not to slosh any into the open jars. When the cooler was sealed, it held the heat long enough for the yogurt to thicken. The process could be shortened on a warm day by placing the cooler in a pleasant, steady sunbeam. It was a tidy, self-contained system of the type that most pleased her—produced with no waste or man-made additives, one batch's last bite begetting, almost magically, the next.

Peg also made good use of her prized possession, the antique wooden butter churn. In the morning, she'd go to the previous day's crock of fresh cow milk and carefully scoop cupfuls of the heavy, yellow cream that had risen to the top during the night. Soon, she learned to let the cream sour slightly before dumping it into the churn. No one at Entropy had ever tasted anything as surpassingly delicious as this sweet, cultured Jersey butter. To eat it slathered and melting over a thick slice of fresh-baked bread—and to reflect that not only the churning of the butter and baking of the bread but also the milking and care of the cow, the grinding of the grain, even the felling of the tree that fueled the oven, all the work of your own hands—the satisfaction in this went bone deep.

For Chris, the experience of long days of hard, physical labor was already turning out to be as fulfilling as he had hoped, a true antidote to the powerlessness he had felt working for the newspaper in Toronto. He had an immediate affinity to the horses and was rapidly becoming expert in tinkering the ever-glitchy farm tools into working order. He hadn't entirely given up on writing, though. In a freelance article for the *Globe and Mail,* he described the cold, wet November night he'd spent trying to prepare one of Entropy's fields for a planned crop of organic oats. The article, titled "If I'm a Nutty Food Faddist, Then You're a Sickly Half-Poisoned Victim of the Agro-Chemical Complex," was both a self-deprecating description of Entropy's efforts ("The potato crop, such as it was, inspired a new definition of ecology: we get half, the slugs get half") and an impassioned argument for the health benefits of organic food. "It's my hunch that the North American food industry has seriously overestimated the strength of the consumer's stomach and underestimated his taste for good, pure foods that haven't been messed around with," he wrote. "If my hunch is right, you may be eating Entropy Acres Oatmeal before too long. If it's wrong," he concluded, "I guess we'll eat it ourselves."

As the next decades proved, Chris's hunch about organics turned out to be correct. But his prediction about the oat crop itself did not—no one ended up eating Entropy Acres Oatmeal because the stalks came up so sparsely, choked out by a plant the locals called "kale," a wild ancestor of today's ubiquitous staple.

Now that spring looked to be on its way, though, they'd have another chance at putting in a different organic crop. The moment the dirt road past the house was relatively free of ice, Eliot decided to start practicing driving the horses.

Eliot had no previous experience with horses, but Peg had showed him how to handle and groom them. She'd grown up riding—her family home included pastures and a small barn— and though her family's two horses hadn't been work animals like these, there were a lot of similarities. The horses' previous owner had shown them how to buckle on the wide leather collars, making sure each pad was properly placed to keep the collar from rubbing the horse's neck when she started pulling. He also explained how to organize the heavy harness in your hands before lifting it over the horse's back and spreading it out over her dappled flanks.

Before long, Eliot had gotten comfortable getting each horse correctly harnessed and bridled. Today, he wanted to try out the solid, ample wagon he expected to rely on for farm work. Remembering which sister preferred which side (Bettyann left, Maryann right), he carefully backed them into position on either side of the wagon's central pole and secured the rest of the harness. Then, heart racing, he climbed up into the driver's seat. He half expected the horses to bolt or to ignore him when he flicked the reins, but instead they amiably jolted off. The wagon's enormous wooden wheels crunched smoothly over the frozen dirt road as if cars had never been invented.

Triumphant, Eliot spent the next few days practicing with the wagon, driving the sisters down the road to the yellow house and turning around at the T-intersection before driving back. It would have been something to continue driving straight over to Myrtle Hill, but that seemed like tempting fate. Still, by the time the snowmelt softened the road into muck and forced Eliot to stop practicing until it dried out, he was confident enough to urge the horses into a trot.

Looking back on it later, it would strike him that he should have been more surprised than he was at this early success. At the time, though, it felt perfectly straightforward: he'd given his life and the state of the world careful consideration and chosen what seemed to him to be the best route forward. The fact that he, a child of the suburbs and a graduate school dropout, was now calmly navigating workhorses along a back road as if "gee" and "haw" were words he'd ever spoken before the previous week—none of this felt at all remarkable. To the contrary: the success with the horses was simple confirmation that this plan he had made, to undertake a fully self-sufficient life, was actually going to work.

Eliot later described his attitude toward his entire learning curve: "There's nothing to do except do it." This echoed the advice Drop City's collaborator Steve Baer offered readers of his *Dome Cookbook*: "You don't need to know that much, you just need to go ahead and try it out."

It might as well have been a mantra for the entire back-to-the-land period. One of the most striking characteristics of the young people who threw themselves into farming and building in the 1970s was their sheer confidence in their own ability to undertake work they'd never even seen performed before. By their own later admission, this was in part the naiveté of those born into families a generation or more removed from farming or manual labor. But to an extraordinary degree, they weren't wrong to trust their own ability to learn as they went along.

In this, it's hard to overstate the influence of the *Whole Earth Catalog*. The *Catalog*'s tagline was "access to tools." To be included in its teeming, oversized pages, an item had to be "1) Useful as a tool, 2) Relevant to independent education, 3) High quality or low cost, 4) Not already common knowledge, 5) Easily available by mail." Before the first issue in 1968, people curious about alternative methods for building, gardening, healing, or producing sustainable energy had to somehow discover information and instructions on their own (not everyone was lucky enough to stumble into Hatch's). The *Catalog*'s contribution was to curate a huge collection of resources, from books to equipment suppliers, presenting ordering information alongside illustrations, excerpts, reviews, and advice from thoughtful, like-minded experimenters, just as a generation's hunger for these resources began to grow. It's still not clear, decades later, how much the *Catalog* merely fed this hunger and how much it actively created it.

What's not in question is that the impetus for the *Catalog* arose directly from the early commune movement of the American Southwest. "The WHOLE EARTH CATALOG got started in a plane over Nebraska in March 1968," Stewart Brand wrote in 1971. "I was returning to California from my father's long dying and funeral that morning in Illinois. The sun had set ahead of the plane while I was reading . . . Between chapters, I gazed out the window into dark nothing and slid into a reverie about my friends who were starting their own civilization hither and yon in the sticks and how could I help. The L.L.Bean Catalog of outdoor stuff came to mind and I pondered upon Mr. Bean's service to humanity over the years. So many of the problems I could identify came down to a matter of access. Where to buy a windmill. Where to get good information on bee-keeping. Where [at a time when they were room-sized machines owned by corporations and the government] to lay hands on a computer without forfeiting freedom. . . ."

Buoyed by inheritance from his father and support from the progressive, nonprofit Portola Institute, Brand's idea quickly gained momentum. Its first iteration was a six-page book list of essential titles ("*Tantra Art, Cybernetics, The Indian Tipi, Recreational Equipment*"). Brand and his wife, Lois, collected samples of each, calling their production The Whole Earth Truck Store.

The "Whole Earth" name came from an earlier project of Brand's. One night in 1966, Brand had dropped acid and climbed up on a rooftop to think. As he sat, shivering, looking out over San Francisco, he noticed that he could see the curve of the earth. "I had the idea that the higher you go, the more you can see earth as round," he explained. He started wondering why photos of earth from space, though they existed, had never been made public. "I started scheming within the trip. How can I make this photograph happen? Because I have now persuaded myself that it will change everything if we have this photograph looking at earth from space." Soon, he printed up and started selling buttons reading, "Why Haven't We Seen a Photograph of the Whole Earth Yet?" but the project felt incomplete. With the Truck Store, he revisited the theme.

Stewart and Lois spent a month driving around the Southwest, shopping their wares to Drop City, New Buffalo, and their early sister communes. After returning to California, the Brands expanded their list and gathered a small publishing staff who quickly put together the Catalog's first issue. Its cover held the striking, now-iconic image of the earth as viewed from space, a fragile blue marble set starkly against a solid black expanse. The pared-down simplicity on the outside of the heavy, lap-sized book contrasted wildly with the explosion of text and illustration within. Its crammed, eccentrically laid out, rough-paper pages juxtaposed log-cabin instruction manuals with physics diagrams, illustrations of snake-bite kits, excerpts from psychology textbooks, reviews of sci-fi series, ads for high-tech calculators and handlooms, Wendell Berry essays, letters from Ken Kesey, and at least once, an entire novel printed in the margin columns. The dizzying array of ideas under presentation invited endless rereading and an experience of perpetual discovery.

In 1971, the *Whole Earth Catalog* won the National Book Award. Or, technically, the version that won was *The Last Whole Earth Catalog*, which clocked in at 446 pages and sold over a million copies.

Despite this success, by 1972, Brand's attention was already turning to other projects—principally, computers. He was an early supporter of the Homebrew Computer Club where member Steve Wozniack would soon present the Apple I; his co-founder, Steve Jobs, would later cite Brand and the *Whole Earth Catalog* as one of his most important influences. Brand's interest in the potential of computers to extend and expand the *Catalog's* flexibility and reach led in 1985 to the WELL (Whole Earth 'Lectronic Link), a computer networking system that let its users communicate with each other in real time. While it was not the first to do this, the WELL became by far the most influential early online network, its culture nourished by Brand's continued emphasis on connection and information-sharing across geographically dispersed communities. His 1968 early-morning airplane epiphany—of an information resource that would connect readers to one another and be "continuously updated, in part by users"—is the direct ancestor of today's internet culture.

But all that was still in the future. During the period that the *Whole Earth Catalog* expanded from the radical, rural communes that were its original audience to a more national, mainstream readership, the back-to-the-land movement expanded too. In 1967, young people seeking out an austere, hands-on life in the country tended to go together, drawing confidence in part from the security of the group itself. For early communes, the information networks they counted on for resources and skill sharing existed in the form of the communal relationships themselves—from people traveling place to place and bringing ideas and practices with them. Brand's innovation of putting "access to tools" in print meant that you no longer needed to actually live with other people or be part of a communal network to benefit from the resources that early back-to-the-landers had been busily rediscovering and developing. Just a few years into the movement, a couple could live alone in a little house on a back road and still have access to tools; they could feel confidently supported by the resources and knowledge of the larger rural counterculture through the pages of the *Whole Earth Catalog.*

Even as the radical commune movement peaked and declined in the early '70s, the waves of back-to-the-landers continued throughout the decade, the balance shifting toward another influx, indistinguishable in every demographic measure from the communards, but who preferred to live as single-family units.

In fact, in the summer of 1971, two such people were in the process of pitching a tent on their own newly purchased acres just a mile over the hill from Myrtle Hill and Entropy Acres. Their names were Larry and Judy. They were my parents.

CHAPTER 10

By the time the maple row at the edge of Myrtle's upper field had swelled into its green, summer glory, tipis and tents had once again begun to spring up as communards old and new arrived for the summer.

All the founders had returned: Nancy, Amy, and the kids from Red Paint; Fletcher and Jason from the Southwest; Jim the Bear from wherever he had gone; Jed from New York, his big truck loaded with supplies; Craig from California.

Craig had been excited to be back in California after a few years away. But as he worked his way through the network of communes that had sprung up along the coast (many of them founded by former Diggers who had been among the first wave of rural communards), Craig was shocked at the level of paranoia he encountered. When he tried to meet up with friends, they refused to talk to him on the phone, which they assumed was bugged, insisting on meeting only in places where they couldn't be easily overheard.

In one or two cases, the paranoia was probably justified. Craig's best friend from high school, still on the lam from the draft board and now going by Jblu, had gotten involved in a radical "direct action group" whose political rhetoric had intensified in the two years since People's Park. One particularly vocal member, a Vietnam vet, had started pushing for the group to arm themselves. Jblu didn't disagree with the politics, he told Craig, but when the man began to make plans for a counterfeiting operation, he decided it was time to split (years later when news came out about the number of FBI informants tasked with penetrating political groups and inciting them to violence, Jblu wondered if the man he knew had been among them).

Craig was also surprised by the emphasis he found among some of the most radical groups on preparing for the coming revolution by stockpiling guns. It's not that this line of thinking didn't exist at Myrtle Hill—Jed in particular, along with some of the other New Yorkers, had both a stronger belief in a revolutionary near-future and a more acute sense of personal vulnerability than Craig did—but this kind of paranoia was not Myrtle Hill's dominant mood.

Though it sometimes lurched to the foreground. One night the previous summer, everyone had been sitting around the fire late when they heard car wheels crunching up the driveway. Unknown headlights cut through the darkness as a tremor of panic shot through the group. Jed and a couple of other New Yorkers reached for their guns.

At many rural communes, it was not unusual for cars of curious rubberneckers to drive by, drawn by eccentric architecture or rumors of nudity. Some late-night visitors arrived hoping (or assuming) that hippie girls' Free Love philosophy extended to them. Even within the same commune, some members tolerated or actively sought out this role as local curiosity, while others resented it.

For city-bred communards who had imagined their rural retreat as a *tabula rasa* for their own goals and projects, it was sometimes hard to know how to interpret attention from the locals they hadn't fully realized would have an opinion about newcomers. Then, too, some remembered their experience in the American South during the Civil Rights movement, where a midnight visit from white men in pickup trucks might really portend violence.

But for anyone living in a remote, unfamiliar place, night visits from strangers could be unsettling—especially if you were stoned, without near neighbors or a telephone, and with flickering firelight the only illumination in the dark woods.

At Myrtle Hill that night, Craig stepped into the darkness to greet whoever had arrived while Fletcher urged Jed to take his finger off the trigger. The visitors, when Craig led them back to the fire, turned out to be a group of local teenagers, more curious than hostile. After a few beers, they went on their way. Everyone exhaled. When Fletcher thought about it later, what scared him was not the teenagers' unannounced arrival but Jed's panicked siege mentality. Every time he remembered Craig leading those kids calmly into the firelight while all around them in the darkness others waited, guns cocked, tense with hostile fear, he shuddered: "It could have been terrible."

The sudden impulse toward rural living that had sent so many in the counterculture running for the hills had always been fueled by a potent mix of pessimism and optimism: the urgent panic of fleeing a coming apocalypse and the equally urgent desire to learn new skills and invent a better way of living. Until his return visit to California, Craig hadn't fully realized how much his time at Myrtle Hill had led him away from a mood of fear and escape and toward the satisfactions of construction and self-reliance. He could hardly wait to get back to Vermont.

His travels had also given him some new ideas to share with the group. One Virginia commune, Twin Oaks, inspired by the behaviorist utopia in B. F. Skinner's *Walden Two*, had developed a highly regimented work system. The commune's members sacrificed a certain amount of personal freedom, but they got a lot accomplished (and, as it turned out, would still be thriving forty years later). No one at Myrtle, Craig included, had any interest in such a strictly enforced system, but, Craig felt, last summer's relaxed approach to work had left them all cold, sick, and scrambling for survival. He never wanted to go through that again.

After a long meeting around the table in the Big House, the dozen communards present finally agreed to a plan: they'd post a chore wheel with daily tasks—milking, dishes, gathering firewood, filling and cleaning the kerosene lanterns—and everyone would sign up for their preferred job, thus striking a perfect balance between personal freedom and group need.

The same balance lay at the heart of the most urgent issue they needed to resolve that summer: the question of whether or not to maintain an open-door policy. After another series of long, earnest meetings, the group finally came to a decision: whoever wished could come and stay at Myrtle, without exception. But only for three days. After that, the commune's permanent residents would politely ask them to move on. If a visitor wanted to join as a full member, including taking a share of the mortgage payments, he or she had to be accepted by group consensus.

This limited-membership policy drew directly from the example of Drop City, whose crumbling, abandoned domes had left Fletcher spooked. But they had another motivating force too, just fifty miles to the north: Earth People's Park.

Unlike low-key Myrtle, the long-anticipated existence of Earth People's Park and its promise of Free Land for Free People made national news in the underground counterculture. One person even reported seeing graffiti—"Old lady got you down? Cops looking for you? Come to Earth People's Park in Norton, VT"—in the bathroom of a bar in Mexico.

The first influx of Earth People's Park inhabitants had arrived in a painted bus the summer before; a few hardy members had spent the winter in the commune's only building, a tiny house that had been previously used as a logging camp. Now, in its second summer, more people had begun arriving, each person or family finding their own little spot in the woods or fields to build a fire and stake a claim. Though some residents later remembered an early spirit of cooperation and mutual support, visitors, especially in later years, found the lack of a central community disorienting and unnerving. The total freedom promised by the land also meant that no one living there was responsible for any fellow resident's behavior. One frequent guest at many of the area's communes remembered Earth People's Park as the only one where he ever felt afraid: "You felt anything might happen to you there."

Myrtle's residents had come to expect a certain number of colorful, transient eccentrics—one round, jolly fellow, with a huge, red beard and a wild light in his blue eyes had returned to Myrtle

Hill the second summer gaunt and angry and fully psychotic; he tried to set the Big House on fire before the men firmly sent him on his way. But this summer's stream of visitors now often included those fumbling their way to Earth People's Park and ending up at Myrtle by mistake. Craig and the others discretely didn't ask, particularly of those with no camping equipment or belongings of any kind, what was motivating them to seek out an undeveloped plot of open land whose woods happened to overlap the Canadian border. Myrtle's three-day policy was in part to protect themselves from the answer.

For Amy, the summer's influx of new people and the return of old friends felt exciting and reinvigorating. As soon as the weather got warm enough, almost everyone moved out of the Big House sleeping loft and back into the plastic-and-sapling lean-tos scattered through the woods. Sleeping outdoors could be chilly and damp, but it was the only way to achieve even a moment of privacy. Amy didn't have a shelter of her own, but she sometimes crashed in other people's when they were away. As happy as she was to see Craig—his presence, to her, was like the sun shining, and it was never quite the same when he was gone—she had also gotten used to the slower pace of winter. Craig, Jed, Jim, and the other men had arrived back at the commune refreshed by their months away and full of plans. Craig and Jed in particular had clearly decided not to let the summer slip by them a second time.

Amy didn't argue with this goal, but she found herself chafing at Craig's push to keep everyone focused on work. She craved time to read and to write in her journal, as she'd done with fever-ish intensity ever since escaping the fire. Amy could see Craig's scorn for those whose work standards didn't meet his own (Pancake, for example, whose preference for reading and meditating Craig could not fathom, although Amy understood entirely). Craig's high esteem mattered to her but she had to meet her own needs too. She quietly took to ducking away into the woods for an hour or two during the day to read or write.

In the weeks they'd spent together wintered in at the Big House, Amy had grown very close to Loraine. Loraine had taken it upon herself to teach Amy everything she knew and was learning in the kitchen; Amy was considered by other Myrtleites and still described years later as Loraine's protégée. But the relationship, at least for Amy, went deeper than mentorship. In the months since she'd arrived at Myrtle, Amy had become acutely attuned to Loraine's every mood. As Loraine's pregnancy advanced, this sixth sense expanded until it seemed to Amy that she was feeling all of Loraine's sensations firsthand. If Loraine was tired, Amy was tired. If Loraine felt nauseous, Amy felt nauseous.

And so, it was no surprise to Amy that she was the first to notice, after dinner one evening, that Loraine had gone into labor.

Amy was with a few others in the small, log-and-tarp sweat lodge they'd constructed next to the spring when she heard Loraine walking up the road from the Big House, chanting and singing in her strong, clear voice. As soon as Amy heard Loraine's song, she knew immediately what was happening. She ran out of the sweat lodge, still naked, to join her.

Loraine's first daughter, Amelia, had been born in a hospital, but Loraine wanted to give birth to the commune's baby at home at Myrtle Hill. The summer's first, urgent press of construction had been to this end: a small, simply designed outbuilding behind the old cellar hole in the middle field, intended as a birthing shack. It had a wood floor and mosquito netting to let the cool breeze through. Its roof beams formed a six-pointed star you could focus on while lying on your back inside; Loraine had dubbed it the Star House. It was there that Loraine and Amy now headed, chanting, with others joining them as they went along.

For her own preparation, Loraine had read every birthing book she could find at the library or borrow from Mildred Hatch's impressive collection. She had spent the winter doing yoga and practicing Lamaze exercises; Craig, when he returned, had agreed to be her birthing partner and practice with her. She had collected special thread and scissors for the umbilical cord and had washed sheets and carefully sterilized them in the oven. She had also enlisted a neighbor friend to act as a midwife. He had read and studied along with Loraine and had attended two previous births—not a lot of training, but Loraine trusted him. Now, someone rushed out to fetch him.

By the time Amy and Loraine reached the Star House, almost everyone at Myrtle Hill—including newly arrived visitors who didn't even know Loraine or the couple of men who were potentially the baby's father—had joined the procession and taken up Loraine's song. As night fell, the chanting went on ceaselessly, both from inside the hut where Hershe, Craig, and the midwife rubbed Loraine's back and breathed with her, and from outside, where the fields were filling up with friends arriving from other communes. No one could later remember how the news had spread so quickly, but this was one of the wider community's first births and a dozen communards from around the region had rushed to be present in support and celebration.

At dawn, just as the birds started singing, Loraine gave two huge pushes and the first baby born at Myrtle Hill came into the world. Someone ran out into the field and blew a long blast on a hunting horn. Loraine named her Rahula. Hershe carried four-year-old Amelia up from the Big House in the early light, half asleep, to meet her new sister. Hershe had only just found out: she was pregnant too.

Loraine stayed in the Star House for another week, nursing Rahula and resting while others brought her food and helped with the baby. At Loraine's request, Nancy had carried the placenta into the kitchen and cooked it up for Loraine to eat—she found it delicious and invigorating. Both mother and infant were perfectly healthy. Neither of them saw a doctor until Rahula was six months old.

For many of those who had been present during the night of chanting outside the Star House, Rahula's birth remained one of the most intensely powerful experiences of their commune years. For Loraine this was true as well, but with a caveat, added later. The beauty and simplicity of the birth had certainly been due in part to her own good health and mental preparation and to the ways everyone present had let themselves be guided by nature and instinct. But to a degree she would only realize later, with the birth of her next child, an equally large measure of credit had to be given to forces beyond anyone's control: the sheer, simple luck of this birth and labor having been uncomplicated.

Rahula was just a week old when a visitor stopped by, asking to talk to Loraine. His name was Bernie Sanders. He had recently moved to Vermont and was writing for various progressive newspapers. Within a few months, he would begin the political career that would make him mayor of Burlington and eventually the only self-proclaimed socialist in the US Senate and a crowd-rallying presidential hopeful. Sanders didn't belong to a commune himself, but many of his friends and many more of his eventual political supporters did.

He had heard through the counterculture grapevine that Loraine's two daughters had been born under drastically different conditions and he wanted to interview her for an article comparing hospital births and home births. As Loraine nursed Rahula in the Star House, he gently peppered her with questions in his thick Brooklyn accent. Loraine was happy to oblige. She liked Bernie and appreciated his thoughtful interest in her experience. This appreciation would only deepen with time. Over the next several decades, well into his national political career, whenever Loraine ran into him, Bernie always chatted with her warmly and never failed to ask after Rahula.

Craig, however, was less enamored with Bernie's visit to Myrtle Hill. It wasn't his viewpoints—Craig would later devote himself heartily to Bernie's mayoral campaign—it was his penchant for sitting around and talking about ideas when there was so much work to be done.

Myrtle Hill's raison d'être, as Craig saw it, was in the doing, not in the theorizing. Even though he agreed with almost everything Bernie had to say, he resented feeling like he had to pull others out of Bernie's orbit if any work was going to get accomplished that day. Endless political discussion was simply not a way they could or should spend their time. The memory of the previous autumn still haunted Craig. He was determined not to let this summer vanish in the same dreamy haze as the first. When Bernie had stayed for Myrtle's allotted three days, Craig politely requested that he move on.

Craig's newfound drive for productivity was rankling others besides Amy. Pancake had never thrived in environments of intense machismo like this summer's construction push. He had no desire to emulate or compete with Craig's commanding charisma or Jed's guns and mechanical know-how or Jim the Bear's system-rigging genius. Even Fletcher, with his short hair and nerdy glasses, had made a film about a biker gang and was spending his time this summer building a tiny, two-story cabin framed on standing trees in the woods behind the Big House. Pancake had zero interest in Free Love, but the group's distain for monogamy, combined with Hershe's vibrant beauty, further complicated his relationships with the other men. Pancake's strategy had always been to duck the commune heavies and stay out of the macho spotlight as best he could. But the summer's all-hands-on-deck pressure had made doing that harder than ever.

The generator Jed had donated to run the power tools was running almost constantly, and its roar was driving Pancake crazy—you could hear it everywhere and it was impossible to meditate. Then one day he had an idea of how he could muffle the sound without interrupting construction. He found a crate and propped it over the generator on a stick. For a while this worked. But when the stick vibrated out of place and brought the crate crashing down, the generator overheated and broke. That night at dinner, Jed excoriated Pancake for his worthlessness in front of the whole group. Hershe snapped back at Jed in Pancake's defense: "This is one of the most beautiful people you've ever met!" But there was no shaking Jed's scorn.

For Hershe and Pancake, the air at Myrtle Hill had been poisoned. "We don't need to put up with this," they decided. They wanted to be somewhere with a healthier vibe, especially now that they had a baby on the way. The only question was, where could they go?

Over at Entropy Acres, they were running into snarls of their own.

Eliot had decided, after carefully consulting Rodale's *Encyclopedia*, that the summer's big project would be a commercial crop of organic carrots and turnips, raised and harvested using only sustainable, horse-drawn equipment.

Eliot had even found a ready market. Peg's father had helped him get in touch with the produce buyer for Boston's Star Markets who'd agreed to take whatever the fledgling farm could produce at twice the wholesale price for nonorganic vegetables. It was a huge coup—Star Market was one of the first supermarket chains in the Northeast to offer organic produce alongside conventionally grown vegetables. Entropy's crop would be part of its inaugural experiment.

On the first clear day after what he judged to be the final frost of the season, Eliot led the two beautiful Belgians to the designated carrot field behind the house. Buoyed by his success with the wagon, Eliot felt confident as he hitched them to the antique plow.

When all the buckles were at last in place and he clicked his tongue and flicked the reins against their sturdy, dappled flanks, the horses started forward—or anyway, they tried to start forward. Neither took a single step. Eliot clicked louder and flicked harder, shouting, "Git up!" as their previous owner had taught him to do. Nothing. Even walking around to the front and attempting to lead them by the bridle got him nowhere. Within a few minutes, he had tried everything he could think of to no avail. The plow had not moved an inch. The sisters didn't seem annoyed or restless, they just simply wouldn't pull. Reluctantly, Eliot unhitched the horses and led them back to the barn. They must have been trained to pull a wagon, he concluded, but just not a plow.

In fact, as he eventually found out, the problem did not lie with the horses. The problem was with the plow itself—it was missing a crucial element, the knife that cuts a furrow into the earth before the plow blade folds it back. Without it, the plow simply offered the horses too much resistance.

Or maybe, as he reflected years later, wondering how he could have missed something so obvious, it was more accurate to acknowledge that the real problem was his own total ignorance of even the most basic principles of the technology he so revered.

Despairing, and with the planting season starting to slip away and with it their only plans for potential income, Eliot and the others did the only thing they could think of—they asked their neighbors, the Johns family, if they could borrow their tractor. While Eliot hated this dispiriting concession to combustion engines, Peg and Chris noted the bright side: the Johns didn't hesitate for a moment before agreeing to help.

The next afternoon, Len Johns drove the tractor over and in no time at all, two acres behind the house had been turned over into furrows of rich, black soil. Coming from the suburbs as everyone at Entropy did, their experience of adult neighborly relations had been marked more by competition and fear of judgement than by mutual aid. For Chris, it was extremely exciting that a neighbor would, without blinking, offer time and the use of expensive, vital equipment to people they barely knew. Peg agreed. What other way could there be to interpret this act of generosity but friendship?

Entropy had the exceptional good luck to have as near neighbors not just the Johns but also Loudon Young and his family.

Loudon's farm lay between Myrtle Hill and Entropy Acres. At the T-intersection where Eliot had practiced turning his horses around instead of continuing straight on toward Myrtle, the rutted dirt road that broke off and cut through the fields ran directly through Loudon's farm. His low, white farmhouse lay a few dozen yards from the elegant old, three-story red barn whose cupola peeked above the treetops.

One afternoon, there was a knock on Entropy's door. The four inside were still getting used to the fact that, in a region where almost everyone worked a farm schedule and phone lines were still not something to take for granted, it was commonly accepted for neighbors to stop by unannounced during the day. The man who stepped into their kitchen had intense features—thick, dark brows and a prominent nose—but these were softened by a friendly smile. They might at first have mistaken him for older, but in fact he was only about fifteen years their senior. His eyes had the unmistakable glint of a well-developed sense of humor. He held up the six-pack of Schaeffer he'd brought along.

The minute Chris and Loudon cracked open beers and started talking, everyone relaxed. If Loudon offered a pretext for his visit, they all knew it was just a cover—after discreetly watching his new neighbors' carryings-on for a few months, Loudon had finally decided it was time to find out what exactly they were up to. As Chris remembered it years later, "Loudon wanted to know what the hell we thought we were doing on the farm next door, and the only way to find out was to ask. Maybe not ask directly; maybe just talk about this and that long enough for the answers to emerge on their own."

Chris and the others could see that Loudon's primary motivation for getting to know them was not suspicion but the kind of empathic curiosity, as Chris put it, "that trumps a lot of the more negative reactions we bring to encounters with people who are different from us." Plus, it only took a few minutes of talking with Loudon and settling into the rhythms of his thick Vermont accent for all of them to realize that they were in the presence of a world-class conversationalist.

Loudon was interested in everything. As he sat in the kitchen, smoking his Camels, the questions he asked and answered revealed how much each side wanted to know about the other's experience. For Chris and Loudon, this casual afternoon visit was the start of a lifelong friendship.

From Chris's perspective, Loudon was the embodiment of the exact skill set he had embarked upon gaining for himself. Loudon had spent his whole life ("so far," as he might correct) on the modest dairy farm that bordered Entropy to the southeast. His daily routine of milking and caring for his several dozen Jerseys and Holsteins was intercut by a myriad of other periodic and seasonal tasks—fixing fences; cutting, drying, and baling hay; planting and harvesting corn for silage; spreading manure to fertilize fields; logging; driving a town snow plow; cutting brush and Christmas trees in winter; and sugaring in spring. In other words, Chris's dream.

Loudon's wife, Arlene, was equally warm and welcoming of her new neighbors. The youngest of the Youngs' seven children was only a few years older than Chris and Ellen's twins. On cold, cabin-fevery days, the Youngs' bright, warm, chaotic kitchen became a welcome destination for Ellen. She bundled up the boys and tucked them into a sled and hauled them a mile down the frozen dirt road to the Youngs'.

Though it was not his own style, Loudon took in stride the college kids' enthusiastic plans for farming according to the instructions they'd read in books. He was especially intrigued by Entropy's dedication to farming with horses. Over the next few months, when Chris or one of the others asked him for advice, he was happy to offer it. "The chief problem," he might say, "is that the horses are smarter than you are." He had worked with a horse years before and loved it, but when it got old and injured, he had never recovered from the pain of having to put it down himself. ("When a tractor suffers its final breakdown," he noted to Chris, "nobody has to shoot it.")

In Loudon's talent for succinct, colorfully worded insights, Chris recognized a fellow wordsmith and a master in the fine art of giving people shit. (One morning after a party, Loudon took one look at Chris's face. "Fuzzy," he said, "your eyes look like two skunks' touchholes in a stone wall.") For Chris, every interaction with Loudon offered a double pleasure—the conversation itself and the discreetly offered advice embedded in it.

For Loudon, a man of insatiable curiosity living in a place without much novelty, friendship with Entropy provided a double pleasure as well: new, young, hardworking neighbors with whom to chat—and a front-row seat on the most entertaining madness in years.

And as Chris considered it later, there was another element that underlay the connection between himself and Loudon. "In the mid-sixties, most Americans saw themselves as embodiments of the straight-ahead, organization-oriented values that had swept them to such affluence in the postwar era. When a substantial part of my generation rejected those values in the rudest possible way, most Americans were threatened, and reacted accordingly," he wrote in Loudon's obituary many years later. "I don't think Loudon saw himself as part of the American mainstream. He felt attached to a much richer culture, the farming culture of northeastern Vermont. It was a culture he liked, and I think he also liked the sense that it was different from the national culture that had left it behind. So his new neighbors had a problem with mainstream values? So what?"

Though it was too soon for anyone at Entropy to realize it, Loudon's visit and his subsequent interest in them was one of their single most important strokes of luck.

For one thing, they badly needed his advice. The problem with learning to farm from books was that no written work, no matter how comprehensive, could ever foresee every pitfall and quirk offered up by land, animals, and equipment. Ideas that sounded great on the page turned out to have unwritten caveats—or maybe it was just that the newcomers' learning curve required not just a new set of skills but also developing what Loudon and Len Johns might just have called "common sense."

For every success that summer—and there were plenty: the horse-drawn hay mower worked wonderfully, for example—there were near-comic, catastrophic setbacks.

Like the radishes. Following a suggestion in Rodale's *Encyclopedia*, Eliot had thought to plant rows of radishes along the edges of their carrot field—being quicker to germinate, the radish seedlings provided orienting row markers that appeared weeks before the carrots' first delicate wisps emerged. It was ingenious and worked perfectly—the radishes were plump enough to harvest just as the carrots came ready for thinning. But the new farmers suddenly found themselves with a problem it had never occurred to them to anticipate—now they also had a huge crop of radishes with no ready market for them. As delicious as they were, snacking made only the tiniest dent in the hundreds of pounds they kept stored in every available tub.

With typical creativity, Peg and the others tried radish salads, radish stews, radish stir-fry, even radish burgers. One afternoon, they invited their friends at Myrtle Hill over for a softball game, Myrtle versus Entropy. Whoever scored a run had to accept a whole shopping bag full of radishes. It was not clear what actually constituted victory.

But radish overdose was the least of their worries. There had been another, more dire, miscalculation.

Though they'd been surpassingly grateful to the Johns family for saving them after their horse plow failed to function, another problem had immediately presented itself: the rows created by the tractor were the wrong width for the rest of the horse-drawn equipment. Not even the wagon could fit between rows, meaning that many of the tools they'd spent the winter accumulating would sit idle all season. Chris was still absorbing this disappointment when a worse realization set in: every bit of labor on their two-acre cash crop would now have to be done by hand.

Starting with the sowing. Carrot seeds are miraculously tiny, prone to getting stuck in every crevice. Walking the rows with bags of seed, bent over to keep the wind from scattering the handfuls before they hit the ground, squinting to see if they'd even landed in the right rows—this was only the first taste of the months of backbreaking labor to come.

As the summer went on, the enormity of the task they'd undertaken continued to sink in. Every few weeks, the entire crop had to be thinned by hand to allow the remaining carrots room to grow unimpeded. This meant hours and hours of bending, neck exposed to the hot sun, grasping feathery tops between the fingertips and extracting tiny, perfectly formed but unwanted carrots one at a time. At first it seemed a shame to waste the thinnings, small as they were, and Eliot brought handfuls of the bigger ones into the house for dinner. But it wasn't long before no one could stand the sight of them, wilting in heaps between the rows.

It was simply too much work for three adults to handle alone, along with the daily care for a menagerie of animals (and especially when Peg's time was often taken up struggling to stay on top of the constant dairy production); Ellen, of course, had her hands full with the twins, pink-cheeked, flaxen-haired, and busily learning to walk.

When Hershe and Pancake, eager to escape Myrtle Hill's summer intensity, asked permission to set up a tipi in the woods behind Entropy's carrot field in exchange for helping with the crop, Peg and the others could not say yes fast enough.

*

One July afternoon over at Myrtle, Craig heard a car coming up the road. It was a baby-blue Oldsmobile, like something a grandmother would drive, scraping its bottom against the ruts. The couple who emerged from the Olds didn't look quite as square as the car, but they definitely weren't freaks. They were both a little older than most of the people at Myrtle Hill. The man was tall and clean-shaven and his hair just brushed the button-down collar of his oxford shirt. The woman's hair hung to her waist in a long, brown braid, but she was wearing an unadorned work shirt and tennis shoes. They looked a little like young professors or social workers. Craig went over to greet them.

Larry and Judy were Myrtle's new neighbors, in an over-hill-and-dale kind of way. They'd arrived in Vermont only recently and were trying to decide what kind of house to build—it had to be something simple, both because it was already midsummer and they planned to spend the winter in it, and because neither of them had any carpentry experience. Their first choice would have been a log cabin—for each of them, a childhood dream—but they'd heard it was already too late in the season to start. The other options, as Larry explained them, were yurt, A-frame, or geodesic dome. They'd heard Myrtle had one of these and were wondering if they could check it out.

As Craig took them over to the dome, offering his usual visitor explanation about Myrtle's goals and philosophy, Larry and Judy took in the scene. There were people everywhere—working or lying in the grass or walking around in eccentric states of dress and undress—more people in one place, Judy realized later, than she'd seen anywhere since arriving in Vermont. Who were they all? How on earth had they ended up in the woods? Larry's eyes lingered for a moment on the chicken shed where someone had evidently been crashing that summer—some bedding blankets and a stump of candle were just visible through the shadows.

Jim the Bear was working at the dome when they ducked through the door. He was happy to stop and answer questions, his appealing, gap-toothed grin flashing beneath his droopy mustache. He explained about Drop City and about Myrtle's aborted attempt to use car tops as siding—this summer's successful innovation had been to abandon that idea and finish the dome instead with scrap-wood slats they got for a few cents each at the local lumberyard. For light and ventilation, they had left many of the dome's triangles uncovered, as windows and skylights. The dome's new mix of materials gave it an eclectic, almost jaunty look, not far from the communards' own mode of dressing—whimsical and multicolored here, practical and work-weathered there.

At first, as Jim explained the process of construction to Larry, Judy listened closely. She was as excited to get started building and learning as Larry was. But after a while, when it became clear that the men did not consider her to be a participant in the conversation—or possibly had forgotten she was still standing there at all—it became harder to concentrate on what they were saying. Her eyes kept wandering upward, to the triangles left open to the arcing clear blue of the sky. The dome felt even more organic and futuristic on the inside than it looked on the outside. The curved, cupping walls held a space somehow both cozy and breathtaking. *I want to live in a space like this*, Judy thought. Larry was still asking Jim questions, but for her, the issue of what they would build was now decided.

Constructing a dome could not be easier, Jim assured them. He sent them off with his own copy of the best new instruction manual for dome builders. What's more, he offered to help Larry and Judy with whatever they needed once they got started. They thanked him and he waved them off, smiling.

The book Jim gave my parents was called *Domebook 2*. It had only been out a few months; their copy was one of the first of a work that would eventually become one of the most iconic documents of the 1970s' back-to-the-land movement. Its author, Lloyd Kahn, was the *Whole Earth Catalog*'s shelter editor.

Three years earlier, in 1968, Kahn had gone to work at the alternative, student-led Pacific High School in the hills of Santa Cruz with an idea to teach students how to build domes. Almost at once, this activity had become the school's central focus.

Before long, students and teachers had put up seventeen domes, scattered through the woods, in a variety of designs and materials. Buckminster Fuller himself visited the campus in 1970, at age seventy-four, and signaled his support by taking a quick nap on a waterbed in the inflated-plastic Pillowdome.

It was Kahn's notes from the school's many experiments with geodesic formulas and building materials that became the basis for his books. *Domebook 2* offered a range of possible designs and materials, along with instructions and detailed commentary by builders. It also followed the *Whole Earth Catalog*'s practice of printing letters, pictures, and advice from readers.

In fact, *Domebook One* had included a letter from Myrtle Hill's Chico, expressing his frustration over the dome-building problems the summer before: "The whole process is clumsy, slow, awkward, bitchy, often a drag to be doing," he wrote.

Jim and the others had designated Myrtle Hill's dome as a workshop for the commune's cottage industry: a candle factory.

Jim had devised a simple but ingenious setup. A woodstove inside the dome held pans of melted wax. Above this hovered a rack, specially designed by Jim, over which a candle maker draped lengths of stringlike wick. You could then lower the rack toward the pan, repeatedly immersing the wicks in melted wax until the candles reached the desired thickness. This method produced dozens of tapers in a single batch.

For block candles, discarded oil cans made perfect molds. By dipping or pouring wax in layers, you could achieve a rainbowy, psychedelic effect that could be highlighted further by carving designs into the finished candle—a creative job everyone loved to do in the evenings. Innovation, as always, was welcome: Nancy had spent a few months experimenting with sand candles. For these, you filled a container with wet sand that you scooped into a bowl shape. Once poured in, the wax seeped slightly into the sand, lending the finished candle a pleasingly rough-hewn look.

Myrtle's candle factory was an ingenious system and created a smart product—everyone, even middle-class straights, needed candles, and the psychedelic look was fashionable. Throughout the summer, Fletcher and Craig made periodic trips to peddle the candles at craft fairs and health-food stores in Boston, New York, and Cape Cod. They unfailingly sold out their entire stock.

Still, it was not as profitable as they wished. They usually ended up with only enough money to resupply the wax and buy a few bags of oats or brown rice. In a pinch, if no generous visitor came through to restock whatever staple Loraine said she needed for the kitchen or if Jed was between trips, Craig dipped into his own savings to cover supplies.

Craig and Fletcher's candle-selling trips were a needed component of Myrtle Hill's economy (as well as being frankly fun for the two men). But Craig was finding that being gone from the hill for stretches of time created its own set of problems.

In another lesson learned from the previous autumn's scramble, as soon as the ground thawed, they had made sure to turn up soil for a garden on a sunny slope in the upper meadow. Beyond a basic organic philosophy of no commercial fertilizers and an effort at a compost heap, the garden had no organizing principle whatsoever. If you liked a vegetable, you planted it. This made for plentiful but chaotic cultivation. It also introduced a less-than-fully-cooperative corollary that revealed itself as the summer went along: if you wanted to actually reap a harvest, it was on you to care for your own crops. So it was that Craig returned from a candle-selling trip to find that the vegetables he'd planted had been ignored by everyone else and were now choked with weeds.

Years later, Loraine was still chuckling over Craig's indignation at this discovery, but it revealed one of the tensions underlying all the work that second summer. Who decides what each person's work ethic and priorities should be? How do you maintain a leaderless system and a do-your-own-thing freedom while also making sure that the group has what it needs to survive?

The chore wheel they'd put up at the beginning of the summer had immediately fallen into disuse, and Loraine and Nancy had once again taken the cooking, cleaning, and childcare upon themselves, now aided by Amy. But even other, seemingly more-desirable jobs presented staffing problems. Some tasks took a lot of practice to master or just weren't very fun. For example, the artistic joys of candle-making were balanced against the sheer unpleasantness of the work. The dome heated quickly, and the melted wax required a daylong fire in the stove—pleasant in cool weather but intolerable on a humid day. The wax itself let off terrible fumes that gave you a headache after a few hours, and the rig for dipping the tapers, though ingenious, was all hand built and forever running into snags that had to be painstakingly untangled.

Even when a project did get under way, there were many obstacles to achieving a focused stretch of work. A crucial tool would break or be mislaid; one person would get started building or organizing and then come back from a break to find someone else undertaking the same job using their own, totally incompatible method. There were also the problems of focus that are to be expected from so many people smoking so much pot so much of the time.

And then there were the distractions of the setting itself. On the long, exquisite summer afternoons, someone would inevitably decide to drive the pickup truck over to a local pond (they could have walked over to the lake en route to Entropy, but its many vacationers put a crimp in the group's preference for daylight skinny-dipping). Anyone who wanted to join would immediately drop what they were doing and pile in. Sometimes the swim break refreshed and energized the whole group. But just as often, those who had undertaken jobs that couldn't easily be dropped—cooking dinner, for example, or staying with napping children or tending the fire under the candle wax—resented having to be martyrs. It was hard not to notice who defined "do your own thing" in a way that benefited themselves more than the group as a whole.

Amy could see Craig's frustration growing each time he returned from a candle-selling trip and found simple projects he'd thought everyone agreed with him were urgent, still left undone. She was sympathetic—she could also see that Loraine and the others mobbed him with problems they expected him to solve the moment he arrived—but she knew from her own experience that it was hard to carry out Craig's vision exactly the way he wanted, especially when he was so often absent. He also didn't seem to notice the way the men's workday ended with talking and passing joints around the campfire while the women continued to cook, clean, and chase after the children until long after dark.

Amy still missed Craig when he was gone, though slightly less since the arrival of LJ. He was twenty-one, broad shouldered, and strong with a brown beard and shoulder-length hair he scraped back in a ponytail. He had played high school football until a brutal hit crushed his windpipe and almost killed him. The injury had left him with a soft, reedy voice and a 4-F exemption from the draft board. He had always been quiet and given to introspection, but his near-death experience—and the fact that it, ironically, was saving him from heading into war like so many of his classmates—had shifted something in him. He had been granted life and he needed to find a way to really live.

LJ was from Cranford, New Jersey, Craig's hometown. This was not a coincidence. LJ's best friend Dennis was dating Craig's little sister Melissa, and it was the three of them who'd arrived together at Craig's invitation. They'd driven north in the '52 Chevy truck that LJ and Dennis had spent the whole previous year fixing up, installing a built-in camper and state-of-the-art eight-track stereo. The three friends had planned a months-long road trip, and Myrtle Hill was the very first stop.

For LJ, life in the country agreed with him right away. He had always loved visiting his cousins' Pennsylvania farm, and at Myrtle Hill he found immense satisfaction in gardening and teaching himself to chop wood for the fire. He was utterly undaunted by hard physical labor, and his skill as a mechanic made him instantly invaluable. While he was slightly disappointed to discover that Craig's descriptions of diligent group work weren't exactly borne out in reality, life at the commune still offered so much to learn. LJ was particularly drawn to Jim the Bear and his inventive genius. Working alongside Jim in the dome, he quickly became one of the summer's principal candle-makers.

Before long, Dennis and Melissa were ready to continue on their Great American Road Trip. But for LJ, Vermont and, in particular, Myrtle Hill, offered the kind of experience he'd been looking for. Despite the vagaries of the communal work ethic, the goal of self-sufficiency appealed to him. He'd also rapidly come to feel at home in the woods.

Besides, he had fallen for beautiful, lively Amy. When Dennis and Melissa packed up the Chevy and headed down the driveway, he watched them go without regret.

With a few notable exceptions, he never left Myrtle Hill again.

CHAPTER 11

Sitting in their field a few miles away, Larry and Judy pored over the pages of *Domebook 2*.

The site they'd picked for their dome was halfway up a long field sloping up from the road, just where it flattened out briefly before climbing even more steeply upwards. The field ran east-west, and they were already planning to face the dome's windows south so that it would collect light all day. In the morning, when they emerged from their tent into the cool morning air and looked eastward down the field, the rising sun caught every tiny dewdrop that clung to the timothy grass, every blade and spider-web glittering and dazzling for the few minutes before the sun rose hot enough to lift it away into mist.

Years later, neither Judy nor Larry could say, exactly, when or how the idea of moving to the country had occurred to them. They had picked it up from the air, by the same invisible osmosis as had thousands of other young, middle-class white people at just the same moment. It would be decades before either of them even realized they'd been part of a huge demographic surge, never mind participated in something called a "movement" without even realizing it. At the time, the idea of living simply and close to the earth just felt like a natural solution to their own particular problems and desires.

Both of them had been in the Peace Corps in Nepal. Larry's group, in 1963, was only the second in that country. He spent

161

two years hiking in the Himalayas, drinking yak's milk tea, and talking to village leaders about democracy. One morning he woke up to the news on the shortwave radio from India that John F. Kennedy had been shot. For three days, he could not get "Jesu, Joy of Man's Desiring" out of his head. The five kinds of intestinal worms he contracted had the positive side effect of permanently ridding him of the baby fat that had plagued him since adolescence. He returned to the States sixty-five pounds leaner, strong, and confident.

The Peace Corps offered him a job training the next group of volunteers headed to Nepal. On the first day, he noticed a beautiful young woman with hazel eyes and a long, brown braid. Judy's face, in repose, slipped into an introspective melancholy that utterly vanished when she smiled. She had a way of tilting up her chin that made her seem defiant and vulnerable at the same time. He offered to tutor her in Nepali; she volunteered to iron his shirts. When they got closer, he gave her his Nepal journals to read. He teased her gently for her subtle Virginia accent; she pointed out that he said toma*h*to like a Boston Brahmin.

When the group went through their military-style physical training, Larry could see that Judy was fast and strong and fearless. In motion, she had a relaxed confidence that turned to silent awkwardness in groups with lots of people talking. When the two of them slipped away for private conversations, though, she emerged smart and thoughtful with plenty to say. Judy had none of the coiffed polish of the co-eds Larry had dated in college—she seemed utterly unaware of her arresting beauty. There was something intoxicatingly feral about her.

For Judy's part, Larry's interest drew her in, to her own astonishment. The male attention attracted by her high cheekbones and curvy figure had always made her impatient and skittish, but this was different somehow. Larry had clear blue eyes and side-parted brown hair. He was prep-school handsome and confident to the point of cockiness. Being around someone so sure of themselves was like standing near a bright light; it made where she was feel a little less in shadow. He was her first real boyfriend.

A trainer dating a trainee was against the Peace Corps rules, but they didn't care. By the time Judy's group got ready to depart overseas three months later, they knew they had something serious.

For the two years she was away, they wrote letters on thin, blue airmail paper. To get the mail, Judy walked two and a half hours to the nearest Himalayan market village on switchback mountain paths that wound past terraced rice paddies, the green striped with blue from the watery, reflected sky. Along with Larry's letters, her mail contained the copies of *Newsweek* her family sent, but rather than bringing home closer, it only highlighted the distance in every way. She didn't know what to make of the trends that *Newsweek* breathlessly reported were storming America in 1967—Flower Children, antiwar marches, marijuana. When she read an article declaring that miniskirts had taken over women's fashion, she wondered if she'd return home to find her plump, Victorian grandmothers wearing them too.

This wasn't the only question she had about her return home after two years away. In their letters, she and Larry had arranged to spend a few days together soon after she arrived back in the States. As Judy scanned for him at the airport, pulse racing, she suddenly thought, "I wonder if I'm going to recognize this guy."

He wasn't worried. They found each other and within a few days it was clear that they were going to be able to pick up where they'd left off. Only now they had an even richer pool of common experiences to draw them together. Almost none of their other friends or family had traveled anywhere outside of Europe or spoke any foreign languages they hadn't learned in school. Larry and Judy had each been through the most profound experience of their lives. It was a source of endless thrill to crack jokes with each other in Nepali. Together, they reinforced each other's newfound identity: traveler, world citizen, adventurer.

Their families, though, didn't seem to notice how profoundly the Peace Corps had changed them. Larry's father, Al, grumbled that Larry was too old not to have a real job by now—at the same age, he himself had been steering his family's dry cleaning business out of the Depression and into prosperity. Larry steeled himself before breaking the news to Al that he had decided on graduate school and an academic career over dry cleaning even though he knew it would likely mean Al's selling the company his French grandfather had founded in 1847. To Larry's surprise, Al took the news calmly. He realized later that Al considered it a mark of his own financial success that his son would have options for his future instead of simply responding to duty as he himself had done. It also may have helped that Larry's chosen graduate school happened to be Harvard.

Judy's parents hardly asked her about her two years in Nepal, though she found out later they'd proudly showed all of her letters to their large circle of friends.

Her father, Eddie, was born in Manhattan, the son of a Republican, German-Jewish garment salesman. Eddie graduated from the University of Wisconsin with a master's degree in geology; then, during the war, he became a defense strategist and an early member of the OSS. Judy and her three siblings grew up on the rambling, ten-acre homestead Eddie had bought in the 1940s on the fast-disappearing farmland of Alexandria, Virginia. Judy's stepmother Kay kept ponies, goats, and chickens and, though she herself had been raised in a posh Chicago suburb, she taught the children to ride, milk, and gather eggs. Eddie cultivated a big garden and a peach orchard. The property included two apartments whose residents became lifelong family friends, the children constantly in and out of each other's homes.

Judy, her older brother, and two younger sisters all attended a local, progressive elementary school, Burgundy Farm Country Day School. Its founders believed that farming and outdoor life played an essential role in children's education. The school itself was on a former dairy farm and the curriculum included chores and animal care. On weekends, parents pitched in to help renovate barns and classrooms—partly out of community spirit and to keep down costs, but also because the progressive founders felt that asking fathers and mothers to stumble through their own trial-and-error learning in the presence of their children provided a healthy antidote to the "Father Knows Best" '50s culture that dangerously discouraged any questioning of authority. In 1950, when Judy was in second grade, several African-American students enrolled, making Burgundy the first racially integrated school in Virginia.

Judy thrived at Burgundy. She was an athletic, energetic child, a tomboy who didn't wear a girl's bathing suit until she was twelve and had no patience for dolls or playing house. She was quick and strong and relished her ability to run and climb faster and higher than anyone else. Once, a boy she'd beaten in a field-day wrestling match refused to say "Uncle." Fuming at being forced to miss other events, Judy sat on his chest for two hours.

Then, when she was eleven, for the first time in her life, a boy zoomed past her in a footrace. Seeing the look of shock on Judy's face, a woman nearby commented, "You'll never beat them again." Even through her humiliated rage, Judy knew she was hearing the truth.

Burgundy only went up through elementary school, so the year Judy reached sixth grade, 1954, she transferred to a huge, suburban junior high. Instead of her childhood uniform of jeans and plaid shirts, she now had to wear skirts every day. The other girls sported perfectly corkscrewed ponytails, but Judy's stepmother refused to let her grow out her awkward, practical bob. Fights over hair were the least of their conflicts. Kay could spend hours encouragingly helping a nine-year-old clean and reassemble a bridle but she had no patience for a sullen, miserable teenage girl. Kay had raised Judy and her brother Peter since they were toddlers, after their own mother had died suddenly. Though she considered them as much her own as their two younger half-sisters, she was temperamentally ill-equipped to nurture two grief-stricken children; following convention, neither she or Eddie ever spoke about their mother, his beloved first wife. One day, rebuffing a teary Judy, Kay told her, "You're too old for hugs." Judy was six.

Soon into her seventh-grade year, her new school sent home a form for families to fill out, asking: *In the case of a nuclear attack, how long would it take for your child to get home? What is your plan of escape?* Judy discussed the questions with Eddie.

She rode a bus to school—it was more than five miles. How long would it take to run that distance in saddle shoes? A hour? More? Judy dutifully wrote down the figures she and Eddie calculated, but a cynical thought asserted itself: "My family will have left by the time I get there." In the case of a nuclear attack, she thought, "I'm done."

Judy spent the rest of high school waiting to escape, first to college, then directly into the Peace Corps. When she returned to Alexandria from Kathmandu, her steamer trunk stuffed with Tibetan rugs and brass bowls, she realized immediately she couldn't stay. Kay still treated her like the sullen adolescent she'd been when she left home. Within a few weeks of returning to the States, she moved into Larry's graduate school apartment in Cambridge. Four months later, they were married.

Larry's graduate program commanded most of his time and attention, so Judy often found herself alone in the city. She was still reeling from culture shock. After two years of living in a remote village where people grew or made almost everything they needed, the supermarket left her stunned and exhausted: What kind of society needed twenty-five varieties of dog food? In the stores and on the street, everywhere she turned her head, ads and signs and slogans clamored for her attention. She started hunting out every park she could find, in search of some sort of landscape, however tiny, some green corner where her eyes could rest.

At night, alone in their sweltering apartment with Larry not yet home from campus, Judy paced the bare, tiny living room like a cage. She would have loved to go for a walk to clear her head, but she didn't argue with Larry's assessment that the dark streets were too threatening for a woman to venture out alone.

Judy found herself fantasizing about escaping the city. She could see it in her mind's eye: a meadow, flanked with pines, sloping down toward the sea.

When she told Larry this idea, he loved it. They began to discuss the merits of buying land. It would be a solid investment for their small savings, more secure than a bank—Larry and Judy did not go as far as some of their more political friends in predicting an immanent systemic collapse but neither were they optimists. Like a lot of people in 1968, they sensed that *something* terrible was about to happen, they just didn't know what. Land, the idea of a little green foothold all their own, was the first anchor in a long time that had let them feel calm.

Rural New England would place them close but not too close to their families. They had just begun discussing coastal Maine in earnest when Larry got a call from an old Peace Corps buddy.

Nick wanted a ride to Vermont. He had a friend who'd found some land up there, and Nick needed to go check it out. Wouldn't Larry and Judy like to give him a lift? He knew they had been thinking about getting out of the city too.

Vermont had not occurred to them, but they were curious and not about to turn down a road trip that would get them out of the city on a beautiful September weekend.

The trip kicked off with an eerie work of coincidence. Nick's friend Nash, who had found the land, turned out to be a Burgundy schoolmate of Judy's—her brother's best friend, in fact. They hadn't seen each since adolescence but Judy remembered the pale, bookish, blond boy she'd known, now grown into a handsome young man. Nash had joined the Civil Rights Movement in 1965, just after Freedom Summer, and had spent the last several years registering voters in rural Mississippi. When the group he'd been working with started to splinter, Nash decided it was time to move on. He was ready anyway for a different kind of hard work—physical instead of political or emotional.

The land Nash had found in northern Vermont turned out to be the greater part of a five-hundred-acre hilltop farm with pastures, hayfields, spruce and pine woods, and a large maple sugar bush. Roger Perron, the farmer, lived in a modern house at the end of the road, but the acres for sale included a tumbling barn and its abandoned 1830s farmhouse, beginning to list gently away from the elderly apple orchard behind it.

My parents and their friends spent several hours walking the farm's contours, guided by Roger. At the top of one old tractor trail that cut up through some steep fields, Roger stopped and they all turned to take in the view. Judy almost gasped. Across the valley, the round, wooded hills had tidy square fields carved into their flanks. On the hilltops and distant hillsides, the maples had begun to turn red and orange, the warm colors clashing gorgeously with the vibrant green of the fields. As Larry took in the vista, he moved his eyes south across the purple horizon to discover, pale in the blue distance, the jagged peaks of the White Mountains where he'd learned to hike as a teenager. All of them stood, taking it in. There was more to see—the sugar bush, loggable stands of timber, free-flowing springs, an old cellar hole or two—but for Larry and Judy, the maple-bright vista across the valley had permanently erased any idea of Maine.

That night, giddy with possibility, the four of them agreed to buy the land together. Larry and Judy had a small nest egg of a few thousand dollars and Nash had about the same. Nick, however, had been working for an aid organization in India, living on next to nothing, and had saved his whole year's salary. He agreed to contribute the entire sum as a down payment. The four of them would own the land in common, that much was clear. The rest of the details could work themselves out later.

At the local bank the next day, the friendly, young manager, Charlie Barrows, listened as they explained their plans. Overseas work would take all of them away for a few years—Nash to Mozambique, Nick possibly back to India, and Larry and Judy to Papua New Guinea, where Larry would conduct his graduate research. But, Larry and Judy assured Charlie, they couldn't wait to return and make Vermont their home.

And now, in mid-July of 1971, they had.

After years abroad, Judy and Larry were both eager to get started on their new adventure. They'd each returned from their travels with a new sense of purpose.

For Larry, it had come in the form of an epiphany. One day, he was walking out of a remote Papuan village when it suddenly occurred to him: every adult here (and probably many of the children) knew how to construct and maintain their own houses, make their own clothes, and raise and hunt enough food for their families. They had an expertise entirely different from his own; and theirs (food, shelter, community) revealed his (theory, argument, concept) to be horrifyingly flimsy by comparison. The fact was, if some catastrophe were to return the world to premodern conditions, these villagers would be fine and he would die immediately, out of pure ignorance. "What's all this education for if I can't even build my own house?" he thought.

Judy had had her own revelation.

In the ex-pat community of Port Moresby, Judy had found herself among the wives. She had tried to volunteer with a family planning program, but her lack of medical expertise meant she wasn't allowed to actually do anything. The cocktail parties where Larry thrived were sheer torture for her. She began to feel like a ghost, haunting her own life.

She was twenty-seven, strong, fearless, and a quick learner, filled with energy she was dying to put to good use but that was slowly curdling into a frustrated rage.

One night, unable to articulate her storm of emotions, she put a hole in the flimsy wall of their apartment's bathroom with her fist. Larry, astonished, wondered if this outburst had been brought on by the copy of Betty Friedan's *The Feminine Mystique* Judy had been reading. It probably wasn't a coincidence, Judy acknowledged, but her sense of impotent anger had been building for months, if not years.

She swore never to feel that useless again.

In their travels, they'd been telling everyone they were from Vermont, assuming correctly that most people they met would not push them very hard on the details. But in truth, they had no idea where the land they'd bought even was, much less how to get there. Sheepishly, Larry wrote Nick and asked him to send directions.

Nash was still in Africa, but Nick had moved to the land—permanently, as it turned out—and started building a cabin. Like them, Nick had grown up in a big house in suburbia. He was a bear of a man, tall with blunt features, a brush of sandy hair, wide shoulders, and strong hands. He was tireless and sharply intelligent but gruff and impatient with anything that looked to him like incompetence.

Over the winter, Nick had encountered the stragglers at Myrtle Hill. He was disgusted that almost all the men had taken off for the winter and had made it his business to drop in occasionally to help with their perpetual firewood crisis (and, unsubtly but unsuccessfully, to let the mostly-female residents know he was available).

In late 1970, a few months before Judy and Larry's return, Nick had written to gauge Larry's interest in the idea of starting a commune on their land. Or at least opening up the property to some interested people he'd met through Myrtle Hill. Larry responded: "Both Judy and I think it would not be a good idea for them to move onto the land. Not now anyway. I appreciate that they might be milked for some valuable labor but they could also lead to all kinds of trouble . . . Besides, we don't want strangers being more familiar with our land than we are." Nick hadn't pushed the idea, but the idea of communal living, in some form or other, still appealed to him.

Before joining the Peace Corps, Nick had gotten a degree in forestry from Syracuse, and he had a lot of ideas about how the three of them (the third being Nash) could best support themselves in their new home while also being good stewards of the land. Since he'd been living in Vermont full time he'd been working odd jobs for local farmers, cutting pulp, and making cedar fence posts. It was hard, physical work but satisfyingly so. With his entrepreneurial mind, Nick had begun to think about how to develop similar businesses that would allow one to make a full living off the land. He knew two things for sure: one, he'd never work in an office again; and two, all his ideas would be easier to carry out with help from his friends.

When Larry and Judy arrived at last, in the baby-blue Oldsmobile they'd inherited from Larry's grandmother, Nick could hardly wait to share the plans he'd made for them all. He'd given their potential living arrangements a lot of thought and come to the conclusion that they'd work best as a team if they lived like a close-knit family. Even if Larry and Nash didn't embrace the idea of becoming a single household as Myrtle Hill had done, they could still build homes nearby one another, the better to share work and resources. He'd built his own cabin on what was obviously the hub of the land, he told them. He had house sites picked out nearby for them too.

Larry and Judy heard him out, but they had different ideas about how they would support themselves in their adult lives. Larry had no intention of scrapping his newly minted doctoral degree in favor of a life of physical labor, as eager as he was to learn how to build a house.

Judy was more personally inclined toward making her livelihood with her hands, and she loved the idea of working in the woods all day, but she had other reservations about Nick's proposed plans: the way Nick looked at her made her uncomfortable. Though it was nothing she hadn't encountered when she was single, she had assumed that marriage—and especially the actual presence of her husband—would place her off-limits to the advances of other men. The discovery that the rules around monogamy and marriage had changed drastically in the counterculture during her years abroad came as an unwelcome shock. Though Nick stopped immediately and forever as soon as she asked him to, she was already exhausted. It had only been three days. The idea of living for the next thirty years cheek-by-jowl with any similarly minded single man filled her with dread.

Larry hadn't particularly noticed the dynamic, but he didn't need any convincing. Nick's flood of plans weren't sitting right with him either. This much was clear: whatever the two of them were going to do, they had to figure it out fast.

They walked up to the field Nick had suggested as a possible house site for them and sat, taking in the view. It was only midafternoon but the summer sun had already dipped behind the high cliff to the west, casting them in shadow. This spot that Nick had identified as the "hub of the land" was also its deepest valley. "If this is what it's like in summer, what time does the sun set in winter?" Judy wondered. If this was the hub, she thought, "I want to be on the rim."

Obeying their instincts, she and Larry stood up and made their way to the main road. Retracing the walk they'd taken with Roger Perron three years earlier, past the barn and tilting farmhouse with its ancient orchard, they found the same tractor trail they'd climbed that day. Halfway up, where the sloping fields leveled out to a meadow, they turned around to see a version of the exact view that had enraptured them then and sustained them during their years abroad: hills, fields, maple hedgerows, and everywhere an exuberant, exploding green.

They broke the news to Nick that night. He took it very hard, predicting—correctly—that the committed, work-sharing alternate family he'd spent the winter planning for would never materialize in the way that he'd hoped. If Nick wanted to make a living off the land, he'd be doing it solo.

Judy and Larry, meanwhile, did not look back. The mutual aid elements of Nick's plan appealed to them, but neither of them had any desire to live communally. Their visit to Myrtle Hill a few days later did not change their minds.

Larry and Judy wanted many of the same things that Myrtle Hill's residents wanted—to build their own shelter and grow their own food; to become more self-sufficient; to create a simple life, close to nature—but they did not share the communards' distrust of the nuclear family or the desire to reinvent the underlying structure of American domestic life. For them, a conventional marriage and a household of two seemed like plenty for the tremendous amount of work they were about to undertake.

"A couple, of any age from twenty to fifty, with a minimum of health, intelligence and capital, can adapt themselves to country living, learn its crafts, overcome its difficulties, and build up a life pattern rich in simple values and productive of personal and social good," wrote Helen and Scott Nearing in their classic, generation-shaping book, *Living the Good Life*. For thousands of young people in the 1970s, wondering how to undertake a life of radical, rural simplicity, the Nearings' book (subtitle: *How to Live Sanely in a Troubled World*) provided a set of clear, inviting, impassioned instructions.

Though *Living the Good Life* has often been called "the bible of the 1970s Back-to-the-Land Movement," the '60s' counterculture generation who embraced it most fully was not its intended audience. The Nearings hailed from a Depression-era generation of back-to-the-landers. Scott was born in 1883, and his involvement with simplicity movements dated all the way back to a turn-of-the-century "single tax" community, Arden. He was a socialist, an outspoken pacifist and held a doctorate in Economics. In 1918, he was charged with treason for critiquing the United States involvement in the First World War. Though he was soon acquitted, he was fired from his teaching job and blacklisted by other academic institutions. Despairing, Scott and Helen concluded their only solution was to build a new life for themselves as homesteaders. In 1932, the Nearings moved from New York to a worn-out hillside farm in southern Vermont.

There, they built themselves a stone house, developed large, organic gardens, and supplemented their income with a seasonal cash crop of maple syrup. In 1950, after turning their syrup-making experiences into *The Maple Sugar Book*, they received a visit from their editor. His wife, the Nobel Prize–winning novelist Pearl Buck, was taken with their way of life and told them that they should write about it. But a few years later when Helen turned in the manuscript for *Living the Good Life,* the publisher had changed its mind. Determined to find an audience, Helen and Scott self-published it in 1954 under their own imprint, Social Science Institute. It's unclear whether the initial run of two thousand copies even sold out.

But by the late '60s, demand had changed. Sales of older back-to-the-land titles had begun to take off, spurred in part by their being listed in the *Whole Earth Catalog.* By then the Nearings had left Vermont and moved to Harborside, Maine, where they continued to build with stone and grow most of their own food. In 1970, Schocken Books reissued *Living the Good Life*, using the Nearings' original 1954 electrotyped plates, but with an added foreword by Paul Goodman: "Today very many young people across the country have decided to try subsistence farming and natural foods for nearly the same reasons as the Nearings told themselves forty years ago," he wrote. "What the young can get from this book is know-how."

The young, apparently, agreed. The reissued *Living the Good Life* sold fifty thousand copies in its first year and was soon translated into five languages. The now-elderly Nearings had written the perfect book for the new homesteading movement.

It's not hard to understand what 1970s readers loved about *Living the Good Life*. In addition to the Nearings' radical politics and the framing of their project as an urgent personal response to a crumbling society, the book itself offered appealing, straightforward-sounding instructions for building and gardening, and a moral rationale that could have been written by the '70s generation themselves: "The society from which we moved had rejected in practice and in principle our pacifism, our vegetarianism and our collectivism," they wrote in their preface. "We hoped to replace worry, fear and hate with serenity, purpose and at-one-ness." Their "4-4-4" philosophy split the day into three periods, dedicated to "bread-labor" (gardening and building), "association" (engagement with community and for social change), and "leisure time." This solution promised not only a life rich in good food and honest work but that most elusive of prizes, time to pursue the life of the mind.

After the book's reissue, the Nearings' leisure time was seriously compromised by the endless waves of visitors who made their way to their Harborside home. Though the Nearings had a practice of making room at the table for whoever stopped by and inviting visitors into the day's work, by the paperback reprint of *Living the Good Life*, they'd felt compelled to add an afterword, asking eager pilgrims to please respect their posted visiting hours "in order that we can maintain our own good life."

As openly as the Nearings welcomed visitors, privately they were generally unimpressed with the young people coming to see them: Scott considered most of them "unattached, uncommitted, insecure, uncertain human beings . . . apolitical, impatient of restraints." Helen observed the dearth of black or working-class visitors and noted that many had been "raised in comfort if not pampered in luxury," though she and Scott both had come from affluent families themselves.

The fact that the Nearings weren't completely forthcoming about their finances in *Living the Good Life* has brought criticism, in some cases by followers stung by the discovery that the Nearings' lifestyle counted on invisible resources—such as inheritance, and Scott's speaking fees from the four months a year he spent on a lecture circuit.

But the difficulties their '70s acolytes found in following the Nearings' version of the good life were not entirely due to the Nearings' very real sins of omission. Scott and Helen were quite specific about the austere, domestic details that made their model work—their vegan diet, for example, was not just a nutritional or moral choice, but a practical one. As they put it, "No man is free who has an animal." Owning chickens, let alone goats or cows, added tremendously to a household's workload and seriously affected its flexibility—milking doesn't allow a single morning off, never mind a four-month lecture tour. The Nearings were also middle-aged, without young children. They enjoyed extreme good health (though again, critics point out a few medical omissions from their work)—and, for people who built huge, stone-walled houses well into their eighties, had spectacular good luck. Scott died two weeks past his one-hundredth birthday while Helen died a dozen years later, at ninety-one, in a car accident.

Their guidebook's sureness of tone made readers feel as though the Nearings' good life was readily accessible, but even Helen and Scott themselves didn't intend their way to be followed unquestioningly. In a 1976 documentary, Scott, pausing as he splits wood, explains his philosophy to the camera. "This is the good life," he says. Then, correcting himself: "This is *a* good life." As far as the Nearings were concerned, other couples between the ages of twenty and fifty with a minimum of health, intelligence, and capital could find their own way to adapt to country living. That couple could build a stone house like the Nearings' or a construction of their own choosing. Including a geodesic dome.

After careful consideration—or as much consideration as they could spare, given that the summer was half gone, Larry and Judy had decided to build a twenty-foot, 5/8 icosahedron. The instructions, which they'd carefully worked out themselves on scrap paper following a formula in the back of *Domebook 2*, called for almost one hundred lengths of 2″ × 3″, cut at various angles.

Larry's brother-in-law, Gene, had a home woodshop in New Hampshire and had offered them the use of his tools. The next weekend, Larry and Judy loaded up the used pickup for which they'd traded the baby-blue Olds—a bright-red Toyota they rechristened "Tomato," a word they each pronounced differently—and drove over. With them was Jim the Bear, who'd offered to come along and help.

Gene was an experienced woodworker and was ready to help Larry and Judy in whatever way he could. It was hard for him to understand what they were doing, however. Jim, with his laidback grin and long, messy hair did not reassure Gene that Larry and Judy were in the hands of an expert. Gene spent the weekend watching in open horror as his guests used his band saw to blithely cut lumber into bizarre shapes. It was clear they had no sense of what they were doing beyond following their sheet of scribbled calculations. At the end of the weekend, they loaded everything back into the truck. Even in her enthusiasm Judy had to admit—it looked like a pile of oversized Tinkertoys.

There's no way these flimsy-looking pieces could ever come together as a viable shelter, Gene told Larry and Judy. He had recently finished renovating an old garage into a house and had a keen sense of the work it took to keep the bitter drafts of a New England winter at bay. His in-laws' casual attitude about their own impending folly alarmed him so much he could hardly speak to them. Finally, as they were preparing to leave, he told them bluntly: "You're going to die."

Larry shrugged this off, undaunted. Judy, though, could not shake the vague sense that they'd been cursed.

Back on their hill a few days later, my parents looked up from what they were doing to see a young man with a thick mustache and glasses walking up the hill toward them. He was thin and wiry and was carrying a backpack and wearing a tool belt. It was the son of a family friend—Judy hadn't seen him in years—who had been hitchhiking around New England, working as a carpenter. His mother had told him what Larry and Judy were up to, so he'd made his way to Vermont. Later, they reflected that the sudden appearance of a near-stranger on a hilltop so remote that they themselves were just getting adept at finding it should probably have surprised them more than it did at the time. But in the 1971 counterculture, people appeared and disappeared unannounced with a fluidity and spontaneity almost unimaginable even a few years later. The intense, fleeting interactions that arose from all this coming and going drew from and contributed to the going ethos: "the universe provides."

Larry and Judy were not particularly inclined toward this kind of mystical thinking, but it immediately became clear that the mysterious carpenter who had arrived so providentially was a godsend. The first thing he did, almost upon setting down his backpack, was to show them how to construct a simple scaffolding by lashing together freshly cut saplings. Their gratitude for this solution was tinged by sheepishness in realizing they hadn't exactly thought through how they'd reach the top of the dome.

In his sparse belongings, he carried a hammer, a saw, and a square. "You can build anything with these three tools," he told them. He showed Judy how to balance a handsaw to achieve a clean, effortless cut—a lesson she never forgot. After a few days of camping out in the field, he moved on. Neither of them ever saw him again.

It was clear by now that, no matter how simple the instructions made it sound, raising the dome's frame was going to be a more-than-two-person job. Judy and Larry set a date and issued an invitation for a dome raising. Family and a few friends agreed to come and help. No one really knew what to expect, least of all Larry and Judy.

The one person who might have shed some insight, Jim the Bear, was nowhere to be found. One afternoon, he had told his friends at Myrtle Hill that he was going into town to run an errand and simply never returned. They never saw him again.

Judy's parents had donated a canvas Army tent for the guests to sleep in. The day before the planned dome raising, Judy and her sister measured a length of sapling for the tent's central support pole. But when they hoisted it into place, the pole fell four inches short. Judy suddenly realized that she and her sister had also measured all the lumber they'd cut for the dome. A sudden cold dread gripped her: *What if the pieces were all the wrong length?* The rest of the doubts she'd been holding at bay flooded in. *What if they didn't have enough people to help? What if the formula turned out to be a hoax or a failure? What if this whole plan was actually as ridiculous and foolhardy as it felt?* But the mood among the others sitting around the fire that night was festive, so she kept her fear to herself.

The next morning, everything was ready to go by 7:00 a.m. Larry had figured that, if they started early, the half-dozen people present could get the frame fully assembled by nightfall. This turned out to be the day's biggest miscalculation.

In fact, the precut pieces—all correctly measured—went together so easily and quickly that the entire structure was standing by 10:00 a.m. As Judy and Larry climbed to the top to secure the final pieces, the frame wobbled drunkenly—for a moment they tensed up, sure it would collapse. But when they slipped the last bolt into place, the structure instantly went rigid and immobile— one more tiny miracle. They tightened the bolt slowly, exalted.

The dome frame looked like it was made out of toothpicks and air. Inside, looking up, the sky appeared carved into triangles of blue, the clouds sliding lazily from one panel into the next. The whole structure seemed light enough to move by hand but was so sturdy that five or six people could all climb up on it together. Judy and Larry and their friends clambered up and down, swung from the beams, walked all around it, took pictures, admired their handiwork, then shrugged their shoulders and, though it was just past noon, cracked open the beers they'd left cooling in springwater, planning on a more appropriate happy hour. There was nothing left to do that day but eat the beans they'd made for lunch and walk down to the lake for a swim.

Myrtle Hill, summer 1971, in front of the dome (note wood panels on top and Drop City–inspired car-top panels on the bottom). Back row (L–R): Fletcher, Jim the Bear, unknown woman, Kathy, LJ; front row: Amelia, Summer, Leecia, Amy, Loraine with Rahula ("the commune's baby"), Dennis and cat, Jason, Nancy holding Kathy's son, Random the dog.

Loraine (without her glasses) in a sunflower field at the Gathering of the Tribes, fall 1970 (photo by Fletcher Oakes).

Craig and tractor (photo by Fletcher Oakes).

Myrtle Hill's Big House and dome from the lower field, ca. winter 1971
(photo by Fletcher Oakes).

Hershe and livestock (photo by Fletcher Oakes).

Riding the bus in San Francisco during the summer of 1967, Fletcher saw a girl come out of a USO wearing a nametag that read "Hi, My name is Fletcher Oakes." He adopted the name on the spot. It became his legal name in the early '70s.

Craig, helping members of the Northeast Kingdom Co-op ("Good Food, Cheap"), ca. 1973 (photo by Fletcher Oakes).

LJ (left) and Dennis, with a Loaves & Fishes truck (photo by Peggy Day).

Eliot, driving Maryann and Bettyann on the road past Entropy Acres (photo by Fletcher Oakes).

Loudon Young (photo by Fletcher Oakes).

My parents, Judy and Larry, in their newly built dome, winter 1971.

Our outhouse (a.k.a. The R. M. Nixon Memorial Hall).

CHAPTER 12

In late summer, Entropy's carrots were finally ready to harvest. Every week, with the aid of Peg, Hershe, Pancake, and whoever else might have wandered over from Myrtle Hill, Eliot and Chris rolled a wheelbarrow down the rows, heaping it to overflowing with freshly pulled carrots before wobbling it back to the barn. When they'd gathered several hundred pounds, they washed each carrot, weighed out one-pound bunches on a scale, bundled them up, and placed each bundle carefully in huge burlap sacks. These they loaded onto the back of Loudon's two-ton farm truck.

It was illegal for anyone but Loudon to operate the truck on open roads, but he'd agreed to drive Chris and Eliot on the weekly round-trip market run to Boston, four hours each way. It was an extraordinary offer but Chris could hear in it Loudon's own eagerness for a rare chance to get off the farm. He'd never been to Boston and he was curious to see the city.

The three men left before dawn, piled into the truck's cab. Soon they were rolling along, Loudon and Chris shooting the shit, chain-smoking Camels, and steadily littering the truck's floor with Schaefer empties. Eliot watched the scenery roll by outside the window. He liked Loudon well enough and appreciated his unfailing generosity, but Loudon's endless, off-color epithets for his Holstein herd bothered him. Where Chris heard hyperbole and affection, not to mention descriptive virtuosity, Eliot couldn't get past the idea that someone whose whole livelihood depended on a working relationship with animals shouldn't speak of them with such disrespect. Eliot recognized the good sense in Loudon's gently offered suggestions, and there was no question he'd saved them from potential disaster more than once, but where Chris eagerly sought out Loudon's advice, Eliot still preferred the ideological purity of the methods he found in his books.

As the traffic got thicker and the buildings closer together, Loudon grew uncharacteristically quiet. The lumbering farm truck felt immense as it wound through Boston's narrow streets, but when they pulled at last into the wholesale vegetable market, it was suddenly dwarfed by semis full of Florida tomatoes and California artichokes.

Eliot and Chris weren't worried about competition, though— almost no one else was selling organics. As promised, Star Market's buyer took every last one of their carrots.

On the day they sold him their last hundred-pound bags, Eliot and Chris broached the subject of the next season. This first crop had been a variety called "half-longs," which Eliot had chosen in a wise, Rodale-influenced concession to their region's heavy, clay-layered soil. Next year, the buyer suggested, they should plant more traditional-looking, longer carrots. "People like longer carrots better, they look better," he told Eliot.

"Yeah, well, you have to admit those are the sweetest and crispest carrots you have ever tasted," Eliot said.

The buyer stared at him, offended. "I never taste anything that I buy," he said. Eliot hadn't realized until then that it was standard practice and sometimes a point of professional pride for produce buyers to choose vegetables only by sight. He began to see how far even the most amenable commercial markets fell from his own food priorities.

Back at home, the carrot harvest finished at last, the group was simply too exhausted to contemplate next year's crop. Chris was convinced his chest had taken on a permanent orange glow, though it was hard to tell if it was because of the carrots or because his fair, freckly skin was so terribly ill-suited for field work. Still, there was no denying that, in terms of market demand at least, their inaugural crop had been a smashing success—they had sold eighteen thousand pounds of carrots, every single one of which had been touched at least four times in the harvesting, washing, bundling, and packing (not even counting the hundreds of pounds of discarded thinnings).

True to his word, the Star Market buyer had offered them twice the wholesale rate for conventional carrots. To the group's dismay, this turned out to be sixteen cents a pound instead of eight. After five months with five adults often working dawn-to-dark, seven days a week, they'd grossed $3,000.

No one could bring themselves to even discuss the possibility of signing on again for another year. Anyway, there was work to be done.

Although the thresher they'd procured in anticipation of growing oats had been sitting disappointingly idle in the barn, the antique haying equipment Eliot had bought turned out to work just fine. In addition to the endless work on the carrot crop, the suburban college kids at Entropy managed to cut, dry, and haul a loftful of hay using only horse-drawn equipment.

The first key decision in haying, Loudon told them, was picking a week you judged would remain rain free so the hay would dry properly in the field. Putting up wet hay, he warned, meant risking not just moldy, inedible fodder for your animals but also a process in which the reproducing bacteria create so much heat the hay can actually spontaneously combust and burn down the barn. The week Loudon chose, with Entropy following his lead, turned out to be hot and bright. Eliot never forgot the thrill of working so closely with the horses that they pulled the mower across the hayfield together in silence, without a single command from him. A few days later they crisscrossed the field again, this time with the tedder that delicately stirred and flipped the drying grass with its long, spidery fingers. Once Chris and Eliot judged it dry enough to collect, they fitted the wagon with a genius 19th-century invention called a hay elevator. The elevator stood upright at the back of the wagon, like a wall mounted on wheels. Four tall slats lined the wall, set at alternating heights. As the wagon moved along the row of dry hay, its motion turned a mechanism that pushed the slats up and down, the fork tines on their undersides drawing the loose hay up and up until it tipped over the top of the wall and fell in tufts down to the wagon below. Eliot drove the horses and Chris stood in the wagon, jolting over bumps as he spread the falling hay into a even layer with a pitchfork. It was hard, strenuous labor, but for both men, decades later it still carried the glow of pride and satisfaction.

The pleasures of working together, when the work went well, made it possible to gloss over other domestic tensions. Entropy's two couples still enjoyed each other's company, but the conflicts to be expected among any set of housemates (especially when the household included two rambunctious toddlers and a menagerie of animals) were compounded at Entropy by the group's status as a sort of semi-commune. Peg, Eliot, Chris, and Ellen had eagerly agreed to share a home and work, but in their enthusiasm to undertake this exciting new life, it never occurred to any of them to discuss how they'd share finances or decision-making. Though none of them would have identified it as such at the time, a troubling pattern emerged.

For example: Peg and Eliot were committed vegetarians while Chris and Ellen unabashedly loved meat. For the most part, their rice-and-bean food budget made meat a luxury item anyway, thus dodging the conflict. But that spring, an affordable source of meat had presented itself when Flash the cow gave birth to a male calf.

On farms like Loudon's, it went without saying that of the calves born to the dairy cows each spring (thus replenishing the year's production of milk), the females went on to a career as milkers while the males became veal. Peg and Eliot had assumed they would just sell Flash's male calf, but Chris and Ellen saw an opportunity to expand their diet—and self-sufficiently, too. Chris also saw it as a question of ethics—if he wanted to eat meat, he reasoned, he needed to be willing to raise and slaughter an animal himself.

But when he and Ellen proposed this idea to Peg and Eliot, the other couple resisted. To Eliot, raising an animal with the sole intention of killing it later was frankly immoral. For him, there was nothing further to say on the subject.

This conflict over the ethics of meat consumption would look familiar to many counterculture households, communal and noncommunal, across the country. Lucy Horton, who traveled the country collecting recipes from communes in 1972, found a general pattern of vegetarianism on West Coast communes while "in New Mexico and later New England, I was surprised to find vegetarianism more the exception than the rule." In Myrtle Hill's first summer, the communards had raised a beef calf named Bullneck. When it came time to slaughter him, they built a kind of scaffold to keep his body from hitting the ground, and led him into place. Then, steeling himself, Fletcher steadied a borrowed .22 rifle and shot Bullneck in the forehead. Either his aim wasn't perfect or they hadn't correctly calculated the thickness of a cow's skull, however, so one bullet wasn't enough. With the calf screaming in pain, Craig took a shot too. Eventually, they slit Bullneck's throat. While Myrtle Hill's meat eaters gained an additional source of protein (though without electricity for refrigeration or a means of salting the beef to preserve it, they had to rent a freezer locker twenty miles away), the group never again raised a beef cow. Craig, for one, had found the experience frankly traumatizing.

At Entropy Acres, though, disagreement over meat ethics was not the biggest problem—the real issue was the fact that the discussion stopped at the first moment of conflict. In this, as in other, smaller, but endless decisions in which Chris's preference contrasted with Eliot's, the latter prevailed nearly every time. Even in his enthusiasm for the whole Entropy project, Chris could not quite forget that this was Peg and Eliot's house and that Peg's bank account paid all the bills. If he and Ellen had had more financial resources to contribute, they might have felt on equal-enough footing to push for things like raising the veal calf. But they didn't. And so, that spring, Chris had swallowed his frustration and resigned himself to another year's diet of beans. All through the summer's work of carrots and hay, he had assumed that his sweat equity would set the balance once the farm became profitable—which is partly why the carrot crop's meager returns had felt particularly devastating to him. How now would he and Ellen ever become equal partners in this project?

Even in this idealistic, anticapitalist, semicommunal household, Entropy's two couples had accidentally defaulted to the same system they hoped to escape, in which decision-making power belonged to those with financial power. If any of them had fully realized this at the time, they all would have been horrified. As it was, though, the dynamic lay entirely unspoken below the surface of their friendship. Eliot kept decreeing what the farm needed next, and Chris kept biting his tongue.

With so much to do, it was easy enough to push frustration aside and keep working. As at Myrtle Hill the autumn before, there was no break between the summer's work and preparation for the coming cold.

Having lived one winter already in the drafty farmhouse, they had a sense of how much firewood they'd have to amass in order to keep from freezing. Getting such a late start—ideally, Loudon reminded them, the wood would have been already drying for months now—meant they'd be burning green wood again, but it couldn't be helped.

Chris would have borrowed Loudon's chain saw in a heartbeat, but Eliot insisted that they stay fully committed to their ideals of working without the aid of combustion engines. Chain saws might be quicker, but they were terrible polluters of the air, both in terms of exhaust and noise. Owning or even using one was out of the question. And so, their hands still stained orange from the carrot harvest, Eliot, Peg, and Chris set out to bring in eight cords of wood using only a handheld, two-man crosscut saw.

Eliot did have a point: despite the grueling work of hauling the saw back and forth at each tree, once you got in the groove it could be a near-mystical experience, to work in a steady, wordless rhythm in the hush of the forest, working up a sweat several times over the course of a chilly afternoon, in service of the wood that would keep you warm again all winter.

And no one could deny the sheer pleasure of working in the woods with the horses. They could drag felled trees from deep in the forest out to the road without tearing huge paths through the underbrush as a skidder would. Working with them took longer, sure, and (being only two-horsepower), the animals couldn't pull as much weight as even a small tractor would, but they intelligently navigated tricky slopes and could pick routes that avoided marshy spots the humans hadn't even noticed. As the men hooked log-grips into place, the two dapple-gray sisters stood patiently, swiveling their ears and flicking their tails at deerflies, waiting for the "Git-up" before moving on. For the rest of his life, Eliot would remember working with horses as like working with a trusted friend.

On days they were cutting wood close to home, Ellen loaded the twins into a toy wagon and came out to help. She and Peg took their turn with the saw, but it was more cumbersome for them than for the men. Later they couldn't say whether this was due to physical differences or merely a lack of practice, but in the interest of time, the women tended to do the work of limbing or hauling brush, leaving the sawing to their husbands.

One afternoon, they carried their saw down the road to the yellow house and turned at the T-intersection toward Loudon's. Instead of stopping in to say hello, they continued another mile, the road becoming more and more rutted as it climbed over a steep hill and then fell sharply on the other side. Their destination lay just beyond the point where it exited onto a well-maintained dirt road: the sugar bush where Nick had invited them to cut wood.

Nick had finished his cabin in the valley where my parents had opted not to settle and was beginning to establish what would eventually become a successful logging business. When he met Eliot and found out that he planned to cut all his wood by hand, Nick thought it sounded nuts but sympathetically invited Entropy to come cut trees on his own property. The spot he suggested to them turned out to be a stand of woods near where Larry and Judy were working on their dome. When Chris, Eliot, and Peg finished their work for the day, they walked up to say hello.

In the weeks that followed the lightning-fast dome raising, it had started to become clear to Larry and Judy how much work they'd undertaken: each facet of the dome had to be covered with a triangle of plywood, but since the prefabricated sheets didn't come large enough, each piece had to be glued to another one and then reinforced with screws before cutting. After the plywood came a layer of tarpaper on the outside, then insulation on the inside, then figuring out the windows (special-ordered panes of triangles and trapezoids). Then after all of that, the cedar shingles they'd decided on had to be measured, hand cut, and applied one at a time over the entire surface of the dome, all while balancing on a ladder leaned against its curves. It was a little daunting.

Judy and Larry had no objection to electricity or telephones, so they'd arranged for the phone and power companies to run a line up the edge of their field, the poles blending in, sort of, with the surrounding trees. Now they could run the old-fashioned electrical saw Larry's father Al had donated. But despite this aid, construction was taking longer than they'd planned. The sun disappeared over the hills earlier and earlier every afternoon.

In thanks for the firewood, Entropy offered to come over and help with the dome when they could. And, despite the many demands on their own time, they made good on this promise. Chris and Peg usually pitched in using whatever method Judy and Larry employed, but Eliot remained true to his principles. He spent hours making holes in the plywood with his own antique, hand-cranked drill. Larry and Judy didn't argue—they were just glad for the help.

And for the friendship. Despite their falling-out with Nick, Larry and Judy were benefitting from the fact that he had gotten to know not just the newcomers at Entropy Acres and Myrtle Hill but many locals as well. Charlie and Lois Barrows became such good friends that Nick had stayed with them while he worked on his cabin. Nick had already developed a reputation among his neighbors as a hard worker—in this region, a category of highest praise. No one seemed to expect that his friends would be any different. By the time Larry and Judy's eccentric confection of a building project became visible from the road, it was clear to everyone living nearby that theirs was a benign brand of crazy.

Friends and family had stopped by all summer to help as well. One of these, a man Judy had known growing up in Alexandria, had accompanied some other friends for the weekend. As the days wore on, Judy noticed him becoming more and more upset. Finally he told her what was bothering him. It was the outhouse. The friend had grown up in rural poverty in North Carolina, the son of a struggling truck farmer. "My father worked his whole life for indoor plumbing," he told Judy. "What you are doing is so disrespectful to his memory, I can never visit you again." He never did.

Most of Larry and Judy's new neighbors had grown up under very similar conditions, but if they shared this sense of offense, they didn't tell Larry and Judy. The neighbors who stopped by to check the dome's progress did offer plenty of advice, however, some of it lifesaving. Donald Perron owned the next farm down the road—a classic Vermont configuration of white farmhouse, red barn, and blue silo, all perched on the side of a steep, rocky, vibrantly green hillside bordered by elegant old maples. Like his friend and neighbor Loudon, Donald's curiosity and interest in other people led him over to my parents' work site regularly. He had an engineer's eye for rigging and simplifying systems. Standing in the field, surveying their work, he'd chew thoughtfully on the ever-present cigar in the corner of his mouth and readjust his cap over his round head before offering, "You might . . ."

Donald's teenage daughter regularly rode over on her pony, just to check out the action—when she stopped appearing, Judy suddenly realized that school must have started. Summer was over. It gave her a lonely feeling.

Meeting Peg, Chris, and Eliot, and later Ellen and the twins, made Judy feel excited and relieved at the same time. It was hard to say why the people at Entropy immediately felt so much more like peers than the people at Myrtle had. They were closer in age, for one, and neither household was rejecting as many elements of mainstream American life as the commune. The best way Larry and Judy could express it was that they and the people at Entropy all had liberal arts degrees (though plenty of people passing through Myrtle did too). Judy and Peg had embarked on a lifelong friendship.

Their affinity for their new neighbors did not stop Larry and Judy from chuckling privately about the two-man saw and the hand-cranked drill, however. In this, they shared the local majority opinion, a fact that was not lost on the residents of Entropy themselves. But Eliot didn't care. Yes, working with a saw and horses was exhausting and slow, but what was that compared with the benefits: heat from trees, gathered with zero reliance on imported fuel, and without the ear-splitting, smelly, messy machines that ripped apart the forest and shattered its stillness. As many of the previous winter's plans had revealed themselves to be more idealistic than practical, here at least was a perfect example of the self-sufficient reality they'd been dreaming of.

One late afternoon after a long day of work in the sugar bush below the dome, Chris and the horses headed home, the wagon laden with logs. He had learned to trust the horses' ability to pick their own route around potholes and washout—if he needed to clear a fallen branch from the road, he could even leave them standing while he walked up ahead and then, without returning to their side, simply call them up to meet him. But the journey over the steep, rutted road that led from the dome, past Loudon's, and back to Entropy could be tense at times. The horses had to work pulling the loaded wagon uphill, and on the downward slope, it was important to monitor their speed to make sure they didn't get going too fast.

Finally, the worst of the hills lay behind them. As Chris entered the section of road that passed through Loudon's farm, he started to relax. He hopped off the wagon and walked a few paces ahead to clear an obstacle from the horses' path. Then he called them up to join him. When they reached him, though, they kept right on walking. And then, without warning, they bolted.

Before Chris even realized what was happening, the sisters were a dozen yards ahead, and then gone, dropping out of sight over a small rise. Chris took off after them, shouting. If they were running for home, they'd have to get around the sharp corner of the T-intersection in front of the yellow house—he didn't think they would make it, galloping at full tilt with the log-filled wagon careening behind them. And too, the road coming from the other way was a blind curve—if a car were to suddenly appear, its driver wouldn't have time to brake before it was too late. He sprinted frantically, fearing the worst.

By the time he caught up with them, though, he was astounded by what he found. Still harnessed to each other and to the loaded wagon, the horses had not made the turn toward Entropy but had charged full speed through the intersection and straight toward the yellow house. Its sloped lawn was scattered with the cut-up chunks of a huge, recently felled maple. The stump lay right in their path. At the last second, the horses had straddled the stump, one on each side and come to a complete stop. By the time Chris reached them, panting, the horses were standing calmly, flicking their tails as though nothing had happened. Miraculously, they were unhurt. He unhitched them, heart pounding, and led them home.

Later, he and Eliot returned to examine the damage. The harness was badly mangled, but worst of all was the wagon: one of its wheels was completely broken. A one-hundred-year-old wooden wheel, spoked and fitted with a steel tire, wasn't the kind of thing you could send away for, not even with help from the *Whole Earth Catalog*.

As he and Chris loaded logs into the pickup to haul them the last few hundred yards home, Eliot ran through scenarios in his mind. Without a wheel, the wagon was useless. Without a wagon, their horse-drawn plans once again became impossible.

This wasn't the first time their antique equipment had crumbled on them. Even thirty years earlier, knowing how to fix a leather harness would have been more or less common knowledge around here. But now, Eliot had found, no one even knew where to begin.

Except for one man. Azarias Raoul Caron was the local blacksmith and farrier. Caron was a French-Canadian man in his late fifties, slight but strong. He wore wire-rim glasses and smoked a pipe and had an innate elegance that made even his simple cap and dark-green work clothes look debonair. Like a lot of farm communities, this area had its fair share of brilliant tinker-inventors but no one came close to Caron. Even decades after his death, he retained a reputation as a once-in-a-century genius. He had a workshop in the village with a forge and anvil at one end and walls crammed with tongs, hammers, files, bores, and many tools of Caron's own invention. Chris took every opportunity to stop by and watch him work, but Caron also made house calls when needed. He had repaired Entropy's harness and hay elevator several times already. This time, despairing, Eliot told him about the broken wagon wheel without much hope. Caron just nodded. A few weeks later, he gave them a call. He'd built a new wooden wheel from scratch, and it worked perfectly.

Eliot never forgot his profound admiration and gratitude for Caron's unassuming master-craftsmanship or his awe at the sheer luck of happening to live a few scant miles from the region's one remaining expert whose skills they so badly needed. But he also never forgot the other lesson that the broken wheel had forced him to acknowledge: true self-sufficiency was impossible.

As he now saw, even if he and his friends could work longer hours or cut wood faster or perfect their cheese recipe or get paid more for their carrot harvest, there would always be something they couldn't do. Something would break, an animal would fall sick. The kind of handmade, labor-intensive life he had dreamed of reviving had, in fact, *never* been fully attainable by one man or even a few families working alone—in his romantic view of the past, he'd forgotten or neglected to understand how interdependent communities have always been. There was a good reason that rural communities delegated the growing of wheat and the grinding of flour to different parties—they were each full-time jobs. Without that depth of community support and knowledge, even the most idealistic experiments in self-sufficiency were never going to be fully free of frustrating setbacks. Successfully working *for* yourself, no matter how much energy and idealism behind the work, was never truly working *by* yourself.

For Eliot, the ideal of total self-reliance had been part of the appeal of Entropy's whole experiment. He loved what he was learning and had a thousand ideas about how to improve, but this new insight left him with mixed feelings. What would it mean to never be free of relying on Loudon or the Johns family or even Azarias Caron? He wasn't sure, but he didn't like the thought.

Chris had also been feeling slightly uncomfortable about how heavily Entropy had been relying on the generosity and expertise of their neighbors, especially Loudon. The examples were endless. The extra flat of broccoli seedlings Loudon had dropped off that spring had been the only ones to thrive in Entropy's garden; they had no idea why. Once, he had taken great pains to come over and help Chris take apart Entropy's stovepipe to bang it free of the built-up creosote that might have risked a chimney fire— Loudon might tease Chris and the others about their eccentric farming choices, but he wasn't about to stand by and let their ignorance become actually dangerous, especially not with babies in the house.

For Chris, the problem was not that all this reliance on Loudon represented a failure of self-sufficiency, it was that it wasn't reciprocal. Aside from providing an enthusiastic audience and a source of entertainment, what could he offer Loudon in return? Chris had been mulling this question for some time. At last, he had an answer.

A few months earlier, right around the Fourth of July, one of Loudon's nephews had shot off a firework that took a rogue twist and landed near the cupola of Loudon's ancient, lovely, three-story red barn. The century-old timbers quickly caught fire and very soon became a full-blown conflagration that spread to Loudon's other, smaller milking barn nearby.

The volunteer fire department did what they could. The house and animals stayed safe, but Loudon lost both barns and all the equipment inside.

It was a devastating blow. For a few weeks after the fire, it was unclear whether or not Loudon would even be able to stay in business. His cows still needed to be milked twice a day, but he had no equipment and nowhere to store the milk; a neighbor took in his herd while Loudon scrambled to find another solution.

Nick, who had been working on his cabin in his valley a few miles away, heard about the fire and stopped by the next day. As soon as he saw Loudon's plight, he got to work putting up a modest, three-sided milking shed out of railroad ties he'd sourced somewhere, covered with the corrugated tin roofing he'd salvaged from the still-smoking ruins. The shed didn't fully solve Loudon's crisis, but it did give him a place to install a little bit of replacement milking equipment, allowing his herd to come home and him to stay in business until the insurance money came in and he could rebuild.

And now, Loudon told Chris, that time had come—and not a moment too soon. Summer was already over and his cows needed a place to live before winter. Loudon had decided to put up his new barn using the traditional method: by inviting all the neighbors to a barn raising.

Chris saw his opportunity to help. With the blessing of his commune-mates, whatever time he had left between the carrots, hay, firewood, and twins, Chris devoted to aiding Loudon get ready. He also made it his personal business to round up as many helpers as possible for the day itself.

Rather than replace the stately, 19th-century, three-story barn that had burned, Loudon had elected to put up a low, arched-roofed, modern barn. Chris helped pour the foundation, watching in delighted awe as another neighbor prepared the cement in the homemade mixer he'd invented using parts salvaged from old state highway equipment.

On the morning of the barn raising, Loudon and Arlene's yard began to fill up with people. All the local families were represented: Loudon's cousins, plus the Johns coming from one direction and the Perrons coming from the other. Myrtle Hill's delegation included Craig, Amy, and LJ; Pancake and Hershe (her belly just starting to show under her work clothes) were still living in their tipi at Entropy, but they were there too. Ellen had pulled the twins in their red wagon so they could watch.

Larry and Judy had also hiked over, at Chris's invitation. It made them a little nervous to lose even one day of work on the dome, there was so much to do, but they didn't want to miss this. They too had been feeling grateful for their neighbors' help and were eager to make themselves useful.

The work that day entailed erecting the barn's frame and its big, beautiful arched rafters. Under the guidance of Loudon and the others who knew what they were doing, the volunteers hammered lumber into the shape of walls or *1-2-3 lift*ed heavy beams into place. In contrast to local custom, Judy, Hershe, and Amy worked alongside the men.

As at any gathering with so many young people, especially one with a mission so uncomplicatedly satisfying as helping a neighbor in need—the mood in the air was festive. In the lulls between work, as Loudon and his cousins discussed the next steps, everyone else chatted. Larry noticed that Chris was too busy helping Loudon to stand around. "The two of them have got a real friendship," he thought.

Craig spotted Larry and came over to say hello. Craig had cut his hair earlier that summer to a comparatively conservative collar length, and the visual contrast between him and his commune-mates struck Larry and Judy. Even in filthy overalls, Judy noticed, Craig's class-president charisma leant him an unmistakable country-club polish.

Judy was introduced to Hershe and Pancake. Though she and Larry thought of themselves as counterculture, the people from Myrtle were some of the first real hippies she was acquainted with. Judy knew that Donald Perron would likely not distinguish much between her waist-length brown braid and Hershe's long, blonde waterfall of hair, but for Judy, the distinctions were all she could see. Living outdoors, working with her hands every day, using an outhouse, and subsisting on an ungodly amount of undercooked soy beans had not previously made her feel particularly conventional, but compared to Myrtle Hill, her style of life was practically bourgeois.

But she sensed other distinctions, harder to define, that seemed tied to the question she'd had in her first shock of seeing so many people over at Myrtle Hill: how had they all ended up in the woods?

To start with: why the pseudonyms? There were plenty of elements of her own past and her own complicated relationship with her family that Judy had hoped to escape by moving so far afield, but nothing that would lead her to live under an assumed name. What could they all be fleeing? she wondered. The draft board? Something worse? She knew better than to ask.

Amy at least left no mystery about her past. As they waited for the next round of work to start, Amy and Judy struck up a conversation. Or, rather, Judy listened, aghast, as Amy poured out the details of the childhood abuse she'd so recently escaped. For Amy, this was just one more opportunity to share her story with a sympathetic listener, something she felt compelled to do over and over throughout those years. For Judy, what struck her even decades later was Amy's matter-of-fact delivery. Judy had never heard anyone talk about sexual abuse, even in the abstract, and to hear this smart, bright-faced teenager speak so plainly about what she'd been through shook her deeply.

It also left her convinced: the commune, for all its eccentricities, had clearly saved this girl's life.

In midafternoon, everyone stopped working and sat down to a huge farm dinner prepared by Arlene. Loudon had slaughtered a heifer to feed the crowd, so there was beef along with greens, biscuits, gravy, and homemade pie garnished with local cheddar.

There was more work to do before evening, but Judy and Larry slipped away. They hated to leave the scene of neighborly cooperation in which they felt spectacularly lucky to have been included, but their own, endless, unfinished work called them home. The sun slipped behind the hills earlier and earlier every night.

CHAPTER 13

One day while Chris was helping Loudon with his barn, Loudon casually mentioned to him that the town might be looking to hire some new school bus drivers. The village elementary school sat up on a hill behind the general store and town hall. Loudon was one-third of the town school board. It had fallen to him to solve this urgent problem. "Maybe you guys should drive the bus," he said to Chris.

When Chris took the idea back to Entropy Acres, the others needed no convincing. They were still reeling from Chris's calculation that they'd performed their summer's-worth of backbreaking labor for an hourly rate of well under $1. Chris told Loudon yes immediately and it seemed as simple as that. Chris, Eliot, Peg, and Ellen were excited. To simplify things, they decided, the job would nominally be Eliot's, though in practice they would all share the driving. Eager to get some practice in, Chris blithely went to pick up the school bus from its previous drivers—who just happened to be their own neighbors, the Johns family. It never occurred to anyone at Entropy to wonder if the Johns knew about, let alone agreed with, the board's decision to find new drivers. At the time, it felt perfectly straightforward. After all, there was precedent: after the horse-drawn plow failed, Eliot and Chris had asked and been granted permission several times to borrow the Johns' tractor. Going to pick up the bus felt like a simple continuation of these neighborly relations.

The four of them were still taking turns practicing backing the bus into three-point turns on a flat field near the house when Loudon called to say that all was not well. A special town meeting had been called to discuss their fitness for the school-bus job. None of them knew what to make of this. They'd never had any interaction with any local that wasn't perfectly cordial. At Loudon's barn raising Chris had worked side by side with some of the same people who were now voicing a skepticism. They didn't want to be paranoid, but it was hard not to hear a certain hostility.

Loudon assured them that they had nothing to worry about. They had to let the disgruntled group air their concerns but then that would be that. The four of them had the full support of the school board.

Before the meeting, Peg, Chris, Eliot, and Ellen sat around the table at Entropy and discussed a strategy. No matter what happened, they decided, they'd follow Loudon's lead. None of them knew what to expect, but the most important thing, they agreed, was to remain calm and united.

The next evening, the school's parking lot was packed with cars. Word had gotten out and everyone, it seemed, had come to show support or to express an opinion—or just not to miss what promised to be a lively night. The meeting was being held in a first-grade classroom. People found seats and settled themselves into tiny chairs, the men's knees awkwardly high. A good portion of the Johns family was there, along with a number of Perrons and several of Loudon's cousins. Charlie Barrows had walked up the hill from his house; Lois was on the school board and was sitting with Loudon. Judy and Larry had driven into town for the meeting and were sitting near the back. Nick was there too, as were Craig and a handful of others from Myrtle Hill.

Though almost everyone in the room, locals and newcomers alike, had spent their day similarly engaged in building, harvesting, or tending to animals, there was no trouble telling the groups apart. Besides the newcomers' long, loose hair on both women and men—in 1971, still a potent emotional trigger for many outside the counterculture—attire was a dead giveaway. Most local farmers wouldn't dream of showing up at a town meeting in their barn clothes; it was a point of pride to appear at any public function freshly shaved, with pressed clothes, clean shoes, and smelling of cologne.

This was perhaps the point of greatest contrast—for the hippies, it was almost a point of pride *not* to take pains with their appearance. Even if they had thought to spruce up at all, which for the most part they hadn't, the locals might not have been able to see the difference. Eclectic taste was part of it—Eliot wore an Indian-style headband a lot in those days, and even Larry owned a dashiki—but there was also the question of hygiene. Eliot had been wearing the same pair of leather pants, a gift from Peg's mother, for weeks on end, to haul carrots, milk goats, and groom horses. The pants were utterly filthy but it never occurred to him to wear something else to the school bus meeting. As Eliot reflected later, "When people used the term 'dirty hippies,' by their standards we were."

There were a number of reasons for this. On a practical level, living without running water made washing a labor-intensive undertaking; showers were a rare treat and laundry even rarer. But more important was the philosophy. For the young newcomers who considered themselves "middle-class refugees," part of the appeal of their new way of life was its contrast with the heavily enforced order and sterility of their childhoods. Rejecting deodorant, fancy soap, and cologne was a way of also rejecting shame about the body and embracing its processes and smells as natural. To this way of thinking, combs and razors were tools intended to unnaturally repress the body's God-given beauty; the choice to discard them was its own expression of purity. Showing up disheveled was a way of indicating that your time and attention were dedicated to pursuits that ran deeper than mere surface concerns. Dirty, patched, ragged work clothes also stood as a defiant contrast to middle-class parents' suits and heels, the dirt itself a proud badge of the hard, physical, nonabstract "real" work that was giving the newcomers so much satisfaction.

But most, like Eliot, never gave a thought to the role their own inherited privilege played in letting them feel comfortable appearing in public so ostentatiously filthy. It's one thing to look and smell dirty because you've made a reversible lifestyle choice in a particular moment; it's entirely another to be so because your life circumstances have robbed you of dignity and control. Part of the '50s' middle-class obsession with hygiene and orderliness itself came out of Depression-era anxiety about poverty. The hippies could reject attention to hygiene and appearance as frivolous trappings because for them, they *were* trappings. They, unlike many of their poor and working-class neighbors, never had to fear that a disheveled appearance could become an obstacle to social mobility or an excuse to discount their value to society. Or to put it another way: they never worried others might look down on them because they felt themselves so securely at the top.

As soon as everyone had settled in as well as they could while wedged into the tiny first-grade seats, Len Johns, who had called the meeting, stood up to express doubts about the newcomers' inexperience. Had any of them ever driven a bus before? he asked. Would they know how to handle it on black ice? Or how to coax it down a steep and winding dirt road? In February?

Chris had to admit, these were very reasonable questions. But it wasn't long before another, more pressing set of concerns started to bubble beneath the surface of the meeting. Finally, Johns addressed them directly: "We don't want you driving our kids," he said. "We have reason to believe that you are growing marijuana."

Peg felt like she'd been punched.

Marijuana had fast become ubiquitous on college campuses and hip downtowns, but in most parts of America it still represented a dangerous menace. For Peg, this accusation from someone she'd thought of as a friend had come out of nowhere and had landed with the weight of distrust and hostility.

And fear: Had the Johns been snooping?

Because it was true. Entropy did have a few plants of homegrown sprouting in an inconspicuous spot, though it was weak stuff and only enough for their own consumption in the evenings (their work was too labor intensive for them to consider doing it high). How had this modest, private supply suddenly become a divisive public issue?

It took years for the whole story to filter down, but eventually Eliot found out how the marijuana rumors began. One of the next farms over from Entropy was owned by a young man who belonged to a big local family. One day, he discovered a pot plant growing in an out-of-the-way corner of his property. The site bordered Peg and Eliot's land and so he came to the obvious conclusion. As it later turned out, the seedling had actually been started by the friend of a friend, a visitor from New York who had planted it without telling his host. But by the time this explanation surfaced, it was far too late for Entropy.

In all of their preparatory kitchen table discussions about what this emergency meeting might entail, Chris, Eliot, Peg, and Ellen had never once considered that they might be accused of a major felony in front of the whole town. Every local they'd met—including, up to this very moment, the Johns family—had seemed to welcome and embrace them. The open hostility in the room took Peg and the others entirely by surprise.

Peg's mind was spinning; she couldn't reconcile the Johns' many acts of generosity, which she'd taken as signs of friendship, with these sudden, deeply unfriendly suspicions and accusations. It wasn't until years later that she realized her mistake. She and the others had failed to recognize that relationships here didn't work exactly as they did in the suburbs, where soliciting or extending help was a kind of intimacy reserved for friends. Here, as in other cold-climate farm communities, the culture made a distinction between neighborliness and friendship. In a region of perilous weather and far-flung emergency services, everyone was vulnerable and potentially in sudden need of help. It was actually dangerous not to maintain good relations with the neighbor whose skidder could pull your car out of a snowbank or whose warm kitchen might shelter your children if your chimney caught fire in the night. Helping each other was a given. But liking or respecting each other? That was something different.

If Peg and the others had a better sense of what was going on nationwide, they might have been less surprised that as representatives of the counterculture they might be looked at with some suspicion.

In the Taos area of New Mexico, relations between locals and the massive, post-Summer of Love influx of hippie communards were so bad by 1971 that the events of the period became known as the "Hippie-Chicano War."

For the most part, this "war" consisted of intense tension and harassment. Local cars sported banners reading "Destroy the Hippies." One observer noted that almost no restaurants in Taos would serve anyone they perceived as a hippie, and many accounts report cars with long-haired occupants being pelted with rocks or chased by children. Occasionally violence erupted. A bus belonging to Wavy Gravy's New Mexico commune, the Hog Farm, was set on fire one night. Someone blew up another commune's bridge.

Some observers noted that Anglo business and civic leaders openly viewed the hippie influx as "a threat to our way of life" and that when they couldn't find ways to stem the hippie tide through the legal system, they quietly encouraged harassment and vandalism. In Taos, Anglo officials cancelled an important Chicano festival citing worry over the surge of hippies—and further fueling tensions.

Hippie newcomers also sometimes fell afoul of locals by not understanding—or ignoring—essential customs. In one widely circulated story, at New Mexico's Drop City spin-off, Libre, a resident was collecting water at a creek with his son one day when a neighbor shot the bucket right out of his hand. The child was understandably traumatized, and the incident sent ripples of fear throughout the commune community in the Huerfano Valley. But the shooting hadn't come out of nowhere. In the desert terrain of the Southwest, water rights were an issue of long-standing controversy and legal precedent. The only person with the right to use what water flowed through a certain area was the person who *owned* those rights—just because a stream passed through or near your property didn't mean you could dip into it or divert it to your own garden if someone else owned the rights. Often hippie newcomers didn't understand this long-standing local system—or rejected it as anathema to their conviction that everyone was entitled to share nature's bounty.

But by all accounts, one of the chief sources of antipathy was the affluent hippies' ability to easily buy land, driving up local prices. Indio, a New Yorker of Puerto Rican descent and one of Reality Construction Company's political radicals, explained the dynamic to a visitor: "Every time a white hippie comes in and buys a Chicano's land to escape the fuckin' city, he sends that Chicano *to* the city to go through what he's been trying to escape *from*, can you dig it? What can you do with that bread out here, man? Nothing. Then when that money's gone, see, the Chicano has to *stay* in the city, cause now he ain't got no land to come back to. He's stuck, and the hippie's free. That's why they don't dig the fuckin' hippies, man."

While there were undoubtedly cases across the country where counterculture newcomers were victims of unwarranted prejudice, in cases where hostilities between communes and their neighbors ran highest, there seem to have been legitimate complaints on both sides.

During their building phase, Drop City enjoyed wonderful relations with their neighbors who helped and supported their building efforts and accepted the newcomers' help in exchange. But when the commune's founders left in frustration over the endless flood of transients, they also abandoned responsibility for the phenomenon they'd put into motion. When Drop City's domes became a haven for biker gangs and drug addicts, the local police and civic leaders had no choice but to step in. "They just left everything sitting there," the local sheriff told a visitor. "The Droppers left us with a mess out here. We had to deal with it. They were gone."

In Vermont, locals' nervousness over the sheer number of newcomers was reaching its peak right around the time of the Entropy Acres bus meeting. A rumor had started that Vermont would soon be flooded by a "hippie invasion" of fifty thousand longhairs. The number was specific and quoted both by worried locals and by the newcomers themselves. One source may have been a 1970 *Yale Law and Social Action* article (Hillary Rodham, associate editor), in which the authors laid out the numbers required for the liberal political conversion of an entire state, specifically suggesting Vermont as a good option (this article provided the basis the next year for another, more widely read piece in *Playboy*, titled "Taking Over Vermont.") A sidebar in the *Whole Earth Catalog* also casually suggested Vermont as a likely back-to-the-land destination, thanks to its cheap property and "Yankee tolerance."

In 1971, the possibility of "invasion" felt real on both sides. Goddard College hired a designated point person—Craig's best friend Jblu, in fact, recently arrived from California—and provided him an office and a budget to prepare the campus and the town for the influx. The Governor, Deane Davis, got so many worried letters that he issued a press release that spring, aiming for a tone of calm: "We have not invited them, nor are we enthusiastic about their arrival . . . I have instructed the police to be scrupulous in the observance of individual rights, that they be courteous, but that they enforce the law."

No one at Entropy had heard these "invasion" rumors and had no idea that they were, in fact, part of a major, lasting, demographic shift under way in the state. To them, this sudden expression of anxiety by their neighbors came as a total shock.

As the meeting in the school continued, several others stood up to echo the Johns' concerns about the dangers of letting drug users drive their children. Loudon fired back, but he seemed to be outnumbered. The tension in the air was palpable.

Then Melvin Mandigo stood up. He was well known in the area for both his skill as a cow breeder and for his conservative politics. He was a Republican state legislator, a tall, slim, distinguished-looking man. Judy, Larry, Craig, and the other Entropy supporters braced themselves for a further condemnation of Entropy's bus bid. But instead, something very different happened.

"I'm ashamed of you," Mandigo said. "I'm ashamed of my town. I'm ashamed of my neighbors. I can't believe what I'm hearing." Judy, Larry, and Craig couldn't believe what they were hearing either. Mandigo went on. "These people have been good neighbors. They built their home. They've come down and helped my wife when she was sick." He built to a finale. "This seems like something that would happen in the South."

Many of the newcomers in the room that day never forgot their shock and delight at the improbability of a local conservative defending hippies to an uneasy gathering of his friends and neighbors. Judy, as a Virginian, had blushed at Mandigo's scornful mention of the South, but his speech confirmed the sense she had about her new neighbors' priorities—that if people perceived you as a hard worker, they forgave, at least publicly, a lot of eccentricity. Later, it occurred to her to wonder how much the mutual whiteness of most back-to-the-landers and Vermonters also contributed to this ease of acceptance.

For a moment, Mandigo's speech seemed to have turned the mood. But not enough to satisfy everyone. For Eliot, things had already gone far enough. Without talking to Chris or Peg, he stood up. "If the community isn't behind us, we'll withdraw our position," he said. "I resign."

The meeting continued a while longer, but no one from Entropy could focus. Without discussing it with any of them, Eliot had single-handedly reversed the decision they'd all made together at the kitchen table a few hours earlier. When everyone unfolded themselves some time later and started to file out the classroom door, the bus-driving job belonged once again to the Johns.

Chris was livid. His yearlong frustration with Eliot's intractability had finally hit its breaking point. He was too furious even to get in the truck, so he walked all the way home from the village—four miles, uphill, fuming.

It was clear that this explosion had been building for a long time, but Chris's fury, as he stalked home, had an element of embarrassment in it too. The worst part, for him, of Eliot's having unilaterally overruled their group decision to stick with the job was that in his sudden resignation, he had appeared to speak for all of them.

To Chris, it was obvious how much Loudon, Mandigo, and their other local supporters had risked socially by standing up for the newcomers in the face of community opposition. In this flame-out resignation, Eliot had clearly given no thought to how that act would affect those local allies and had left them no opening to save face in the community. To Chris, Eliot's casually tossing aside the job that others had lobbied for on their behalf was an act of disrespect—and, worse, one in which Chris was now implicated. He didn't want to be part of any group that would treat Loudon or anyone else with so little regard.

By the time Chris got home, still fuming, it was clear to him that his time in the collective life was over. He was through for good with letting others speak for him.

A short time later, he, Ellen and the twins moved out. Entropy Acres, the communal farming experiment, was dead.

CHAPTER 14

C raig left the school bus meeting with a mix of feelings. The drug accusations against Entropy had surprised him too and he felt for his friends' anguished shock. But in a way, Myrtle Hill's more extreme unconventionality had better prepared him for a skeptical response from the locals. He was proud of the fact that his group had already weathered several potentially hostile overtures and had come through not just unscathed but also with new allies.

One of the most important was the town constable, Will Urie. Urie and his wife lived near Myrtle Hill. Both were pillars of the community, but like Loudon Young saw themselves as belonging to an older, regional culture that remained defiantly outside of the American mainstream. Like a lot of local families, the Uries heated with wood and produced and preserved as much of their own food as they could. Long after most of their neighbors had moved to milking machines, they still milked their cows by hand. From this perspective, the newcomers' choice to do the same didn't look bizarre or like a threatening rejection of established values.

Earlier that summer, Craig had answered a knock at the Big House door to find Constable Urie, accompanied by a well-dressed couple. Urie greeted Craig politely but he looked uncharacteristically tense. As soon as they saw Craig, the couple suddenly began shouting, "We want our daughter back! You kidnapped her!" Urie didn't flinch, but he also continued to stand between them and the door. Calmly, he said, "Well, Craig, is Sarah here?"

In fact, she was. Myrtle Hill was connected enough to other networks of communes that they'd been receiving a steady flow of runaway suburban teenagers. Some were just bored and looking for adventure, but some had the haunted intensity of those truly staging an escape.

Across the country, communes were struggling with their role in what had become a nationwide crisis. A few months later, in early 1972, the Senate Judiciary Subcommitee on Juvenile Delinquency would put the annual number of American runaways at somewhere between 500,000 and one million. While some scholars found these numbers high, they also noted that nearly all the runaways they encountered in their studies had experienced violence of some kind in their home—verbal, physical, and sexual. In the early 1970s, the social services tasked with child welfare didn't even have formal mechanisms for asking children about their home life; their policies were oriented entirely around the goal of returning runaway teens to their parents' care.

To many in the counterculture, already questioning the premise of parental authority and the sanctity of the nuclear family, the assumption that all children were safest in their own homes seemed dangerously misguided. Most communards were sympathetic to runaway teenagers' motivations—many were only slightly older themselves and could see how close "running away" could be to "dropping out."

But for a commune's adults, the presence of underage teenagers posed serious conflicts and in some cases, true danger. There was real weight to the list of criminal charges that could be brought against the adults in a group where minors were doing drugs and having, even consensual, sex: statutory rape, providing controlled substances to a minor, abetting truancy, kidnapping. But even putting these aside, the very presence of children in groups of adults to whom they were not related invited unwanted scrutiny from authorities. Local law enforcement might overlook naked gardening or even drug use, as long as it remained discreetly hidden from public view, but no sheriff could ignore frantic phone calls from a parent who suspected that her lost child was being sheltered by a group in his jurisdiction.

As Constable Urie stood patiently waiting for his response, Craig thought about the dilemma that faced him. The girl had showed up a few days earlier and was now hiding upstairs, listening. Myrtle's three-day stay policy, Craig was finding, was much easier to enforce with adult men he felt fine about redirecting toward Earth People's Park than with frightened teenage girls who arrived, as this one had, full of stories about the horrors of her home life.

For a moment, Craig didn't know what to do. Hide the girl to protect her but damage, perhaps dangerously, what was currently a cordial relationship with the constable? Or hand her over and betray any number of communal ideals, chief among them the belief that the commune should be a place of escape and healing?

Craig could see that there was no point in lying. Urie already knew the girl was there. But that didn't mean Craig had to let her go easily. "Yes," he said, folding his arms. A few others had come to stand behind him and they folded their arms too.

"Well," the constable said, "Her parents are here and they're mighty concerned about her. We'd like to talk."

Craig was about to respond when Sarah herself decided to come downstairs. As soon as she saw her parents through the half-open door, she started screaming. "I don't want to talk to them! I hate them!" Craig braced himself. The situation was clearly about to escalate. It was hard for him to imagine Urie using force, but if it came to that, he wanted to be prepared. He could feel the others behind him tensing as well.

Urie, though, remained perfectly calm. "Why don't we talk," he said again. "Let's sit down and have a cup of coffee and talk it over." Craig could see that he was serious. He was so surprised at this mild, plain-spoken approach that he couldn't help but respond in kind. He opened the door wider and let the three of them into the low-ceilinged room. They all sat down at the big table, facing one another.

Hours later, they were still sitting there, still talking. Craig was amazed by Urie's patience. His commitment to finding a compromise had quieted all of them. The mood was still charged,

but the anger between Sarah and her parents had ebbed, replaced by tears and expressions of regret. The parents, once they
calmed down, weren't monsters after all, Craig could see. At last,
Urie suggested that everyone might sleep on it before deciding if
Sarah would return home. He convinced her parents to spend
the night in a motel and come back to Myrtle Hill in the morning. "We'll talk to Sarah," Craig assured them as they left.

The next day, amid further tears, Sarah's parents promised to
make some important changes, and Sarah climbed into the car
of her own will. For Craig, the whole episode had been a miracle,
but no part more so than watching Urie work. The idea that a law
enforcement officer was capable of mediating an emotional conflict with such deftness and grace—and to such a happy result—
impressed him deeply. More than many of the other things he'd
learned in his time in Vermont, Urie's example had taught him
skills he would use for the rest of his life.

Of course, he might have felt less open to compromise and more
fiercely protective if authorities had ever showed up looking
for Amy.

Amy was the group's obvious exception to any self-protective
policy for handling teenage runaways. She had long since been
accepted as a full adult member of the commune. She was aware
that her mere presence, never mind her full participation in the
group's Free Love practices, posed a danger to Craig and the
other adults, no matter how fully she felt she was acting of her
own, mature free will. She was grateful that none of them ever
for a moment let her feel like a burden. It helped that nothing
about her appearance attracted attention since she looked and
seemed much older than seventeen. It also helped that "Amy"
wasn't her real name. And that her mother had no idea where
she was.

She'd taken pains to erase her tracks. Occasionally, when Amy
heard that someone was headed someplace far-flung—Florida,
Oregon, Chicago—she asked them to take a letter to drop in the
mail when they got there. In this way, she could let her mother
know she was safe without a postmark revealing her actual

whereabouts. She later found out that her mother had followed one of these false leads. She had left Amy's four younger siblings in California to spend a few days hunting fruitlessly for Amy on the streets of Seattle.

In fact, her mother needn't have worried. Amy was thriving at Myrtle Hill. Like the others, she appreciated the satisfactions of hard, physical work and felt grounded by its obvious connection to her own daily survival. She'd found a few babysitting jobs, which let her save enough to cover her share of the mortgage, cementing her place as a full, communal member. As it seemed to her years later, she probably couldn't have designed a better environment to counter the horrors of her childhood than the one she stumbled into—a community that offered unconditional love and sympathetic listening, a sex life over which she had total control, and long days of hard work mixed with time to read, reflect, and write endlessly in her journal.

When Craig started preparing to leave for what was now accepted as his annual winter trip to California, Amy couldn't help feeling a little sad. The goodness he saw in her and his admiration for her ability to embrace joy and life after everything she'd been through helped her see these qualities in herself. They were already developing the loving friendship they'd maintain for the rest of their lives. Amy knew she'd miss him. It helped, though, that LJ was planning to stay through the cold months.

The Big House was crowded with children and, it appeared, would remain so throughout the winter. Red Paint, the communal school, had lost momentum over the summer and hadn't started up again in the fall. When the school's main teacher, Summer, was suddenly stranded with nowhere to live, she and her four-year-old daughter Leecia came to stay at Myrtle Hill.

Summer was tall and willowy with dark, boyishly short hair, a shy smile and fierce political opinions. She came from a working-class family in the South with a long history of formal and informal communal living arrangements—orphanages, a boys' ranch, homes shared by multiple branches of extended family. She held a deep suspicion that nuclear families were destined to fail in caring for the needs of their members. Communal living, with its philosophy of shared parenting, even when murkily defined, felt right to her—better for the parents, especially young, single mothers, and better for the kids who could benefit from the love, teaching, and example of more adults than merely the two flawed people who had happened to give them life.

Loraine, Craig, and others at Myrtle Hill shared this conviction, though stripped of theory. When Summer started talking about Marcuse, Loraine's eyes glazed over. Summer's radical politics would have fit in better at a place like Franklin—she never forgot her appalled shock at hearing Loraine once casually express a mild ambivalence about the Vietnam War, to which Summer was fervently opposed—but Franklin was undergoing their own interpersonal upheavals, so she accepted Myrtle's invitation to stay. Summer was always on alert to avoid any expression of middle-class comfort. And whatever else you could say about Myrtle Hill in the winter, there was no danger of its being labeled bourgeois.

Five-year-old Amelia, of course, was delighted to have a friend her own age, especially a girl. She and Leecia spent hours inventing elaborate games in the woods and, on rainy days, coloring at the big table, pressing their crayons against the hot stovepipe because melted wax made brighter colors on the paper. When they were hungry for a snack, Loraine scooped them handfuls of raw, rolled oats mixed with a dollop of honey.

Loraine taught them how to identify edible, wild greens, and Leecia loved the responsibility of gathering the whole group's dinner salad. Collecting eggs from the chicken shed was also fun, though it meant risking an encounter with the children's nemesis: the demonic, hyperaggressive, toddler-sized rooster. If one of the kids wandered into what he perceived as his territory, he charged at them, hissing, wings spread, his beak stabbing startlingly high. One day the rooster chased Amelia until she dashed into the outhouse to escape. But rather than drifting away, he stood guard outside the door, trapping her in the close, smelly space. Amelia screamed for Loraine until Nancy finally appeared to chase the rooster away and set her free.

This turned out to be the rooster's last act. The mothers decided to bring his reign of terror to an end. That night, the commune's nonvegetarians enjoyed a delicious chicken dinner.

The kids also found other, less constructive, forms of entertainment. Years later, Amelia could still remember her delight at watching toys and spoons sink beneath the frothy surface of the yeasty-smelling crocks of fruit the adults were fermenting into wine. Amelia was more mischievous than Leecia—she had less direct parental oversight, now that Loraine was doubly distracted by the new baby and her ongoing role as head cook and herbalist—but also more fragile.

One Christmas, Amelia's grandmother gave her a toy camper-trailer with moving parts that you could take out and set up. It made a clicking noise when you pulled it behind you on a string. It was one of the first brand-new objects she had ever owned and she loved it passionately. All the toys belonging to the commune were to be shared by all the kids, that was understood, but what about special presents from a grandparent? Amelia hoped that this might constitute a reasonable loophole in the communal philosophy, but she didn't dare ask. Even if she had been able to get permission from the group to keep the toy to herself, where would she have put it? There were no private cubbies or boxes in the children's corner of the loft. Even their clothes were piled together and worn by whoever fit in them or pulled them on first. As it turned out, Amelia was right to fear what would happen. Whether out of carelessness or unsupervised mischief, the other kids soon scattered the precious toy's parts far and wide and threw the camper itself into the woods. The only part Amelia managed to recover was the bottom. She pulled it around constantly, clicking.

Sometimes the contrasts between the stated philosophies of communal life and its actual practice were more obvious to children than to adults. It was undoubtedly true that having more grown-ups around meant that it was easier to find someone with the time to tie a shoe or help with a project. For Amelia, the attention offered by Amy, Summer, and Nancy was especially welcome. But a philosophy only went so far. For the most intimate and essential moments of need—a skinned knee, a nightmare—there was never a question of who you'd call to for help. As loving and supportive as the other adults could be, in the middle of the night, there was never any substitute for your own mother.

For Myrtle Hill's mothers too, the ideal of communal parenting had its limits. Arranging for childcare never posed a problem, even if you wanted to go away for a week or more at a time, but others' shared responsibility for your children sometimes stopped surprisingly short. The laundry nightmare presented by a bed-wetting phase in a house without running water, for example, fell to the mother alone.

For certain essential questions of childrearing—what children should eat, what constitutes appropriate play, how they should be educated and disciplined, how much sexuality and violence they should be exposed to—philosophical differences can cause major tensions even between just two parents. In a communal family where the parental role was expanded to a group of non-related adults who themselves sometimes struggled to get along meant that these same tensions were often intensely magnified. Many once-fiercely committed communards can identify the moment the communal experiment ended for them as the moment they saw another adult reprimand their child in a way that they found unacceptable.

Nancy's last straw turned out to be something simpler.

That fall, the Myrtle Hill kids came down with a standard childhood complaint: head lice. What makes for a serious inconvenience in more conventional homes, requiring the entire household to undertake careful, medicinal shampooing, and a thorough laundering process, became a full-blown crisis at Myrtle Hill. Before long, everyone was scratching their heads. Even in the dim kerosene-lantern light, you could see other people's scalps crawling.

Earlier that fall, Fletcher had hit on an ingenious solution to the group's hygiene challenges, a place where the doors were never locked, the residents welcomed longhairs and the showers were hot and plentiful: college dorms. Once a week, the group started arranging for enough cars to take them all to the local state college, forty minutes away; en route, they stopped by the laundromat and filled whole rows of washers to capacity.

For several weeks, this innovation worked perfectly. But then the lice epidemic struck—once-a-week showers and trips to the laundromat were no match.

After weeks of thinking she'd finally eradicated the lice from her own and her children's hair, only to feel her stomach drop when her fingers discovered yet another tell-tale crop of nits, Nancy decided she'd finally had it. She'd never fully shaken an illness she'd contracted at Red Paint the winter before and her ill health and low energy had frustrated her all summer (a doctor later told her it was probably hepatitis). The failure of the communal school disappointed her deeply. There had been elements of its politics she hadn't fully embraced—for example, the guy who'd insisted on marching the children around chanting "Ho! Ho! Ho Chi Minh! Vietcong are going to win!"—but she'd believed passionately in the mission of the school itself and had worked hard to help it get organized. More than two years into her communal experiment, she couldn't help but notice: none of her many ideas about water recycling or alternative education had born fruit. Despite Summer's observation that *none* of the women's ideas gained any traction with the men, even many years later, Nancy still felt this as a personal failure.

The amount of work it took to live day-to-day at Myrtle Hill had begun to overwhelm her, and the prospect of spending another winter in the Big House was more than she could contemplate. Her marriage with Fletcher had more or less ended months ago—he had spent the summer in his treehouse hideaway behind the Big House and was now planning to spend the winter elsewhere. The lice epidemic was really just the final blow.

When she hugged Loraine goodbye that fall, Nancy couldn't say exactly when she'd be back. The answer, as it turned out, was never.

The lice drove out pretty much everyone else who had other options. By Thanksgiving, the Big House residents had been reduced again to Loraine and her two daughters; Summer and

Leecia; and Amy and LJ. Despite LJ's impressive mechanical abilities, the group was once again wintered in with no working vehicles.

The summer's haphazard garden had allowed them to put away a better larder this year, but the communal workforce had drifted off before they got organized enough to undertake a serious firewood effort. Hoping to avoid the crisis of the winter before, someone had arranged to buy several cords of cut wood to be dumped at the end of the driveway. Though it would have taken the group only one afternoon to haul and stack it closer to the house as Loraine had suggested, somehow this had been one of the many planned tasks that had fallen by the wayside. The first snow buried the pile permanently. For the rest of the winter, one of LJ and Amy's daily jobs was to haul a toboggan and a shovel out to the end of the driveway and chip free enough firewood for the day. It was strenuous, tedious work, but at least you got warm doing it.

The "wood mine," as they affectionately began calling the pile, was also the spot where the kids waited for the village school bus in the morning. Leecia, at four, was technically too young for kindergarten, but she badly wanted to go to school with Amelia. When her mother forged her birthdate on the registration papers, the teachers looked the other way. Summer realized later that they were probably as eager as she was to offer Leecia long schooldays in warmth and comfort. The commune's children were not the first, nor the last, local children for whom school was a crucial respite from the harsh conditions of rural poverty.

Across the country, it was the presence of women with children that provided many communes with their most essential and reliable source of support: welfare. Food stamps and government commodities sustained countless (possibly the majority of) communal groups.

Collecting welfare was a choice that prompted controversy both within groups and with the wider community. As Oregon communard Elaine Sundancer put it, "We want to drop out, but we're buying our food with money that comes from the same government that is fighting the Vietnam War. I want good vibes in my food, but I'm eating Vietnam for breakfast." Within communes, political positions varied widely: Was participation in this, or any government program, an acquiescence to a hated, death-machine of a system? Or was accepting need-based help actually a healthy endorsement of socialism and a critique of capitalism? Was accepting cheese and powdered milk a shameful admission that the self-sufficient ideal had failed? Or was doing so the ultimate scam, an impudent fuck-you to the bourgeoisie and a pleasant way to horrify one's well-to-do family? For many commune parents, though, politics took a backseat to a more straightforward rationale: without subsidized food, they couldn't be sure their children wouldn't go hungry.

At Myrtle Hill, the welfare decision fell to the mothers without much controversy. But in some groups, signing up for a government program actively endangered certain members by opening the door to scrutiny that many, especially those sought by the draft board, had spent years trying to elude. This conflict often sparked a gender divide: women became much less sympathetic to men's need to duck the feds the moment their children complained of hunger or were diagnosed with malnutrition.

In rural regions where huge hippie influxes were quickly followed by a surge in the welfare rolls, the issue helped to fuel tensions with the local population. In Oregon, according to one observer, rural communes enjoyed good relations with their neighbors until the Governor "threatened to raise state taxes to pay for soaring welfare costs, and public tolerance of the newcomers decreased." In at least one community in Hawaii, locals frustrated by one communal group's reliance on public support greeted a second newly arriving group with overt hostility and violence.

Some municipalities, however, were swayed by the opposite argument: the residents of the California open-land commune Wheeler's Ranch had long been denied food stamps by the county until one of the commune's leaders, Snakepit Eddie, successfully convinced officials that offering benefits would drastically reduce the area's incidents of shoplifting.

The welfare question sometimes sparked a deeper, more emotional outrage for those who, understandably, resented many communards' middle-class backgrounds and education and identified their poverty as a perverse choice. When the founders of Colorado's Drop City first applied for food stamps, they had a sympathetic administrator who helped them maximize their available resources. When he was fired, his replacement did not share his attitude toward the college-educated artists. "YOU HAVE NO RIGHT TO BE POOR!!!" he shouted at them in frustration one day. As Peter Rabbit reported it, the communards' reaction probably didn't increase his sympathy: "We fell out the door laughing hysterically."

Though different individuals and groups had different standards for acceptable levels of hardship (cold toes and outhouses: yes; starvation: no), there was no question that, at least in the early days, young, middle-class back-to-the-landers regarded an austere, physically difficult life as morally purer than the comfort in which they'd been raised. "The poverty of your hip commune or household is no cousin to the poverty of Holiday Inns or college campuses. There is, often enough, in the psychedelic household, an aura of being in the hands of the Lord, as if anything could happen and we could deal with anything when it comes along," Raymond Mungo wrote from Total Loss Farm in 1970. This romantic conception of poverty—made possible, as many have observed, by the participants' childhood affluence and generational distance from *actual* poverty—was openly reflected in the counterculture press. "If you understand how to do it, you understand that poverty is sensual, poverty is turned on, poverty is thrilling," said Timothy Leary in the widely read 1967 *Oracle* interview that followed his Southwest commune tour. Peter Rabbit, commenting on the same article, noted the irony: "It said how strong and beautiful and honest and groovy and turned-on Drop City and Buffalo were because we had to work and scrounge so hard. He really dug how poor we were. Poverty, beautiful poverty. We wondered if the *Oracle* paid him for that article."

But no matter what ideas had led them to seek out a life of "voluntary primitivism," not many cold-climate communards would describe their winters as sensual, turned-on, or thrilling.

And for some, like the women and children in Myrtle Hill's Big House, the conditions were not even particularly voluntary.

That winter, Leecia suffered from a series of chronic ear infections. Summer had no insurance and no income. The only affordable health care she could find was the free clinic run by a teaching hospital in Burlington, two hours away. But with no working vehicles and no public transportation, Summer had no way of getting Leecia there.

An elderly local man named Bailey Frank had made friends with the communards and started dropping by. He soon offered himself as an essential source of support for Myrtle Hill's near-abandoned mothers. He lived a few towns over and made his living as the author of a syndicated astronomy column called "The Skies Today." He always arrived on the hill bearing candy for the children and treats for the dogs and seemed to have an uncanny ability to show up just when the communards were facing the point of crisis.

For the rest of the winter, he drove Summer and Leecia to her frequent doctor's appointments in Burlington. Neither mother nor daughter ever forgot Frank's unassuming generosity or their own luck in winning his friendship. Without him, Summer knew, Leecia would have gone deaf.

CHAPTER 15

For my parents, at work on their dome, the first snows came shockingly early.

The dome's roof was still more tarpaper than shingles the first morning they emerged from their camper-trailer to find everything coated in a crisp layer of white. The snow melted by midday, but it left them spooked. Every night, before they stopped work, they began covering the dome with a sheet of plastic. The icy sheets that slid off and crashed to the ground when they hauled the tarp off each morning grew steadily thicker and sharper.

Even with the heater in the camper running full blast, Larry and Judy awoke each day to the sight of their breath coming in white puffs. Only the thought of how much work still lay ahead hustled them out of their warm sleeping bags and into the frosty morning. It was too hard to handle the shingles with gloves on, so Judy's fingers spent whole days stiff and bloodless, even when she took breaks to thaw them. Finally, they decided that, no matter how unfinished the dome, that space couldn't be colder than the uninsulated trailer. It was time to move in.

The two of them planned to announce this decision to Larry's family over Thanksgiving dinner.

Larry's parents, Al and Lois, had sold their suburban Wellesley house and retired to New Hampshire, to a lovely old farmhouse and barn on forty wooded acres. The property included a working sawmill, its huge wooden waterwheel powered by the sluice over the millpond dam. Al had devoted his retirement to puttering about in his woods and outbuildings. He took a childlike delight in his model-train and music-box collections, but he still presented a stern and imposing figure. If his son's rural adventure appealed at all to his own passion for wood-working and spending his days outdoors, smelling of pine pitch and sawdust, he never admitted it aloud. "Happy to be out of the pig pen?" he would brusquely ask Larry and Judy when they arrived.

Al did not know what to make of Judy, with her long hair and work pants and frank, unflirtatious style. Whenever she tried to help him and Larry with an outdoor project—even stacking fire-wood, much easier than the work she'd been doing every day for months now—Al would fix her with a stare. "Doesn't Lois need you in the kitchen?" *No,* Judy wanted to say. *I'd be much more helpful out here.* But it was easier to be polite so she headed back inside.

Every meal hosted by Lois was an opulent affair, but none more so than Thanksgiving. Even when the guest list included only family, she set the table with heirloom china and polished silver, the ornate tureens and pickle plates laden with food. Like the rest of the house, every detail of the table's decor was a result of Lois's handiwork: she'd arranged the elaborate centerpiece, embroidered the tablecloth and the monogrammed linens—she'd even hand-carved the chairs and upholstered them in her own needlepoint with the help of her mother.

It would have been overwhelming for any daughter-in-law. Though she often felt wildly out of place in her homemade, Indian-paisley blouses, her long braid in sharp contrast to Lois's perms and curls, Judy did her best to help in the kitchen. She struggled to make small talk, but Lois gracefully drew out their common interests: literature, songbirds.

Judy could appreciate the meal's handmade care. In her own childhood home, her stepmother Kay had been impatient with shopping and preparing meals—or any domestic task, really, that kept her indoors and away from the physical outdoor work she much preferred. Starting at the age of eleven, one of Judy's chores had been to prepare breakfast for her father. Since then, she had always been inclined to view food preparation as a form of female drudgery. But Lois had an artistic flair for domestic work and a highly appreciative audience in Al. First among his many rules of table etiquette was the edict that no one was to begin eating before Lois was seated and had raised her fork. In Lois's kitchen, for the first time, Judy understood how creating a meal was not unlike a symphony: hours of diligent preparation leading to a moment of performance, followed by disappearance into the ether.

Lois's Thanksgiving menu was a smorgasbord of dishes and ingredients forbidden in a counterculture larder like Judy's, but after months of eating undersoaked, saltless soybeans, neither she nor Larry was about to let principle stand between them and a meal of creamy, ham-flavored spinach, marshmallow-topped yams, or ambrosia salad with Cool Whip.

And besides, both of them were in a good mood as they watched Al carve the turkey, elated at their progress on the dome. The decision to move in had proven brilliant. The dome's potbellied woodstove had been an immediate improvement over the paltry heat of the trailer's space heater, and for the first time in weeks, they had gone to bed warm. There was still a lot to be done, of course, but, as Larry cheerfully explained to his family, he was sure now that they'd be comfortable through the winter.

None of Larry's confidence or Judy's preparations had changed their brother-in-law Gene's opinion about their chances for survival. He could see that their minds were made up and had stopped trying to dissuade them, but not one of their assurances had made a dent. To him, they still sounded suicidal. He sat at the dinner table in silence, listening to their plans, so upset he could hardly speak.

On Sunday afternoon, as Larry and Judy prepared to leave, Lois packed them a paper bag of leftovers. Al came back from rummaging in his barn insisting they accept some supplies he'd decided they urgently needed. He handed Larry two pairs of antique snowshoes and two long raccoon coats like the ones he probably wore to college football games in the 1920s. Larry and Judy put up no resistance, eager to be on their way.

A few hours later, as they passed through the White Mountains, it began to snow. By the time they got to Vermont, they were in a full-blown blizzard.

At the foot of their hill, they pulled the truck as far off the road as they could. There were three feet of fresh snow on the ground. The walk up the hill was only a few hundred yards, but it might as well have been miles. Sheepishly, they fished the coats and snowshoes out of the back of the truck and put them on. By the time they got inside and lit the fire, they were exhausted. But not too exhausted to acknowledge that Al's eccentric gifts had turned out to be vital. They didn't dare ask themselves if Gene might have been right too.

In any case, it was too late. The experiment was under way.

To Judy, living in the dome felt like living inside an eggshell.

In the morning, she and Larry awoke to wind-tossed spruce boughs bouncing into view through the little triangular skylight over the loft bed. Sitting up, Judy looked around to see if anything had changed overnight. Every day brought some new surprise—often wonderful, sometimes dismaying. The huge triangle window on the facing wall looked out across the snowy field, past the ancient farmhouse and orchard and off south toward the distant mountains.

The loft itself stuck a third of the way into the dome's otherwise open space, suspended on its open side by chains anchored to the triangle-frame's strong vertices. Larry had attached a homemade ladder to the loft with leather straps so that it could be swung out of the way each morning, hooked to the bottom of the loft by a latch made from a sturdy, crooked branch.

Judy and Larry hurried into their clothes. Mornings could be chilly, since they were still learning how to bank the fire so it burned slowly all night. The firewood supply was stacked neatly just outside the door. Their neighbor, Donald Perron, had tipped them off that fall about where and why to buy cords of dry wood. For this, Larry and Judy thanked him anew every time they coaxed the night's embers into a new day's hot, snapping fire.

Donald's milk house also supplied the milk for Judy's tea; Larry preferred black coffee, which he prepared cowboy style by pouring boiling water over an inch of grounds in a tin cup and jiggling it gently until they settled to the bottom. There were no tables or chairs, mostly by choice ("We were *against* furniture," Larry explained), so at mealtimes, Judy rolled Japanese tatami mats over the rugs, and they ate leaning against the pile of over-sized bolsters that served as a couch. The old barn down the road was about to collapse, and Judy had salvaged its grooved, silver boards to cover the dome's inside walls. On them, decora-tive Nepalese kukri knives hung next to masks from Papua New Guinea and a poster of Ganesha in an ornate, gold frame.

Through one of the windows, they could see the birdfeeder Larry had hung from a low branch, and they watched the tiny, bold, black-capped chickadees dip and swoop. Once the birds knew where to find the food, Larry learned, you could remove the feeder and stand perfectly still in its place, offering up a palm-ful of sunflower seeds. Before long, the chickadees got used to the new arrangement and lost all fear. You could pass a whole morning like this, arm outstretched, frozen but exhilarated, the tiny wild birds alighting in a soft, thrilling flurry on your bare fingertips.

Filled now with belongings, the dome risked becoming as cramped and cluttered as any studio apartment. It helped that the huge windows and round, high, white-painted ceiling always felt expansive. In one "corner" of the round, open space, there was a tiny bar refrigerator, a gas-fueled two-burner hotplate, and rope-and-plank shelves that held large glass pickle jars full of whole-wheat flour, oats, bran, and beans.

Any kind of washing, from dishes to bathing or for Judy to shampoo her waist-length hair, meant hauling a pot of water a dozen yards over a snow-covered path from the spring, heating it on the tiny hotplate, pouring half into the tub with soap, and reserving the other half for rinsing. Dumping the dirty water would have meant both of them lugging the sloshing, unwieldy tub through the snow (too close to the house and the dishwater food scraps risked attracting skunks and porcupines), so Judy had devised a drain system: a black pipe led from the tub under the floorboards and safely away from the dome. For a few weeks she applauded her own cleverness until the system's major drawback appeared. The pipe became enthusiastically embraced as a convenient route to indoor warmth by an endless stream of field mice. She killed twenty-four mice inside the dome before she finally changed the system.

Other innovations that had at first felt so clever were now backfiring as well. Only a few weeks into winter, it became clear that one family friend whose advice they'd relied on heavily had been egregiously mistaken about a few key areas. They'd followed his instructions on building the dome's supporting platform, but its proportions turned out to be all wrong. In the first (fully predictable) winter thaw, the snow that had fallen around the platform's edge melted and immediately ran under the dome, like coffee pooling under a cup in a saucer; when the weather turned cold again, the insulation they'd carefully layered under the floor, now soaked, froze solid for the rest of the winter. They piled on another layer of rugs and hoped for the best.

The mice and the frozen floor and the fact that the big triangular window fogged up instantly and wept a constant stream of condensation that decorated its inside sills with a row of tiny icicles overnight—all this was disconcerting, to say the least. In some ways, living in the dome felt like camping. Except—as Judy kept realizing with a shock every time the outside world made incursions into her living quarters—that they had no other home to return to. This was their life.

Judy tried not to think about Gene or the others who had told them they were crazy, but the perilousness of this Vermont adventure was impossible to ignore. The thermometer Larry had nailed to a tree regularly registered daytime temperatures well below zero; in January, if the days reached single digits, it felt like cause for celebration.

At night, once they climbed into their loft bed and turned out the lights, the darkness was total. One twenty-below night, Larry lay in bed looking out in the direction of the pitch-black windows, at the blackness beyond. It was warm under the covers, even as the fire in the stove dwindled, but listening to the wind buffet the dome, it suddenly came into stark relief: there was only the thinnest shell between him and a wildly frigid night. The strengths of that fragile shell were the result of his work, but so were its weaknesses. This was, of course, the "real" experience he'd been looking for, but for the first time, it was stripped of all abstraction: he was responsible, as he had never been before, for the only barrier standing between himself and freezing to death in his sleep.

The only exceptions to the dome's no furniture policy were Larry's writing desk and chair, tucked under the small triangular spy-window that looked out toward the road. All winter, Larry sat down for several hours every afternoon to work on his novel, a political thriller set in Papua New Guinea. Judy couldn't stay in the tiny space while he worked, so she spent most of her time outdoors, skiing across the snowy fields.

The snow seemed to change daily. In the woods, one day grainy chunks might stick to the bottom of her skis and make for an impossibly slow slog but the next, a crust might have formed three feet above the forest floor that allowed her to navigate otherwise impenetrable brush with ease. In fresh powder, whole dramas were visible in the tracks left by animals—a squirrel's panicked zigzag from tree to tree; a deer's delicate path toward some cedars whose bark had been hungrily stripped; a fox's ruler-straight trail, punctuated by the snowy scuffle where she'd nosed for a sleeping vole; the tiny, racing mouse prints that suddenly vanished in a puff, plucked into the sky by a hawk. In the open fields on clear, cold days, the trees spilled shadows blue as ink at the edges of the white expanse. On those days the snow sparkled brightly enough to make her squint. A mittenful revealed each crystalline flake, distinct and intricate, miraculous.

Just as locals had found in earlier, carless centuries, winter, counterintuitively, turned out to be the easiest time for visiting neighbors. The most direct route between the dome and Entropy, the rutted dirt road that ran past Loudon's, spent half the year buried in snow and the other half muddy or bone-rattling. If Judy wanted to drive over and see Peg, in any season, without ripping off her muffler, she had to take the long route, eleven miles through town instead of one directly over the hill. But in winter, the snow's even blanket made any path possible for skis. On her long afternoons, when her cheeks were flaming and her fingers became too numb to grip her poles, Judy glided across fields and through the woods to knock on Peg's door.

Very often, Peg joined her on these long treks. They cut through pastures where the snow piled so high they could easily coast over the tops of the barbed-wire fences. Peg loved to find the spots where the wind banked the snow into drifts high enough for them to rest against, their faces almost warm in the weak sunlight filtering through the frigid air. One week, the temperature stayed at forty below for days on end. They went out anyway, the snow squeaking beneath their skis.

Just as Entropy Acres was a haven for Judy on the afternoons when she had to leave Larry alone with his (increasingly frustrated) novel writing, so the dome became a welcome retreat for Peg. For one thing, the small round space was nice and warm compared to her own drafty, underinsulated farmhouse. The big windows shed a daylong pool of sunlight on the floor. To bask in these beams, out of the wind and bone-chilling drafts, reclined against a bolster, cup of steaming mint tea in hand, was very close to heavenly.

Occasionally that winter, Larry and Judy invited Peg and Eliot for cramped dinner parties in the dome. They piled brass bowls with Nepalese curry and lentils-and-rice *dal bhat*. Cross-legged on the floor, Peg and Eliot gamely followed Judy and Larry's lead, delicately scooping mouthfuls with the fingertips of their right hands. After dinner, tea, and, very often, a passed joint of homegrown, Larry hung a white sheet in front of the dome's windows and balanced a slide projector on the desk. Then he clicked through photo after photo: hillsides striped with terraced fields and capped by spired temples; women bent over in rice paddies, their dark clothes decorated with brightly colored piping; young girls with heavy gold nose-rings balancing earthenware pots on their hips; water buffalo with foot-long horns, painted and festooned; plump, solemn children with kohl-rimmed eyes, decked out in pink and red and gold for a festival; and everywhere, in every photo, the icy peaks and breathtaking vistas of the Himalayas.

To Peg at the time, the images showed an ideal version of the life they were all trying to make for themselves—happy people eking out a simple, joyful living close to the earth. Larry and Judy shared this view to a degree—their admiration for what they saw as the self-sufficient dignity of these same farmers and villagers had started them wondering how to change their own lives, after all. But Judy and Larry's romanticism was tempered by having lived in the Third World long enough not to take certain First World stabilities for granted. Walking one afternoon in a remote part of New Guinea, Judy had stepped on a stick that had snapped up and punctured the skin above her ankle quite deeply. It hadn't hurt very much but an hour later her whole leg was swollen and inflamed. By dumb luck, she and Larry had been on their way to visit an American missionary's clinic, so she'd been able to get antibiotics in time, but if she hadn't, she might have lost her leg or worse. During the years Judy lived in Nepal, the child mortality rate there was 50 percent for children under five. Most of them died of dysentery and other preventable diseases. The mother in the family she'd lived with had been pregnant with twins. Both babies had died shortly after birth; Judy never found out why.

She had found herself thinking about those babies a lot during the winter hours she had to herself. Now that they'd gotten the dome finished, the question of what came next had begun to loom. A few weeks earlier, Larry had gotten a job offer that promised to take them overseas again, this time to Indonesia. As exciting as this was, whenever Judy contemplated repacking a steamer trunk with iodine tablets and two years' worth of bras, she felt panicky. Later she realized how much she must have been dreading a repeat of the furious, impotent uselessness she'd felt when she put her fist through their apartment wall in Port Moresby.

But that winter, as she spent her days skiing through the maple woods and trying to picture herself far away, in another humid jungle, the image that haunted her was of those babies she'd seen ill and dying from diseases long-since vanished in the West. She wanted interesting, productive work abroad, but she wanted kids too, they both did. Could she and Larry really move to wherever the work took them and still be sure of keeping a tiny baby safe and healthy? She knew that as a privileged Westerner, she would have tremendous resources unavailable to most others, but it would still be hard.

While she was in Nepal, Judy had contracted an amoeba that threatened to attack her organs. The Peace Corps doctors determined she would have to leave her village to avoid further exposure. In Kathmandu, she had stayed with some Peace Corps friends, a couple with a small baby. When their son learned to crawl, they asked everyone to leave their shoes outside the house and scrubbed the floor with Clorox every day. It had worked, the baby had remained healthy, but Judy couldn't forget the parents' stress and exhaustion. She wasn't sure she was prepared to spend years in a state of constant vigilance and fear.

Larry understood, but he had to tell the Indonesia people something soon. He was waiting for her to make up her mind.

As it turned out, the person who helped Judy decide not just about this trip but also about her whole life's direction, was Hershe.

Hershe and Pancake had pitched their tipi in the woods behind Entropy's front field, in a clearing across a small stream. Living there under the trees had provided them the peace and quiet and undemanding solitude Pancake had missed in Myrtle Hill's Big House.

The tipi was surprisingly large, twenty-two feet in diameter. Hershe and Pancake had cut long saplings for its support poles and Pancake, who was over six feet tall, could walk around easily inside.

To serve as an entryway, they'd built a kind of long wigwam out of bent saplings covered in leftover Earth Day plastic sheeting. They stacked their firewood here, next to the barrels in which they stored their food. It was also where they left their snowshoes before pushing aside the hanging blanket door and entering the tipi itself.

Inside, the tipi felt pleasantly spacious. The circle comfortably encompassed a double bed up on a platform, plus a small wood-burning cookstove. For the floor, Hershe had carefully spread a layer of hay over the open ground, then laid down another sheet of plastic, then a thick layer of rugs. Under bare feet, each step gave slightly with a cozy softness.

Once the nights turned truly frigid, Hershe and Pancake had added a few more winterizing touches. Hershe wrapped hay bales in plastic and, encumbered a bit by her growing belly, stacked them around the tipi's outside perimeter as a buffer against cold drafts and later, the deep-drifted snow. Pancake helped her tie the corners of a wool blanket to the tipi's support poles high over their heads. This lowered the ceiling, which was too bad, but it worked very well to trap the heat. The tipi had a liner reaching six feet up the inside wall, and she stuffed this with more hay to insulate it further. In one spot, they'd had to cut a hole in the canvas to put the stovepipe through. The pipe was ringed by an aluminum insulator to keep it from getting too hot, a level of precaution Hershe felt perfectly comfortable with, though it sometimes made guests nervous.

By the time Hershe had prepared the space to her satisfaction, the tipi felt downright cozy. In exchange for their ongoing help with Entropy's animals, Peg and Eliot had given Hershe and Pancake a set of excellent down sleeping bags that zipped together into one. On twenty-below nights the tipi wasn't exactly warm by central heating standards, but it was no chillier than Entropy's upstairs bedroom, and far less drafty.

The Entropy farmhouse's perennial heating problems aside, Peg's kitchen offered her neighbors a different kind of warmth. Judy was not the only one to arrive at Peg's doorstep with frost-thickened eyelashes in search of a hot mug of tea and Peg's sympathetic ear. Amy walked three snowy miles over from Myrtle as often as she could and openly worshipped Peg. Whenever they could finagle a ride, Loraine and Summer packed up the children and brought them all over for the exquisite bliss of a hot shower.

Hershe and Pancake, of course, dropped in to the house whenever they needed a break from the tipi. Perhaps inspired by Larry and Judy's Nepalese curry dinners, Hershe and Peg decided to host a series of what they were calling "gourmet international meals." In late January, they invited everyone they could think of to come over to Entropy for a Mexican feast.

The afternoon of the party, it started to snow. It looked like it might turn into a blizzard, but the women decided to go ahead with the party anyway. Peg was busy in the kitchen when Hershe stepped through the door, eyes aglow. She had begun labor. Some guests, hoping to beat the snow, had already begun to arrive. There was no need to cancel the party, Hershe assured Peg. They could just move it to the tipi. This birth could be just as festive and celebratory as Loraine's birth with Rahula had been a few months earlier. Anyone who wanted was welcome to come down to the tipi and join them.

By good luck or providence, one of the early-arriving guests happened to be the person Hershe had selected as a midwife, a friend with bright-red hair and beard who'd recently returned from a tour in Vietnam as a medic. The only birth he'd attended before was his own child's, but Hershe felt confident in his abilities. Plus, he was really just there as backup. She'd seen how little Loraine's midwife-friend had appeared to do. Like Loraine, Hershe had read her way through Mildred Hatch's lending library of books on natural childbirth. Many of these emphasized that it was the laboring mother and not the doctor who was chiefly responsible for bringing the baby into the world. Hershe was strong and healthy and unafraid of pain or hard work. If anyone could handle this, she could. Someone drove off to pick up Loraine from Myrtle Hill, and Hershe walked back to the tipi through the falling snow to continue her preparations.

One of Mildred Hatch's books had recommended keeping hard candy on hand for the mother to suck on if her mouth got dry during labor. Hershe had decided to replace the hard candy with homemade maple fudge. She spent the rest of the afternoon cooking energetically between contractions, finishing the huge batch of potato salad she'd intended for the party's potluck, and boiling syrup and cream together for fudge.

By the time Judy and Larry made their way across the dark field and ducked through the tipi's blanket door several hours later, they found a more hushed scene. Hershe had moved to the bed and was moaning rhythmically. She was completely naked but didn't seem to notice either the cold or the half-dozen people now crowding the tiny space. Even those standing right next to the woodstove had their coats on. The hurricane lanterns hanging from the support poles bathed everything in a yellowish glow. People had stopped bothering to kick snow off their boots and the normally pristine rugs were now muddy and sodden. The smell of snowmelt mingled with the scents of boiled syrup, wood smoke, and kerosene.

Peg was crouched against the wall next to the stove. When Larry ducked back out, Judy moved beside her. LJ had come over from Myrtle Hill with Amy and Loraine and was sitting behind Hershe, rubbing her back with his large, strong mechanic's hands. Loraine sat on the floor, nursing baby Rahula. She was singing and chanting beautifully but forcefully in an effort to bring the mood in the tipi to the same ecstatic state of energy and calm as at Rahula's birth. This time it wasn't as easy.

For one thing, it was hard to get everyone focused. Not all the guests could fit inside, certainly not comfortably, and it was too frigid outside for them to linger nearby in supportive presence. The snow had stopped, but the temperature had dropped, sharply. The guests kept going back and forth to the house, particularly the men. The path through the snowy field was tricky to navigate even with flashlights, and people kept missing the little bridge over the stream and soaking their boots.

There were other obstacles too. One of the dinner party guests was a young man who'd brought his sixteen-year-old girlfriend, a junior at the local high school, down to the tipi. She was palpably terrified—no one else knew yet, but she was pregnant too. Her boyfriend had suggested she come watch as a way of reassuring her about the wonders of childbirth, but it was not working. Despite Loraine's valiant efforts to chant the group into focus, the room's energy was pulled toward the girl's abject fear.

From her spot on the floor, Peg watched Hershe labor with a mix of awe and fascination. She'd never seen real childbirth before—she found it messier and more intense but also more profoundly moving than she had imagined.

Next to Peg, the cold seeping through the tipi's walls and her layers of parka and sweater, Judy was biting back waves of terror. She could not stop calculating and recalculating: the tipi sat half a mile off the road, which was itself twenty-five miles from the nearest medical facility. It would take an ambulance forty-five minutes to arrive and the same to get back to the hospital—longer if the roads hadn't been well cleared. Hershe's labor seemed to be going well, as far as Judy could tell, but what if something went wrong? Who here had enough experience to know what to do? Her own sense of helplessness frightened her.

After what seemed like years, Larry appeared through the blanket door to collect Judy, Hershe still moaning long streams of white breath. Most of the others had left as well, but Peg stayed, frozen against the tipi's canvas for another few hours. Loraine rocked Rahula and sang rhythmically. The tipi's air grew close with the smells of amniotic fluid, and then vomit as Hershe began throwing up the candy she'd eaten earlier. Finally Hershe stood up and gave a huge bellow. The medic-midwife reached out to catch the baby as it emerged, fat and slick. In the frigid air, the tiny, warm, wet body steamed.

Pancake cut the umbilical cord, and someone wrapped mother and baby snugly together. Later, Hershe reflected that this birth had gone more or less exactly as she thought it would. It would have been nice to have the chanting work a little better, but she had still been able to concentrate in the way she needed to. And there had been a tiny, wonderful miracle at the moment of birth: amid the adults' sudden excitement, six-month-old Rahula, in Loraine's arms, made a noise that sounded distinctly like, "Hi!"—a clear greeting for a new and, as it turned out, lifelong friend.

Hershe and Pancake named the baby Jethro. Both he and Hershe were fine.

The person who left the tipi forever changed that night was my mother.

Judy's hours of crouching, cold and afraid, had left her determined never again to find herself in a medical situation feeling so utterly helpless.

She was entirely sympathetic to Hershe's decision to eschew the hospitals and doctors that seemed to have replaced the body's every natural labor and birth process with systems of their own devising. When Larry was born, for example, his mother Lois has been knocked completely unconscious with scopolamine, which prevented her from remembering anything about the birth. It was hours before she was allowed to hold him, and then only for a few minutes before the nurses took him away to feed him. That system, so entirely sure of itself, left no room for a woman to obey her own instincts during labor or even to request whoever she wanted as support. Stories floated around the counterculture about couples who tried to thwart a hospital's policy of barring fathers from the delivery room by handcuffing themselves together. For Judy, like Hershe and Loraine and so many others, everything about this felt terribly wrong.

Their decision to seek out an alternate birth experience for themselves and their babies felt entirely consistent with the wider social revolution under way, another example of rejecting the practices of the postwar society that assumed everything man-made was superior to everything naturally occurring. Many elements of Western medicine came under suspicion during this period, but none more so than modern obstetrics. How had the doctor become more central to healthy birthing than the mother herself?

Judy shared this critique, though she couldn't forget her experience living in places where access to even just a little more Western medicine and hospital support would save thousands of lives. She was not prepared to reject all medical expertise, she just wanted a more flexible, more woman-centric version of it. And, she now decided, she wanted that expertise herself.

If women like Hershe were going to walk away from hospital births and trust themselves and nature to what felt to Judy like an extreme degree, they'd need better, more sympathetic sources of medical support and expertise than was currently available. And maybe, Judy thought, she could be one of the people to provide it. It was exactly the kind of exciting, necessary, creative professional work she'd been wondering how to find. The night in the tipi had made up her mind. She would become a midwife.

All over the country, at almost the same moment, other women were having similar experiences with far-flung home births—in snowed-in cabins, on high desert mesas, in remote canyons—and coming to conclusions very similar to Judy's. Most famously and influentially, Ina May Gaskin.

Ina May, as she is known in her best-selling guides to natural labor, childbirth, and nursing, was teaching English in San Francisco in 1968, having recently returned from the Peace Corps in Malaysia. She and her husband became regular attendees at Stephen Gaskin's pan-theological Monday Night Classes and then joined Gaskin and his wife in what they called a "four marriage," an arrangement that eventually pared down to just Stephen and Ina May.

When Stephen decided to take his classes on a countrywide lecture circuit, several hundred of his devotees followed, in a caravan of painted school buses and converted bread trucks. One night, after the caravan had stopped to rest near Evanston, Illinois, a man appeared at the Gaskins' door. His wife had gone into labor and he was looking for help.

Ina May, like a number of women in the caravan, was pregnant herself. She had been talking to many of the others about their previous birth experiences. Her own first birth had been traumatic. She had entered the hospital confident and feeling strong, but the doctors had given her an episiotomy and used forceps without talking to her about it, which had left her feeling assaulted and shaken. During their long hours on the road, she and the other women had begun reading the best source they could find about natural childbirth, a Mexican midwifery manual.

That night, she watched as Stephen talked to the worried father-to-be with confidence, but she knew him well enough to see that, despite his experience as a medic in Korea, he didn't really know what to do. "I'll go," she offered.

As she sat with the woman laboring on a bed in the back of the bus, the manual's advice helped Ina May to understand what was happening. But, out of superstition, she and the other women had skipped a chapter about what to do if the baby wasn't breathing. When this baby emerged, blue-faced and still, she suddenly realized with horror how little she really knew.

Someone raced to fetch Stephen. He arrived in time to give the baby mouth-to-mouth. It worked. Just a few minutes later, the baby was wailing and ruddy, safe in her mother's arms.

For some in the group, this had been nothing short of a miracle performed by their leader and spiritual teacher. But Ina May knew how much they owed to pure luck. For her, it had been a wake-up call.

Ina May knew this would not be the last time her group would face this kind of crisis. She felt that it would be irresponsible to continue supporting home births, as she planned to do, without gaining the serious expertise needed to keep mothers and babies safe. And so she started collecting and learning to use basic obstetric equipment as she and many of her commune sisters began reading everything they could find. By the time the lecture tour ended, eleven babies had been born.

For the rest of the five-month lecture tour, all the babies but one were born safe. Ina May's own son was born two months prematurely at just three pounds. He did not survive.

By 1971, when Stephen and the rest of the group decided to move from San Francisco to the Tennessee acres that would become The Farm, it was clear that the new commune's mission would include a serious commitment to natural childbirth and midwifery. The birthing house was one of the first buildings they constructed. Between 1971 and 1980, The Farm's midwives delivered more than two thousand babies; nearly one thousand more have been born there since.

As Ina May threw herself into learning, she talked to both sympathetic and unsympathetic obstetricians and to midwives from every background she could find. But mainly, as she put it, "I learned by listening to women." She noticed what conditions and experiences helped laboring women to relax and feel confident and paid close attention to the emotional and psychological elements of labor that conventional medicine most often ignored.

Over the next decades, Ina May, former academic, began to amass a spectacular library. She especially valued obstetrics manuals from the 19th century, whose authors had grown up on farms and had lots of practice confidently resolving complicated births on creatures other than humans.

But one of The Farm midwives' greatest sources of learning, as for so many back-to-the-landers, turned out to be their own neighbors: the Ethridge Amish community. Midwives there had refined their own home-birth practices over several centuries—under the same no-electricity, no-running-water conditions that felt so novel to the communards. The intensive collaboration between the two groups of midwives continues to this day.

This proximity to a thriving home-birth tradition, plus The Farm's huge numbers, both of birthing women and interested midwives, made it an ideal learning environment for Ina May and her commune sisters. What made Ina May the most famous midwife in the world, though, was not just her rapidly growing expertise and ability to share this knowledge with others but also a stroke of simple good timing.

Around 1975, one Farm member received an inheritance, and the group decided to invest it in the means for a cash sideline: a printing press. This appealed to them as a method of producing salable materials (books) with relatively little overhead. Plus, it offered the group and its effusive leader an outlet for culture-disrupting ideas. Now all they needed was material. Ina May decided to turn some of what she and the other midwives had learned into a book. *Spiritual Midwifery*, a collection of findings, observations, personal stories, and advice, was exactly the text thousands of readers had been hungering for. The book, now in its fourth edition, has remained steadily in print since its first run in 1975. It has been translated into twelve languages.

When Judy told Larry about her new determination to become a midwife, he supported it completely. Unlike Ina May and her self-taught colleagues, though, Judy preferred to enter the profession through the more conventional route of first becoming a registered nurse. It would take a few years to earn this degree, which would mean Larry turning down the Indonesia job and remaining in the States.

He didn't mind—he had recently run into a former Harvard classmate at work on an interesting new undertaking. There was poverty program money available for projects that provided people in rural areas with access to higher education, the friend explained. After talking it over with Judy, Larry accepted his friend's invitation to join the team designing what would eventually become the Community College of Vermont.

Both Larry and Judy were eager to get back to some form of gainful employment. Like many middle-class back-to-the-landers, my parents had entered into their adventure with a vague idea about escaping the confines of a cash economy but without any definite plan for how they might actually achieve this. Whenever the subject of money came up, one of them would narrate the fantasy again: what if there was a leather bag, like an old-fashioned mail bag, hanging from the apex of the dome, full of money? And any time they needed cash, they could reach up and grab a handful. Really, they reasoned, only half-joking, there was only one obstacle to making this a reality: figuring out how to get the money into the bag in the first place.

Though their day-to-day life cost next to nothing—endless meals of soybeans hadn't even made a dent in the fifty-pound bag they'd bought at Hatch's—they had both been watching anxiously all winter as their savings account steadily depleted. Neither of them, they realized, would be able to relax as long as their finances remained unstable. Larry's return to conventional, professional employment was coming sooner than he'd imagined it might in his back-to-the-land fantasies, but he had no regrets. He was proud of his graduate degree and interested in the ideas it offered. He saw no reason why a professional life of the mind couldn't coexist with a life close to the earth.

By April, a month when most parts of the country were relaxing into spring, the snow around the dome remained stubbornly waist-deep. Both Larry and Judy had developed an acute case of cabin fever. The air had softened slightly and picked up a quickness that made staying indoors unbearable, though going out was even more difficult now than it had been in February. The snow was far too wet and heavy to ski or snowshoe but it was still impossible to walk; driving was its own nightmare as the dirt roads softened into pudding.

The endless winter had made one thing eminently clear: the dome was too small. If Judy and Larry were going to stay in Vermont as they'd decided, they'd need a bigger house.

As lovely as their current meadow was, Judy and Larry had been in such a rush to get started building that they hadn't actually given much thought to the dome's location. Basically, they'd just picked a sunny contrast to Nick's valley and a spot as far back from the road as still qualified them for free phone lines from Ma Bell. Now they had time to be more deliberate with their choice of house site.

Judy had emerged from winter more convinced than ever that it would be essential to their mental health to maximize daylight exposure. With this in mind, she and Larry headed up, toward the spot where they'd paused on their walk with Roger Perron that first afternoon several years before, turning to admire the hillsides and gather in the vista that had stayed with them through their years abroad.

Walking up to reexamine this view, they crossed through a long field that sloped down toward the maple sugar bush whose colors they'd admired in autumn and from which Donald Perron had just finished collecting sap. They'd been up this hill before, but now they noticed something new: at the field's top edge, just before the spruce forest engulfed it, there was a small ledge.

While the snow still stood in crusty drifts everywhere else, here alone it had already melted away.

The location appealed to them immediately, both for its practical merits—it was warm, south facing, with a beautiful view—and for its sheer romance. What could be less suburban than siting your house in a spot chosen by the sun?

They had found the site for their new home.

Now all they had to do was figure out how to move the dome.

CHAPTER 16

My parents were not the only ones who emerged that spring into a new vision for their future.

One afternoon a few weeks after Jethro was born, Hershe heard footsteps crunching through the snow and looked out of the tipi to see a woman she didn't know picking her way through the frozen, knee-deep drifts. Not only was she not wearing snowshoes—by far the easiest way to get across the field—she was wearing a skirt and pumps.

By the time the woman reached the tipi, she was thoroughly miserable. As Hershe helped her take off her snow-sodden shoes and shredded pantyhose and settled her near the stove to warm up, the woman introduced herself as a home health nurse. Her job was to check up on potential cases of child endangerment.

Hershe fixed her a steaming cup of herbal tea and began talking. While she talked, the woman gazed around, taking in the cloth diapers hanging from clothesline strung ingeniously from the tipi's support poles, the rugs, the big bed with its cozy nest of zipped-together sleeping bags and the baby himself who snoozed snugly in a hanging cradle and woke to nurse. After listening to Hershe deliver what she remembered later as an hour-long lecture on the philosophy and science behind natural childbirth, vegetarianism, and organic food, the woman at last stood to go.

Hershe helped her start back across the snowy field and waved her off. In the nurse's rounds visiting mothers with babies in the remote, rural poverty of northern Vermont, Hershe's tipi might have been the most eccentric home she visited, but it was probably far from the coldest or most dangerous. The visit apparently put to rest any questions about Jethro's safety. Hershe never saw the nurse again.

The rest of the winter passed uneventfully enough. At some point, a neighbor's cows discovered the insulating hay bales that Hershe had carefully stacked around the base of the tipi, and their soft munching became a steady background noise. By the time the snow melted, the bales were gone. Hershe and Pancake were ready for a change too. As soon as it got warm, they decided to repitch their tipi back over at Myrtle Hill.

They noticed it right away: the commune's vibe had changed.

Craig, Jed, and other men who'd left for the winter had returned, plus the usual flow of friends and visitors, but the intense, macho emphasis on construction that had alienated Pancake the summer before had now evaporated, replaced by a mellower but slightly disorienting anarchy.

The lack of focus was partly good news, a measure of the group's victorious exit from the panicked mode of the last two summers. They had accomplished a lot. Myrtle Hill now boasted a barn, finished house, and a functional candle factory, plus two outhouses, the Star House, and a clever, gravity-fed outdoor shower that Jed and some others had built using a hillside spring they'd found in the woods behind the upper field, a few hundred yards past the point where the commune's road disappeared into the trees. The men had gotten the idea for the shower from the *Mother Earth News*: after catching the spring water in a barrel at the top of the slope and leaving it to heat in the sun for several hours, you came back to shower in blissful warmth, if no one had beaten you there first.

In the absence of catastrophic deadlines, however, smaller irritations they'd previously brushed aside now began to assert themselves. Where the garden's lack of central planning and haphazard tending had been previously been a source of amiable eye-rolling, now the disorder sparked actual conflicts. Everyone had their own idea about how to amend the soil and what to plant where. Loraine relished the freedom to cultivate herbs wherever and however she pleased—she didn't mind it when mint and comfrey proliferated and took over—while Hershe preferred orderly, well-tended rows.

As always, the group regularly gathered for the long meetings in which they hashed out issues and, theoretically anyway, came to consensus about what to do next. No one had ever loved these, but they believed in the process and thus stayed engaged—even when a discussion about whether or not to put doors on the outhouse veered into a blunt, honest, encounter-group airing of individual members' personal hang-ups, as identified by their comrades. That intense, personal feedback was never easy to take, but knowing your friends were critiquing you from a place of love made it easier. This year, though, the meetings' tone of respectful patience had notably eroded. In the middle of discussions, people got up and walked away, and no one went after them to bring them back. As Pancake put it later, "Things were not as friendly . . . Less was getting done, more arguing was going on."

For their wheat, the group had decided to buy only whole berries, which had to be ground into flour by hand in a crank grinder. This made for lovely, dark loaves of bread but it turned baking them into an entire day's work for Loraine. When the loaves finally emerged from the woodstove's oven, steaming and fragrant, they were often devoured instantly. When one guy discovered that Loraine often tucked a loaf or two away, out of the feeding frenzy, he got pissed and started shouting. What gave her the right to single-handedly decide what happened to the group's bread?

Loraine, ducking conflict, did not say what she thought: What gave him the right to prioritize his own immediate hunger? She shouldn't *have* to hide the bread to ensure that the children would have breakfast in the morning.

There were a lot of little frustrations that Loraine wished later she'd dared to express. For example, insisting on the dogs' and chickens' total freedom from leashes and pens meant that the barefoot children were constantly stepping in shit. Loraine couldn't get over how many city- and suburban-bred people thought of everything in nature as automatically pure and clean. It was like they'd never heard of germs.

For example, the staph outbreak. Suddenly the children's cuts and scrapes would not heal for weeks on end, and the adults developed strange, disturbing rashes. The only one unaffected was Loraine. She was also the only one not drinking milk, which was how she figured out that the problem stemmed from a couple of guys not bothering to sterilize the equipment properly when they finished milking.

The staph episode—which she did bring up in a meeting to the improvement of everyone's boiling habits—left Loraine with a surprising, not totally welcome insight: maybe her Depression-escapee mother's obsession with hygiene hadn't been a total crock after all. As Loraine saw it, this whole communal experiment had been a furious effort to cast off the endless bullshit piled upon them by their parents—but now, she saw, buried in the bullshit here and there lay little nuggets of important truths. How the hell were they supposed to tell the difference?

For everyone at the commune, other new questions arose. For example, what should a productive day look like? Though in actual terms gardening, animal care, crop production, and firewood collection were no less life-sustaining than the previous years' construction projects, they somehow lacked heroic urgency. Simply put: for many at Myrtle Hill, it turned out that the chores of maintaining daily life—the "real work" they'd imagined for themselves during so many nights around the campfire—felt, in practice, uncomfortably close to drudgery.

LJ and a few others made an attempt at starting up candle production, but by now it was clear that this would never be the serious commercial operation they had dreamed of, so it was hard to stay motivated. Plus, fixes to the factory's glitchy rigging had become more and more haphazard after its inventor, Jim the Bear, had disappeared. They'd gotten a postcard from him in the mail, addressed to the whole group: "Living free in Mexico," it read, signed, "Jimmy July." LJ missed Jim, who'd been a mentor to him in the few weeks they'd worked together.

But LJ too had emerged into spring with a new plan. His winter amid a houseful of women and children had left him with a new insight: perhaps privacy—or at least peace and quiet—wasn't as expendable as communal groups had generally assumed. It was a philosophical shift then starting to creep through the wider counterculture. Doors: not so oppressively bourgeois after all.

If LJ wanted to stay at Myrtle Hill—and, despite the winter's hardships, he was very clear that he did—he couldn't spend another winter in the blanket-walled communal sleeping loft. He kept thinking about the cozy getaway Fletcher had built himself behind the Big House the summer before: a tiny two-story, 6′ × 8′ treehouse, suspended just a few feet off the ground on living trees. It was just big enough for a chair and a little stove downstairs, and a bed in the loft above. LJ had admired Fletcher's design, and he now also admired his motivation. He began pondering how he might construct himself a similar hermitage. In fact, he had already begun gathering materials for a tool shed in the middle field. As soon as spring arrived in earnest, he began planning how to expand the shed into a cabin of his own, near where the first summer's cook tent had been, a few yards from the old cellar hole.

When Jed noticed what LJ was up to, he decided to undertake a similar project. His family's business had kept him in New York all winter as usual, but the idea of building his own house appealed to him.

For LJ, Jed starting to build was great news. Jed excelled at jerry-rigging and troubleshooting and had far more building experience than LJ—not to mention his generator and power tools, with which he remained extremely generous. Another guy, August (Summer's ex-husband) had begun a cabin of his own too, deeper in the woods. The three men agreed to collaborate, aided by several of their friends.

Where LJ planned a very simple, low-cost cabin—16′ × 16′, built entirely from the perfectly good lumber he found at the local dump, refuse from the nearby Ethan Allen furniture factory— Jed's design ran a little grander. He picked out a spot in the woods above LJ's cabin, back where the road that divided the upper and middle fields disappeared behind the trees. After cutting and clearing the top of a west-facing ledge, he began framing a gorgeous, one-of-a-kind house—tall, multitiered, and filled with windows that looked out over the hills toward the sunset.

It was only later, after he had started looking back to try and identify exactly what had precipitated the end of things at Myrtle Hill that it occurred to LJ: in this, the commune's third summer, all this house construction meant that most of the group's able-bodied and committed builders now focused their time and attention not on group plans but on individual projects. At the time, his and Jed's decision to build private houses at the top of Myrtle's road, only a few hundred yards apart, felt practical and exciting—just a natural continuation of the commune's "do your thing" ethic and not the irreversible step it turned out to be.

In fact, LJ would still be living in that same cabin forty years later. And though he would try not to hold himself responsible for failing to guess the future, all those years later he would still be regretting the choices he made that summer, for himself and for his family.

There were some other new tensions at Myrtle Hill that spring.

Jed had arrived not just with his usual truckload of supplies but also with a new companion. Clever, funny, raunchy Jed, with his thick glasses and crazy hair, now had a serious girlfriend, soon to be his wife. Lilith was a fellow New Yorker, with long black hair, dark eyes, and pale skin. She had a full-time job teaching at an inner-city school, so she mainly came up to Myrtle in the summer. Hershe, when she met Lilith, thought she could have been beautiful if she didn't look so miserable about being in the woods. To Loraine, Lilith's demeanor looked less like unhappiness and more like distain.

But Loraine herself admitted how hard it could be for visiting women to feel comfortable at Myrtle Hill. During the summer, Fletcher and Craig had sometimes returned from candle-selling trips with pretty girls who visibly struggled, in their bright dresses and perfect hair, to match the men's description of communal utopia with the muddy, hectic campsite to which they'd arrived. It was not their fault, Loraine knew, but she could not resist a kind of gentle hazing. She sent girls in leather flats struggling up the hill with overflowing buckets to empty into the compost heap. "How do you turn on the stove?" asked one woman who'd wandered into the kitchen to help.

"Oh, you push the button . . ." Loraine gestured vaguely before slipping away, leaving the woman to fiddle with the wood-burning cookstove.

This was unkind. Almost immediately Loraine felt guilty. But when she confessed to Hershe what she'd done, Hershe thought it was hilarious.

From the start, though, Loraine's relationship with Lilith was more complicated. Part of it was a simple question of clashing personalities. Loraine thought of herself as shy and timid, but no one who knew her failed to recognize the force that lay behind her sweetly myopic gaze. It was generally understood that Myrtle Hill's kitchen and larder fell under Loraine's purview, and for most people this posed no conflict. But where Hershe preferred working outdoors and Amy liked her role as sous-chef and the men simply didn't concern themselves with cooking or cleaning, Lilith, somehow, had a harder time navigating the not-quite-fully-shared nature of the kitchen. It didn't help that her own personal force was every bit as strong as Loraine's but without any veneer of shyness.

And even Loraine had to admit, even years later: it could not have been easy for Lilith to join a community and to live alongside the women who had shared several blissful Free Love summers with her (now-monogamous) husband.

Whatever its sources, the tension between the women was uncomfortable and everyone felt it. Amy noticed a bright side, though: where Hershe, yet another unabashed alpha-woman, had sometimes butted heads with Loraine, that was now over. Their mutual discomfort with Lilith brought Hershe and Loraine firmly into a permanent, lifelong alliance.

Loraine's clashes with Hershe had followed from differences of style or preference, fueled by their own strong wills. But

with Lilith, there was something about the way she held herself apart—above, it seemed to Loraine—that filled Loraine with
a hot, angry resentment. At the time she didn't have the political perspective to see how her rage might have stemmed from
Lilith's refusal—with its implication of free choice—to shoulder
the commune's domestic burden as fully and uncomplainingly
as Loraine had.

From the commune's first season, Loraine had noticed that the
men considered their workday over at dinnertime while the wom-
en's continued until they fell into bed exhausted. But it wasn't
until that third year, when Summer began talking about wom-
en's lib, that Loraine began to think about this pattern in political terms.

That summer, the *Whole Earth Catalog* printed an essay
called "Women in Communes" that described Myrtle Hill to a T.
Its author recounted the attempts by women in her group to
change the gendered division of labor by simply choosing, after a long day in the fields, to chop wood instead of doing the
dishes. "Our experiment was a colossal failure," she wrote. "If
we went gathering wood at dinner time, the men cooked—for
themselves only. They washed their own dishes, but never the
pots and pans that the food came from." She went on, "A lot of
dusty old myths were dragged out and shoved in our faces . . .
'You don't work fast enough . . . Before you learn to drive a tractor, learn to get the dishes clean (I don't want you fucking with
my tractor, baby.)'" This last line kept the women at Myrtle Hill
laughing for weeks.

Loraine was amazed to find out how many other women shared
the same frustrations and humiliations that had felt so personal
to her. Early on, some communal groups had romanticized "traditionally" gendered work. In the early days of New Buffalo, a
resident recalled, "none of the women . . . wanted to be liberated;
the 19th-century image of aproned, long-skirted womanhood appealed to them." When a visiting woman asked to work in the
fields, neither the men nor women would let her; the women also
denied a visiting man's request to work in the kitchen.

But in most places, like Myrtle Hill, the pattern just snuck up on them. Explaining the starkly gendered roles at one early commune, a male observer explained that it was not by design but just what happened when "everyone does what they enjoy doing." Suddenly women started questioning this assumption. As one put it, "Even though the women may have embraced and enjoyed their tasks, they were not tasks that were coveted."

In the back-to-the-land context, men and women alike were yearning for more satisfying, hands-on work than their parents' lives had offered. In addition to being higher status, outdoor work like building or farming had tangible, productive outcomes you could stand back and admire at the end of the day, unlike the endless, thankless cycles of cleaning and cooking with their fragile, fleeting end products. As communard Vivian Estellachild wrote, "I was really quite tired of kitchen work, serving men visitors, illness and babies . . . One morning as I was starting a fire in the stove one man came in, said he was in a hurry, and that I had better let him do it. I screamed to be allowed to do something. To learn some skill besides the ones I had learned all my life—babies, dishes and cooking."

Learning new skills, after all, was central to the appeal of going back to the land, for men and women alike. But women moving not just into new practices (handling a crosscut saw) but also into new spheres of work (the outdoors) often felt their learning curves come under more scrutiny than their equally inexperienced male comrades'. As women tried out jobs forbidden to them as girls, they ran up against overt criticism from men but also against their own gendered expectations. Struggling with an axe taught some women that they needed more practice or better fitting tools, but led others to conclude that they somehow inherently weren't fit for the job.

The same dynamics occasionally worked in the other direction too. One of Elaine Sundancer's commune-mates asked her to teach him to sew. Watching him struggle, she noted, "His hands moved so slowly. It took an effort not to say, 'Here, let me do that for you.' It was a shock to realize that a needle and thread were as strange to him as a hammer is to me."

To encourage this kind of mutual growth, some groups insti-
tuted job rotations specifically designed to challenge gendered
patterns. At one of these, the women were just heading out to the
fields when a man on his first kitchen shift came running after
them, panicked: "Hey, look, you can't leave all the *kids* here, I've
gotta cook!" The women just looked at each other and laughed.

For those women, as for Hershe and Amy, working outdoors
doing hard, physical labor taught them their own strength and
further pushed aside their girlhoods' myth of daintiness. Taking a shot at the "men's" work of building and fixing left many
women with the sense that, while some jobs were always going to
be easier for those taller and stronger, many others were no more
difficult than traditional women's work and in many ways much
more satisfying.

For Loraine, though, her desire for a creative and physical
realm of work was fully met by her role as the commune's head
cook. For her, as for many other women and men, the counterculture kitchen provided a new frontier, rich for experimentation, with new ingredients, techniques, and priorities, where
food production bore almost no similarity to their mothers'
appliance-aided work. Loraine found tremendous personal and
intellectual satisfaction in inventing and mastering what would
only later be recognized as a distinct, new American cuisine.

Loraine's burgeoning feminist consciousness didn't turn her
from the kitchen, but it did bring her another, dismaying insight.
As she began to see how unquestioningly she'd undertaken the
role of the commune's "chief cook and bottle washer," dutifully
serving the men while also expecting them to solve problems
and bring home the oat bran, she suddenly saw how she and the
others had unconsciously reproduced the gender patterns of a
conservative, 1950s household.

In trying to grant herself the maximum amount of freedom
to live her own life, she had moved to the woods, adopted a new
diet, new medicine, new shelter, new models of how to be a parent and friend and lover. She'd sought out and helped invent an
entirely new, radical form of family. And still, despite every effort to the contrary, she had somehow managed to become her

mother. When she heard herself snap at Amelia in Nelly's sharp, frustrated tone one day, Loraine was horrified.

The problems of her upbringing had not been solved, as she had hoped, by simply walking away and starting over in the woods. Maybe, she was beginning to understand, the problems weren't inherent after all to the structure of the nuclear family. If she and her commune-mates had somehow managed to import their parents' destructive, oppressive patterns almost wholly unchanged into this fresh and radical setting, those patterns and problems must lie deeper, within themselves. It was a sobering thought.

Suddenly, every interaction raised intense, new questions. The communal meetings' encounter-group personality critiques now became openly antagonistic. When Summer suggested the women begin meeting together, alone, to discuss their experience, Loraine embraced the idea.

The men, however, did not. Craig recalled his hurt astonishment when the women announced they wanted to counter what they saw as the men's dominance in meetings by holding their own. "What? Why?" he asked.

Summer remembered the dynamic more bluntly. One weekend, she invited a friend who belonged to a radical women's collective in Burlington to the commune for a visit. The woman hadn't particularly talked politics while she was at Myrtle, she just wanted a few days in the countryside. But when her friend returned home, Summer recalled Craig scolding her: "We don't want any more of those feminist women here, those man-haters."

For Craig, the arrival of women's lib in the communes was like night and day. Every conversation between men and women suddenly turned strained and political. Free Love shut off like a faucet. To him, the women's insistence on separation felt like a rebuff to the communal ideal of togetherness. He was stung by their anger and *you, you, you* accusations, which made him defensive: "I thought it was *we*."

It took many years and marriage to a feminist for him to understand: what had felt at the time like a bolt from the blue aimed directly at destroying his little utopia was actually the explosion following years and centuries of the pent-up rage that had been there along.

Craig's return to Myrtle Hill that spring had been troubling for other, less political reasons.

His acknowledged role as the commune's leading visionary had always been a complicated one for him. On the one hand, he saw it as central to his communal contributions to enrich the isolated community by bringing ideas, connections, and collaborations back from his travels, and he was often frustrated when the others didn't follow through on one of his plans or visions in his absence.

On the other hand, the assumption, shared by him, that the group wouldn't undertake any major decision without his input meant that every time he returned from a trip he was barraged by problems that others clearly expected him to solve, the flip side of the same "Wait 'till your father gets home" dynamic that Loraine had noticed. He helped LJ and Jed with their houses, but his heart wasn't in it. He had hardly been at the commune a week before he was already frustrated and exhausted.

Plus, a new idea had caught hold of his restless attention. His best friend Jblu—still ducking the draft board and living near Goddard—had gotten involved in an exciting new venture that appealed to Craig: sourcing and supplying whole grains, dried goods, and organic produce to locals and rural freaks at the cheapest possible prices. It was happening in counterculture hotbeds all over the country. Jblu and other organizers were calling them food conspiracies.

Craig could feel it—the center of the action was shifting again. He wasn't about to miss out.

For Amy too, it was time for a change. The winter had been a hard one for her.

She had begun the season ready to pass the cold months reading, curled in warm sleeping bags with LJ. Where Craig thrilled her with his idealism and bright-burning charisma, LJ had a calming gravity that settled her. Like her, LJ seemed much older than his years. He was quiet but sure, his strong hands equally capable of building a cabin, fixing a truck, or shushing a crying baby. Amy, though she wouldn't have put it this way at the time, had begun to think of him as her boyfriend.

Then, a few weeks into the long Big House winter, Loraine had approached Amy with a request. Since LJ was the only resident man, would Amy be willing to share him?

Amy said yes. At the time, both she and Loraine were acting on what they believed was the group's Free Love ethic. Both of them also remembered the first summer's exhilarating sexual openness and what had truly been for them a jealousy-free experience of community and connection. Why should this time be any different? Later, both Loraine and Amy admitted how poorly they'd predicted the intensity of their own emotions.

One night, when LJ was with Loraine in the Star House where she'd been staying with Rahula, they looked up to see Amy's stricken face in the window. Loraine felt terrible. Amy was still a teenager, six years her junior, and desperately in need of stable relationships. Up until now, Loraine had offered just this by taking Amy under her wing in the kitchen and treating her like a protegée. Loraine told herself that she had done what she could to act in good faith by asking Amy's permission in advance before she got together with LJ. In the context of Myrtle Hill, infidelity was technically impossible. But immediately, and for many years afterward, Loraine felt herself guilty of a serious betrayal.

At the same time, though, it was hard to regret her move toward LJ: of all the commune's men, including those who were possibly Rahula's father, only LJ, who'd arrived after her birth, showed any inclination toward full-time fatherhood. From the moment he arrived, he had thrown himself fully into helping care for the baby. All winter he had rocked and played with her. Loraine found his uncomplicated affection for her child intoxicating.

For his part, LJ liked that Loraine was a mother, and he admired her skill with herbs and in the garden. She was clearly the best equipped of anyone at the commune to handle this way of life. His first interaction with her had been the day he arrived, sick with a stomach ailment from brushing his teeth in Lake Champlain a few days earlier; Loraine had cured him with a cup of mint tea.

Myrtle Hill's Free Love philosophy had enriched and complicated the lives of its residents—Loraine's in particular—but this still came as its most surprising twist: over their long, snowed-in winter in the Big House, Loraine and LJ had fallen truly, fully in love.

Amy, ever perceptive, could see the intensity of Loraine and LJ's connection. She loved them both enough not to get in the way.

But that didn't make spending all winter in an open, blanket-walled sleeping loft with them any easier. Jealousy was a new sensation to her, and she did not like it. Worse, she couldn't help but feel that, aside from Craig, she'd lost the two people closest to her. So Amy spent as much time as possible at Entropy's kitchen table that winter, partaking in the tea and sympathy that had become Peg's specialty.

Amy had celebrated her eighteenth birthday in January, freed at last from the danger of being caught by authorities and sent back to California against her will. When a friend offered her a ride to the West Coast, she decided it was safe to risk a visit. After arriving in California, she checked in on her mother and siblings, but as soon as she saw that they were all right and let them see that she was too, she moved on again. At her grandmother's house in Arizona, she stayed long enough to get her GED before returning to Vermont.

When she arrived back at Myrtle Hill, she discovered that Craig had moved out. That spring, as his frustration at Myrtle grew, Craig started escaping over to Entropy more and more often. Peg listened to him with a particular understanding. She too had felt the discomfort of financially supporting a communal project, however freely and generously that support was given.

She and Eliot had never really recovered from the aftermath of the school bus meeting and the blow of Chris and Ellen's departure. Both of them working full time could barely keep up with the milking and animal care. Their marriage was fraying. Neither of them would even consider the prospect of another summer's worth of farming with so many fewer helpers. They wanted to go away on a trip to help get their minds straight, but they couldn't leave the animals. Now, Peg saw a possible solution.

When Peg suggested that Craig come live at Entropy, he said yes. And once Amy came back, he invited her to join him. She agreed at once.

The two of them weren't really leaving the commune, they insisted. They were just taking a little break. And, though they both remained full members, continuing to go to meetings, paying their share of the mortgage, and staying involved even through the years of trouble that were soon to follow, theirs was more than a little break. Neither Amy nor Craig ever lived at Myrtle Hill again.

CHAPTER 17

The third-summer growing pains at Myrtle Hill would not have surprised a lot of other communards.

At the end of his nationwide commune tour, Robert Houriet noted, "Everywhere, a screaming need for privacy, to be alone in a place called your own, one that was sacred and noncommunal. Everywhere hassles and marathon encounter meetings that couldn't resolve questions like whether to leave the dogs in or out. Everywhere, cars that wouldn't run and pumps that wouldn't pump because everybody knew all about the occult history of tarot and nobody knew anything about mechanics. Everywhere, people who strove for self-sufficiency and freedom from the capitalist system but accepted food stamps and handouts from Daddy, a corporate sales VP. Sinks filled with dishes, cows wandering through gates left open, and no one to blame. Everywhere, instability, transiency. Somebody was always splitting, rolling up his bags, packing his guitar and kissing good-bye—off again in search of the truly free, unhung-up community."

For many in the late 1960s, the whole point of the communal experiment had been to find an "unhung-up community," somewhere it was possible to live "truly free." But as time went on, the two priorities of personal freedom and communal self-sufficiency often came into increasingly irresolvable conflict.

In a letter he titled "All Asshole Farm Exposé," Ken Kesey complained about the lack of cooperative spirit he saw on his Oregon farm the summer he opened it up as a commune. "We have very little sense of community here, except in desperate moments when everybody <u>must</u> help. Most of the time, most of us are 'pigs at the trough'. . . I believe that the decay, the pigs-at-the-trough feeling, is caused by the INSTABILITY." For Kesey, the last straw came when he walked into the barn and found someone's sleeping nest accessorized with a burned-down candle stub in a singed hay bale. Ahead of the wave as always, Kesey packed the whole group off to Woodstock in his famous bus; when they came back, they found his farm closed except to a few close friends.

As quickly as they had become ubiquitous, within just a few years rural communes began to vanish. Though an exact count is as impossible now as it was then, the most reliable figures indicate that the numbers peaked between about 1970 and 1973 and began to decline precipitously shortly thereafter. One contemporary scholar noted that by 1975 there seemed to be several thousand fewer rural communes in operation than just a few years earlier—though he also noted that the remaining number still totaled far more than in all other eras of American history combined.

Myrtle Hill would have recognized Peter Rabbit's description of the turn toward anarchy at Drop City: "While everyone is working together on actual construction the energy is centered, there is fantastic high spirit, everyone knows what he is doing all the time. But after the building is done comes a time of dissolution. There's no focus for the group energy, and most hippies don't have anything to *do* with their individual energy."

As it turns out, this question of "focus for the group energy" may be the single most important factor determining whether a particular commune survived or failed. In her groundbreaking study of utopian communities, sociologist Rosabeth Moss Kanter found that groups with a central, agreed-upon focus and a clear set of expectations for members' behavior and participation survived much longer than those without. The key factor determining the fate of each group, she concluded, lay in "how strongly they built commitment," a process of "detaching the person from other options and attaching him to the community." In Kesey's all-caps phrasing, in other words, a group's survival depended on how strongly they countered INSTABILITY. For this, Kanter found, a group's central focus is crucial. "The clearer and more defined a group becomes to a person," she wrote, "the easier it is for him to concentrate commitment there."

Published in 1972, Kanter's study drew from the examples of older utopian groups like Oneida, Brook Farm, and the Shakers. While her work has lately come under scrutiny for relying too heavily on narrow definitions of "success" and "failure," several of the contemporary communal groups she featured, including The Farm and the B. F. Skinner-influenced Twin Oaks, are still in existence almost fifty years later. While those groups have undergone major changes, they've managed to retain a crucial, central philosophy that both sustains enthusiasm for the members' shared work and informs consensus about what, exactly, that work should be. As Kanter put it, "Commitment is not only important to the survival of the community, but it is also part of the essence of community. It forms the connection between self-interest and group interest." It helps people avoid being assholes.

For spiritual or religious communes, of course, this focus and consensus often came straightforwardly, as part of the group's jointly held beliefs. It's maybe partly for this reason that so many commune observers in the mid- and late '70s report higher numbers of religious and spiritual communes than the more freeform groups of earlier in the decade. A few groups whose focus centered on the dictates of a single, charismatic leader developed (and occasionally deserved) reputations as cults—especially when "commitment" was enforced by coercive rules or a remote location that defied escape.

But for secular groups like Myrtle Hill, undergoing their own, disorienting postconstruction dissolution, the challenge remained: how to find a focus for their group energy? None of them realized how much the community's survival depended on it.

By the time LJ's cabin and Jed's house were finished and winterized enough to live in year-round, the commune's population had thinned substantially, its permanent members now spread out along the winding road: from the lower field's Big House and dome, all the way up past LJ's cabin in the middle field to the top of the hill where the road disappeared into the trees on its way to Jed and Lilith's.

When Summer returned to Myrtle Hill with her daughter Leecia after a few months away, ready for another crowded season in the sleeping loft, she was shocked at the change.

A new family had moved in and for a while had had the Big House all to themselves. They welcomed Summer and Leecia, but Summer resented feeling like a guest in a house that was no more theirs than hers. Though three times as many people had lived in the same space in past years, to Summer the house now felt crowded and uncomfortable. As she put it later, "I was not a happy camper." Summer's political and personal preference for communal family structure remained entirely unchanged, but in this, she saw, she now stood alone. Not only didn't Loraine or anyone else any longer express anger at the oppressive bourgeois values inherent in the nuclear family, but worse—nuclear families had, overnight, become Myrtle Hill's new normal. She and Leecia moved into a tent and lived there for a few chilly weeks as Summer seethed. Finally, the two of them left.

Next door to the Big House, at the top of the lower field, the dome was undergoing yet another makeover. Another new guy, Terry, was converting it, hoping to get it winterized enough for a home. Terry was a funny, friendly guy but he had come home from Vietnam shaken and drifting. A friend of a friend had invited him to visit Myrtle Hill; after a week Terry knew he needed to stay. Working with his hands and living under the trees was restoring his ability to feel calm.

In the dome, he'd cleared out the now-defunct candle-making equipment and put down flooring over the open, packed earth. After tearing off the leaky, drafty, unsealed car tops, Terry re-covered the dome's sturdy frame with plywood, tarpaper, and wood strips. On the west side, looking out across the lower field, he left triangles open for a window in the shape of a huge, six-pointed star.

Terry's partner in all this was Hershe. Her marriage with Pancake had not managed to survive the many ways that life at Myrtle Hill agreed with her but not with him. Later it would seem to Jethro that his gentle, intellectual father just hadn't been prepared for a life of relentless work and extreme austerity or for the interpersonal complications brought by communal living and Free Love. And too, Jethro noted, when Pancake finally decided he'd had enough, he had other options: "My dad could just hop on the interstate and head back home to Connecticut. And that's what he did."

"Whereas my mom had no safe, comfortable home to return to." As Jethro put it, "She had no 'back' to go."

For Hershe, Myrtle Hill was home. And for Jethro, raised there in the dome next to the Big House, it was also the context for his whole childhood, the place that would shape his character and where he'd form some of the best and worst memories of his life.

Jethro was lucky to have a friend his own age living right up the road. Rahula shared an upstairs bedroom with her sister Amelia in the cozy cabin that LJ was already starting to expand to accommodate his growing family. The cabin's kitchen smelled of baking bread and the oregano and onions Loraine hung from the rafters to dry. Its front porch faced the old cellar hole, and its windows looked out across the road to the upper field, taking in the line of ancient maples and the old stone wall that ran along its border. In the field itself lay the gardens; up above, at the edge of the trees, was the spot where the buck deer had emerged that first day. From the kitchen's back window, the road to Jed and Lilith's was visible, but not the house itself.

To get there from Loraine and LJ's, you had to continue up the road for another fifty yards as it passed back into the woods and curved around a bend. There, in a clearing, stood Jed and Lilith's house. Though modest by most American standards, it was a mansion compared to everything else at Myrtle. Jed had designed it with three bedrooms, skylights, front and back decks, an interior full of clever built-ins, and what his neighbors later described as a bomb shelter. The house sat with its back to the road, facing out to the west. Jed had cleared trees on the slope below to gain the luxury of the hill's only expansive view— out across the valley, over Loudon Young's fields toward Entropy Acres and the gently rolling hills beyond.

*

Entropy Acres, the communards soon started to joke, should change its name to "Myrtle Hill Annex for People on the Way Out."

But Craig did not see himself this way. Even though he no longer lived at Myrtle Hill, Craig's vision and enthusiasm still guided the whole group's attention. His new project, the food conspiracy, had taken off like a rocket—though now, like most people, he was calling it by its straight moniker: a food co-op.

Myrtle Hill, like Entropy Acres and my parents and many of the other counterculture residents in the area whose eating preferences ran to brown rice and tamari and organic broccoli, had struggled with where to find these ingredients. The best local source had long been Hatch's. But now, even in the backwoods nationwide, other options had started to appear.

Between 1969 and 1979 as many as ten thousand new food co-ops sprang up across the country, with an annual gross of $500 million. They followed in a tradition that dated all the way back to 1844, when a group of striking weavers in England organized a cooperative store to supply themselves with basic goods. Each member had one vote, and the group divided all surplus profits evenly. More recently, the 1930s and 1940s saw a proliferation of co-ops of all kinds, supported by the New Deal. When that funding ended, many food co-ops went under; by the early '70s, the few that remained had morphed either into stores nearly indistinguishable from supermarkets or into "old-wave" health-food stores run by what one '70s-era co-op founder described with distain as "hypochondriac food faddists," obsessed with "dipping desiccated wheat germ crackers into yeasty carrot juice cocktails." But in places like the Twin Cities, a hotbed of both '30s- and '70s-era cooperatives, those "old-wave" co-ops—and the members themselves—often offered essential foundation and support for the "new-wave" cooperatives suddenly appearing around college campuses and in the abandoned storefronts of battered downtowns across the country.

Goddard College in Plainfield, Vermont, had just such an "old-wave" co-op that had foundered gently since the 1940s. Craig's friend Jblu had recently decided to devote himself to rebooting it, and Craig had been helping so much that he might as well have been taking co-op-starting lessons. He couldn't wait to get his own organization up and running. When he got himself a federal grant through VISTA—a Johnson-era program that supported local projects aimed at fighting poverty and provided grantees with a small stipend, plus travel expenses—it allowed Craig to devote himself entirely to his new plans.

Craig's co-op, like many others, started out as a buyer's club. One of his biggest allies, yet again, was Lois Barrows. She had quit her job at the bank a few years earlier and had recently started a business making a new, hit treat: granola bars, marketed under the label Our Little Leader. She welcomed Craig's promise of cheap, high-quality ingredients. Craig and Lois, along with any other interested households, sat down once a month to organize a bulk order of dried goods. Eventually, with help from Craig, other localities put together similar orders. Before long, there were whole networks scattered across the region, organized in each tiny hamlet by one "neighborhood coordinator," responsible for collecting her neighbors' orders and getting them in to Craig. The new co-op's motto: "Good food, cheap."

The demand for inexpensive, organic rolled oats in northern Vermont turned out to be surprisingly high. Once all the orders came in, Craig and Jblu drove down to Boston to procure the goods.

For this adventure, they preferred huge Army trucks, which they somehow arranged (the details remained vague) to borrow from the National Guard. The trucks only went about forty miles an hour, so the trip took them twice as long as it would otherwise. But the visual irony of a huge military vehicle piloted by two freaks—one a still-on-the-lam draft resister, no less—was too delicious to pass up.

Their main destination in Boston was Erehwon, the pioneering natural food store started by two early macrobiotic educators. There, they loaded up the truck with brown rice, molasses, nutritional yeast, honey. From the city's import markets, they bought nuts, dried apricots, and figs. When they extended their rounds to New York, they brought home cheese, olives, and spices still too exotic for local supermarkets: turmeric, ginger, cumin.

These orders became larger and larger as the co-op network expanded across Vermont and eventually New England. As demand for the products grew, co-op organizers began to seek out other sources. Craig and Jblu, on behalf of their growing network, brokered a deal with nearby Cabot Creamery (itself a longtime cooperative) to buy massive wheels of cheese. Soon, at an amazingly low price, members could take home huge, plastic-wrapped chunks of pale, sharply fragrant cheddar.

Before long, Craig's co-op had expanded enough to justify opening a physical location. The village storefront next door to Lois Barrows' granola-bar operation had sat empty since its previous tenant, the A&P, had moved to a bigger, freestanding building years earlier. All the grocery-store equipment remained—shelving, scales, old coolers. It was perfect.

Now the neighborhood coordinators had a place to gather when Craig returned from the city with a truckload of goods. The stated goal of the co-op's monthly Breakdown Days was to prepare individual orders for delivery—slicing up the huge wheels of cheddar and Yarlsburg, pouring tamari into one-quart containers, sorting raisins into bags—but the mayhem of scooping and slicing was fueled by too many passed joints and too much laughing for anyone to mistake them as strictly business. For a lot of members living isolated on back roads, the co-op's events—Breakdown Days, but soon picnics and contra dances too—quickly became the center of their social life.

At the same moment that Myrtle Hill, like many of its regional sister communes, began to splinter and evolve, the co-op became the hub of a new network—one that included noncommunal and ex-communal households. The co-op's founders, often supported as they worked by their own communal living arrangements, put in place many of the structures and resources that attracted and supported the later, much larger waves of noncommunal back-to-the-landers. As Jblu put it to me later, "Communes fed the co-ops with human resources . . . Then folks like your parents and other independent living folks signed up in big ways. And they were the anchor for the co-ops, really. Their numbers were far bigger than the commune numbers. And they had money. Jobs, imagine that!"

While many of the co-op's new members would readily have described themselves as counterculture or even hippies, its numbers also included a good many members who fervently would not.

Craig had devoted himself specifically to attracting this last category of membership. He took the community and antipoverty elements of the co-op's mission seriously. Resuming the long, rambling, backwoods drives of Myrtle's first summer, he started going door-to-door once again—this time, not in search of junked cars, but to ensure that everyone he could reach would know where to find good food, cheap.

Amy accompanied Craig on a few of these missions. The presence of a sweet-faced young girl probably helped open a few doors (though Craig's collar-length hair had him looking relatively square these days as well). But Amy went along mostly because she loved to watch Craig engage with people. He deliberately sought out the farthest-flung homes he could find. Not much shocked Amy at that point, but even her winters in the Big House and many years of living without running water or electricity had not prepared her for the extreme poverty of some of the households they visited. She could see, now, the difference between the college kids who'd spent some nights crashing in Myrtle's chicken shed and the multigeneration family who appeared to be living with their chickens not by choice. Craig talked to everyone the same way he talked to her. "Hi," he'd say when they opened the door. "Can I come in? I'm Craig."

In tin-roofed shacks and comfortable farmhouses, he explained the co-op. Sometimes he got only a polite frostiness, but very often his enthusiasm pulled people in. Amy watched skepticism melt from their faces as he piled bags of dried fruit and nuts on the table and earnestly explained the health benefits of whole grains. Some of the people they visited had never tasted dried apricots before. He asked them what kind of products they'd like to see—chocolate, pecans—and let them know when the co-op started carrying them. He also made sure the co-op sold products from locals' small businesses—maple syrup, jam, pickles, pies, fresh eggs.

For the rest of her life, as she sought out and invented a career for herself, Amy remained grateful for her front-row seat on this direct, engaging, successful approach to community outreach and collaboration.

The co-op offered Amy another life skill as well. She and Craig, still living at Entropy, had been joined there by Craig's sister Melissa and her boyfriend Dennis, LJ's best friend. Seeing a niche in the co-op's inventory, Melissa and Amy had decided to start a business making granola. They installed a pizza oven and started baking massive batches. Other co-ops around the state began asking to carry it, and soon they were making between one and two tons of granola each month. For Amy, this experience later formed the basis of a long, successful career as a caterer.

Loraine too started a small food business with a friend. "Old Mother Breads" baked whole-grain loaves, cookies, and bars. Loraine's years of cooking for the commune had taught her how to prepare food on a massive scale. The recipe-tweaking required by the group's preference for coarse grains, natural sweeteners, and nonchemical leaveners (baking powder was verboten), plus the frequent scarcity of key ingredients, had fostered her trial-and-error ingenuity. She'd spent her entire commune years inventing and perfecting recipes and collecting them, along with those from friends, in a well-used notebook.

A lot of people, it turned out, wanted to eat dark, crusty, whole-grain bread but didn't want to have to make it themselves. Aside from co-ops and health food stores, the only place you could buy bread like that was in ethnic neighborhoods in cities—local supermarkets carried only variations on Wonder Bread. Loraine brought her loaves to different co-ops around the region. They sold out as fast as she could make them.

In other parts of the country, other back-to-the-landers were having a similar experience turning their personal food adventures into small businesses. Starting in the 1970s, some portions of the American palate began to shift toward flavors and ingredients once relegated to macrobiotic restaurants and ethnic cuisines—rice instead of potatoes, honey instead of sugar, steamed or raw instead of boiled vegetables.

Even in the counterculture, though, this dietary shift had arrived suddenly. Food historian Warren Belasco notes that the food emphasis among radical groups of the late '60s ran entirely to how to eat as cheaply and simply as possible—in Drop City's first years, its members prided themselves on a diet cobbled together from government commodities and dumpster-diving. Right up until 1969, Belasco found, counterculture publications still offered recipes calling for processed foods like powdered mashed potatoes and canned cheddar cheese soup—then never again, "except in contempt." Books like Francis Moore Lappé's 1971 *Diet for a Small Planet* connected food choices like vegetarianism and organics to the political and ecological values already in place in the counterculture.

As Belasco puts it, "Whiteness meant Wonder Bread, White Tower, Cool Whip, Minute Rice, instant mashed potatoes, peeled apples, White Tornadoes, white coats, white collar, whitewash, White House, white racism. Brown meant whole wheat bread, unhulled rice, turbinado sugar, wild flower honey, unsulfured molasses, soy sauce, peasant yams, 'black is beautiful.' Darkness was funky, earthy, authentic, while whiteness, the color of powerful detergents, suggested fear of contamination and disorder."

As radical politics shifted away from street activism, people in the counterculture looked for ways to express protest more personally, in their daily lives—the same impulse that led many of them to go back to the land. Eating Wonder Bread, then, wasn't just bad for your health or newly unfashionable, it implicated you in the corrupt, racist system you still felt you were trying to overturn. "To make clean bread, [Wonder Bread's] bakers removed all colored ingredients (segregation), bleached the remaining flour (suburban school socialization), and then, to prevent discoloring decay, added strong preservatives and stabilizers (law enforcement). Brown breads had shorter life spans, but at their peak seemed suffused with innate character," Belasco notes. "The color contrast externalized white radicals' estrangement from sanitized suburban life"—just as fully as did building a wood-heated cabin and relying on an outhouse.

By the late 1970s, in small towns and big cities across the country, consumers interested in trying out the "natural foods" recipes they started to see published in magazines and cook-books like *Laurel's Kitchen* or *Moosewood Cookbook* suddenly had access to ingredients that had been rare and fringe-y only a few years earlier. At the heart of this growing demand for pesticide-free, whole, nonprocessed ingredients—a demand that has proven to be even more robust and mainstream in the 21st century than even in the 1970s—were back-to-the-landers, city people with ties to both to organic farmers and urban markets, who knew how to how to source and sell food in both directions.

Today, supermarkets are full of product lines with back-to-the-land origin stories (though many are now owned by giant con-glomerates). Mo Siegal began collecting wild plants in the Rocky Mountains in 1969 before Celestial Seasonings grew into a na-tionwide brand. Photographer Burt Shavitz abruptly fled New York City in 1970 and worked a series of odd jobs before some-one gave him the bees whose wax would later become ubiquitous beauty products. Toms of Maine founders Tom and Kate Chappell left Philadelphia for Kennebunk in 1968. Cascadian Farms Or-ganic, one of today's biggest organic labels, was started in 1972, its story goes, "by an idealistic, 24-year-old grad school dropout who just wanted to make a difference in the world." The founder of the soymilk company Silk first learned how to crush and strain soybeans while living at an ashram in New Hampshire.

One of the founders of Stonyfield yogurt, Sam Kayman, was a political radical whose early passion for local, organic food sys-tems was fueled by his conviction that America's cities were on the verge of collapse. He, along with the commune writer Rob-ert Houriet among others, spent much of the early '70s help-ing organize New England's organic vegetable farmers—most of whom were recent back-to-the-landers like Entropy Acres' carrot-growers, and new to agriculture—into a regional net-work that would arrange markets for their products. This effort eventually resulted in NOFA (Northeast Organic Farm Association), an organic farming regulatory body and advocacy group, one of the nation's first. NOFA was responsible in part for helping define federal requirements for the food label "organic." Its organizers also contributed to the rebirth in cities and towns across the Northeast of regular, organized farmers' markets, a priority initially inspired, according to Houriet, by Mao's *Little Red Book*. Kayman's yogurt company originally served as a cash sideline to support his nonprofit, organic farming school.

At least one counterculture entrepreneur later admitted that, though he'd spent years loudly rejecting his capitalist father's priorities and work life, he had nonetheless inherited an excellent business sense and a deal-maker's confidence (not to mention capital and a Rolodex of influential connections). Craig, Jblu, and many others entering wholeheartedly into the counterculture food scene drew on their personal relationships—one set of friends in the city and another in the country—to find markets and sources in both directions. This feet-in-both-worlds position, plus the fact that they thought nothing of hopping in a car to crisscross the country at a moment's notice—plus their own, ever-present, apocalypse-driven urgency—made them bold about brokering exchanges of goods across huge areas.

Craig and Jblu had begun working with David Hatch, who, rather than worry about the new co-ops' competition with his family's natural food store, fully embraced a collaboration. A friend in Florida told Hatch that hotels down there served an unbelievable number of pancakes for tourists' breakfasts and clearly promised a limitless market for maple syrup. He and Craig at once bought up every barrel they could from their Vermont neighbors. When they arrived in Florida in the middle of the night, the friend met them at the truck. "I made a big mistake," he said. "They're using syrup, but it's Log Cabin, it's not real maple syrup. They're used to paying 1/10th of what real maple syrup costs." After a moment of deliberation, Craig and Hatch dumped the barrels of syrup on their friend's lawn and left him to find a more amenable market. When their truck headed back north, though, it was laden with fresh oranges for the co-op.

As Craig and the others sourced products from farther and farther afield and worked out exchanges with groups in other places—Maine potatoes, Minnesota oats, Montana wheat, organic grains from Deaf Smith County in Texas—it quickly became clear that one truck was not enough. They'd already replaced the slow, attention-attracting Army wagons with a refurbished mail van, but it was way too small. Then a friend of Craig's named Carl Giamba decided to invest some of his inheritance in an eighteen-wheeler. Before long, he'd expanded his fleet into the Loaves & Fishes Trucking Company. For the huge network of co-ops that now connected across New England, Loaves & Fishes became the chief transportation resource. It also became the main employer for residents—former and current—of Myrtle Hill.

LJ (now sporting a fashionable, droopy David Crosby mustache) and his best friend Dennis, along with their buddy Terry who was fixing up the dome, all got their trucking licenses and began driving for Loaves & Fishes. Hershe ran the office and kept the books. The company's offices were where Jethro learned to walk.

Hershe also started another food project with support from a VISTA grant: the Northeast Kingdom Community Cannery. She filled a storefront near the co-op with commercial stoves, steam-jacketed kettles, and canning supplies. The facility was open to anyone needing to preserve large amounts of produce. (Hershe and Terry themselves once canned seven hundred pounds of corn in one day.) As part of its mission, the cannery also offered classes and hired local young people to make products like apple maple butter, dilly beans, pickled beets, and succotash, which they sold through the co-op. Hershe joked that her canning experience dated all the way back to her summer job as a teenager in Hawaii, sorting chunks of pineapple on the conveyor belts at Dole.

And Myrtle Hill hadn't lost its urge to cook for the masses at big events. One summer, they drove to New York state, to a huge concert at Watkins Glen where they offered free vegetarian food to the 600,000 concert-goers. They also got permission to set up a concession booth at the local county fair, serving vegetarian chili and date bars alongside the hot dogs and fried dough. And when an avant-garde theater group called Bread and Puppet moved from the East Village to a local farmhouse and started putting on an annual circus that drew crowds in the tens of thousands to the tiny community, Myrtle Hill was there, selling roast corn from the very first summer.

In food, Myrtle Hill had succeeded in finding a crucial focus for their group energy. No one was getting rich or even doing more than just barely scraping by—as Terry put it, "the pay was sparse and the work was many," but working at the co-op, the cannery, and the trucking company had other benefits. Chiefly, keeping the group together.

In explaining his own move away from communal living, Ken Kesey cited "the great statement" made by his friend Babbs: "We don't want a commune, we want a community." Myrtle Hill would have agreed. While they had found that they were happier not living together, no one was ready to give up on their connection to one another or on their interdependence. At least in their daily work, they remained all together.

Or almost all. Jed and Lilith, now that their house was finished and comfortably winterized, had begun spending more time at Myrtle Hill. Like everyone else, they came to the now-erratic monthly meetings and took their share of the mortgage payments. Jed even covered Amy's at least once when she came up short. Like the others, they planted gardens, though Lilith's canning efforts didn't share Loraine and Hershe's survival-driven volume. But neither Jed nor Lilith worked with the co-op. Their jobs in the city had apparently left them comfortable enough not to. Later, no one could even recall if they'd been members or not.

There was one project, though, that did, at least briefly, tie Jed and Lilith to some of the other households living on Myrtle Hill, one more thread that still bound them together.

As Loraine explained it later, it was a practical consideration that led to the decision to grow marijuana. Like almost every other counterculture household in the region, Myrtle Hill had quietly grown a personal supply for years. Expanding this production slightly into a modest cash crop, the thinking went, would help with a nagging concern: money for taxes.

The irony in this was not lost. And, least for Loraine, the outlaw thrill held part of the appeal. They'd be breaking a law, but a law they didn't believe in anyway. Plus, like a lot of rural hippies, they'd gotten really good at cultivation.

It was a calculation a lot of individuals and groups were starting to make all over the country. But it was a decision whose impact proved hard to predict. One ex-Myrtleite put it bluntly. "Marijuana broke everyone apart," he said. "That was when trouble started."

CHAPTER 18

It took Larry and Judy two summers to prepare the sun-warmed ledge up the hill from the dome for their new, bigger, family-sized house.

Now that they weren't rushing to beat winter, they had time to undertake the structure they'd each envisioned since playing with Lincoln Logs as children: a bona-fide log cabin.

As soon as the snow in the woods had thinned enough to walk without snowshoes, they started scouting trees. What they wanted were tall, straight spruce, at least ten inches in diameter at the base. Cedar would have been the best, but there was not enough around, and they'd heard that balsam fir, of which there was plenty, would not last as long. Donald Perron helpfully suggested that the best place to look would be deep in the woods, where the young evergreens, forced to compete for light, grew straight up toward the sun.

When they found a suitable spruce, Judy climbed forty feet up and looped a rope around the trunk. Once she was back on the ground and holding the rope a safe distance away, Larry started the chainsaw, its roar ripping through the silence of the woods. The air filled with the sweet, mingled smells of spruce pitch and exhaust as he angled the blade into the trunk. At the first sharp crack of the toppling tree, Judy tugged the rope to encourage it to fall toward her and away from the thickest part of the canopy. As soon as the tree crashed to the ground in a soft explosion of needles and muck, Larry got to work limbing it with an axe.

Then came Judy's favorite part: debarking. Standing beside the log, she made a small cut in the bark and inserted the spoon-like blade of an old-fashioned-looking tool called a spud. Later in the season, after the sap stopped rising, the bark became all but glued to the wood, almost impossible to remove. But in early spring, the spud slid the bark off in long, satisfying sheets, revealing the wood underneath, as smooth and pale as the inside of Judy's forearm. It remained some of the most satisfying work of her life.

Later they'd come back with a tractor (or Entropy's horses, a few times) to haul the logs out of the woods and into a field. Once dry, the logs turned a beautiful, glossy russet. It took a while, but eventually my parents had amassed enough for the whole house.

The other major prep work was clearing the site and digging the cellar hole. Loudon and Donald, who, as always, came over to offer opinions, couldn't imagine why Larry had chosen to build on a ledge inaccessible to the skidder that might have cleared the brush in a heartbeat. Larry explained cheerfully about the sun and the melting snow and that this was the only spot where his beloved White Mountains appeared like a dream in the distance. He and Judy were committed to their romantic and lovely choice of location and were not daunted by the physical labor ahead of them.

But as usual, their neighbors had a much more accurate sense of what exactly that labor would entail. After the scrubby trees had been cut and hauled into the woods, each stump had to be pried out of the ground individually. After the stumps came the rocks.

To distract them while they worked, Judy propped up a portable radio and tuned in to the Watergate hearings. Nixon seemed a thousand miles away, the trial a dreamlike abstraction in the context of their aching muscles and blistered hands. When the trial ended, Larry and Judy continued in silence—shovels against rock for days on end. Occasionally, during the long afternoons, Larry looked up with the disorienting sense that he had slipped through time to an earlier century.

This slow, backbreaking labor was the same labor, Larry realized, that had been performed with many fewer resources on a far greater scale by earlier generations of settlers. The field his house would rest atop had been cleared of its trees in much this same way by some long-departed Yankee more than one hundred years earlier, with axes and horses instead of chainsaws and mini-tractors. To city-bred eyes like his, the open, emerald fields that made Vermont's hills so iconic had always represented a bucolic antithesis to work-driven hubbub. Now, pausing in his work to guzzle from the jar he'd filled with spring water, he gazed out over his neighbors' fields with a new appreciation for the hundreds of years of toil that had made such a landscape possible.

For Larry, progress on the house was only part of the work he was doing. The education project his friend had offered him a few months back had turned into a full-time job. He was helping to establish an entirely new institution: the Community College of Vermont. Larry was its founding dean. His CCV work was exciting and intellectually rewarding, but it meant his spending long workdays in Montpelier, over an hour away. Since Judy's nursing classes wouldn't start until fall, she spent the long summer days alone, working on the house.

Pulling stumps out was satisfying work but grueling—it could take all day to free just one. The small tractor Larry's father had donated, not much bigger than a riding lawn mower, was helpful but it brought its own perils—more than once, the front bucked up suddenly and sent Judy flying. Each time as she picked herself up off the ground, she pushed aside the thoughts of what might have happened if the angle had been slightly different and the tractor had toppled over on her, of how many hours it might be before anyone found her.

Bored one day as she ate her lunch, she flipped on the TV in the camper-trailer that still sat parked near the dome. Before long, she found herself rushing to get to the trailer every day in time for *As the World Turns*. As she worked alone, day after day, she found herself genuinely worrying about the characters' problems: *would Liz would ever tell Paul that Dan and not he was the father of her baby?* By the time Judy's shovel hit ledge and she could dig no further by hand, her biceps had grown so much that she had to cut slits in the cuffs of her short-sleeved blouses to put her arms through.

To open the rest of the cellar hole, they hired a man to come blast it out with dynamite. Some friends came and brought their children to watch. As the man set the charges, they all retreated to what they thought was a safe distance. The explosion kicked stones into the air, which flew unsettlingly close to where they sat in the grass below. The dynamite had done the trick, but when she walked up to examine its work, all Judy could see was that the hole she'd spent weeks clearing of rocks was now completely full of brand-new rubble. "Oh God, this is . . ." She didn't finish the thought. The hole took the rest of the summer to clear.

At last, it was time to move the dome.

Somehow or other, my parents needed to lift it from the meadow where it sat, and transport it two hundred yards straight up the steep hill to the ledge where the new house would be. This ought to be possible, Larry was almost certain. The dome certainly *looked* portable. Its tidy, compact sphere was no bigger than a mobile home, though a very different shape—not to mention hand-built by novices.

As he and Judy brainstormed possibilities, it was hard for Larry to judge when an idea crossed the line into the ridiculous— the whole idea to move the dome was madness to begin with. But so had been deciding to build a house with no experience, following an obscure mathematical formula published by a hippie high school. And that had turned out all right.

So the possibilities were endless. Could you park a crane halfway up the hill, one big enough to pluck the dome from its meadow and swing it through the air before dropping it neatly into place? He ruled this out because, among other concerns, there was no level spot between the old and new house sites on which to safely rest a huge piece of equipment. The image of the dome floating through the sky appealed enough, though, that Larry actually looked into what it would cost to rent a strong-enough helicopter (too much). A cheaper option: they could round up seventy-five hippies to just pick the dome up and carry it straight up the hill.

As usual, Larry asked his neighbors for advice. For Donald in particular, the challenge appealed immediately to his engineer's mind. The dome wouldn't be much heavier than a similarly sized barn, he figured, so a small crawler should be strong enough to pull it. His brother Norman had one that might work. With Donald's assurance that he could enlist his brother's help, Larry and Judy invited everyone they could think of for the Great Dome Moving, Columbus Day weekend, 1973. As they had with the dome raising, they decided to treat it like a party. That way, Larry hoped, maybe they could once again coast on sheer optimism over the project's many, potentially catastrophic unknowns.

Saturday dawned a perfect Indian summer day, the sky a deep, high, October blue and the air full and balmy. It was an auspicious start.

Less auspicious: the moment Loudon, Donald, and Donald's brothers showed up with the crawler, they took one look at the spruce-log travois that Larry and Judy had carefully built and began shaking their heads. Larry started to explain how he'd read that nomadic Plains Indians used poles lashed together at one end like this to haul their belongings, but his neighbors weren't listening. They had already begun inventing a better alternative.

Donald was visibly enjoying himself, grinning around the unlit cigar clamped perpetually in the corner of his mouth. He had driven over on his big green tractor, loaded up with a pile of equipment that he thought might come in handy—chains, logging tackle, old tires, chunks of 8″ × 8″ wooden beams—and had fully embraced the problem-solving challenge of this audacious, foolhardy project. Plus, like Loudon, he had long since learned not to miss the action where hippie building schemes were concerned. Within minutes, the men had added another log to the travois and wrapped the whole thing in heavy logging chains. It had lost all traces of the delicate simplicity Larry had conceived for it, but he was not about to argue—there was no doubt about who was in charge.

Once Donald was satisfied with the rig, he began easing the
bucket of his tractor under the edge of the dome to lift it. Judy
held her breath as her teacup of a house tilted askew. She prepared herself to watch the shingles affixed over so many icy days
start molting off in sheets. But the dome held tight. Before long,
it was perched atop its log raft, belted in for the ride. Donald
declared that it was time to start pulling. His brother Norman
started up his crawler and backed it into position.

At the last second, one of Larry's CCV coworkers, a tall, wild-
eyed, red-haired young man, volunteered himself to ride up
inside—to keep an eye on things, he said, though everyone understood it to be a joyride. Donald and the others didn't seem
to mind, so Larry gave him the okay. He stood on the dome's
floor, with his feet wide and his hands high, spreading himself
into a kind of flimsy human brace. At least, Judy thought, there
would be a witness for the moment when the shelves inside came
crashing off the walls.

Slowly, the crawler sputtered its way uphill, drawing the sil-
very sphere of the dome behind like a spider's egg sac. When
Donald or Loudon called instructions to Norman or signaled him
to stop so they could duck in and make adjustments, Larry listened in, nodding. Judy could hardly bear to watch, though she
kept her face stoic. Over the crawler's harumph echoing back
from the trees around the field, she listened for the sound of
windows popping, the walls crushing inward, all her hard work
crumbling before her eyes.

To her it felt like years before the crawler came to rest at the
top of the hill but in truth it was scarcely more than an hour.
Miraculously, not one windowpane had cracked. The dome was
sturdier than it looked. Its lone occupant jumped down, shaking
out his arms, triumphant.

By now, the air was summer-warm and everyone was working
in shirtsleeves. Children chased each other around the field in
t-shirts while their parents helped carry tools and belongings up
the hill.

All that had to be done now was to slip the dome off its platform and over the cellar hole. In theory, this would require a

motion like sliding eggs out of a frying pan onto a plate, except that in this case, the eggs were a house, the spatula was a tractor bucket, and the plate was a thin foundation edge ringing a gaping hole.

The dome had slid halfway into place when one of the support logs snapped. With a sickening lurch, the dome suddenly toppled toward the chasm and came to rest at a vertiginous angle. Judy stopped breathing.

Removing the cigar he'd been chewing all morning, Donald hopped into the hole to get a better look. It wasn't good, but at least the dome wasn't going to fall further. That being the case, he suggested, they might as well break for lunch.

Donald's wife Carolyn had brought over a huge stockpot of homemade stew, and she ladled portions onto tin plates, aided by my grandmothers, Kay and Lois, who'd come to help (Kay in sneakers and jeans, Lois in a polyester pantsuit). To keep morale high, Larry went ahead and tapped the keg of beer with which they'd hoped to toast victory at the end of the day. While Larry and Donald discussed next steps, Judy tried to listen but the men were talking only to each other. Around her, everyone was chatting, eating, and drinking in the warm sun as the children climbed over the log piles scattered across the field. But Judy couldn't concentrate on anything except the seasick list of the dome.

A lot of friends, old and new, had turned up to help. Charlie Barrows, the banker-selectman, was there. Nick was away, but Nash, Judy's childhood friend and their fellow landowner, had recently returned from Africa and had started building his own house in a high field on the far side of the property from Nick's. Nash had just introduced Judy to his girlfriend Mariel, a tall, graceful dancer he'd met in New York. She had taken a Greyhound from the city to help them build. Judy liked Mariel right away, sensing, perhaps, the start of a long friendship.

It would be good to have some more women around. Peg had left the summer before and Judy still missed her.

Under the strain of trying to work a self-sufficient farm more or less by themselves, Peg and Eliot's marriage had come apart.

Eventually, both of them had moved on. Peg still owned the farmhouse that would forever be known as Entropy Acres, but she had left it for the last time. She'd entrusted the property and animals into the good care of Craig, Amy, and Dennis, making Entropy, truly now, a Myrtle Hill Annex.

But among the children playing in the field below the toppled dome that day were a pair of towheaded twins. Chris and Ellen had returned—this time, permanently.

Chris had not lost an ounce of the determination to swear off communal living that he'd formed the night he stalked home fuming from the school bus meeting. But the intervening years had left him with another, equally strong determination: he wanted to live in Vermont. Specifically, he wanted to live in a community with his friend Loudon.

Ellen agreed. Their time away had made them both realize how rapidly they'd come to love not just the hills and fields and wild, green beauty of their adopted home but also its people.

Their plan to return, though, had not included specific plans for how they'd make a living. Chris admired many elements of Loudon's life, but the summer Chris had spent buried in carrots had taught him that he himself would make a terrible farmer.

He did love helping Loudon during sugar season, though. So many elements of making maple syrup appealed to him: the intuitive, clever designs of boiling pans and gravity-fed tanks; the fire-feeding and the beer-fueled sugar house camaraderie; the long, outdoor days as the season passed from bitter to balmy—all in service to a product whose only purpose was pure pleasure.

If Chris could have found a way to support his family as a sugarmaker, he would have done it in a heartbeat. But he didn't see how it could work: local farmers normally sugared as a sideline, one more way to supplement their cash income in a season where not much else was happening. At the time, Loudon didn't know of anyone in the area making a full living on it. And there was a bigger problem: most sugarmakers tapped their own land, occasionally arranging to expand into a neighbor's otherwise unused sugar bush in exchange for a few gallons of syrup. Chris simply didn't have enough cash to buy or lease the acres of trees he'd need to support a viable business. He resigned himself to a future of permanently assisting Loudon.

In his quest to find a livelihood, he began accepting pretty much anything he was offered. This led to a series of thrilling (to him) but imperfect odd jobs—working on a road crew after a flood, cutting balsam brush (its persistent, fragrant pitch prompted Ellen's veto: "If I'd wanted to sleep with a tree, I would have married a tree," she told him).

Then one day, he got a call from an old friend, a guy whom he'd known during his *Toronto Globe and Mail* days. The friend had recently decided to invest in starting up a local, rural newspaper and was looking for a suitable market as well as for a partner to run it. Was Chris interested? Chris wasn't sure. He'd sworn off desk jobs, and everyone at Entropy remembered him declaring loudly more than once that the last thing the world needed was another fucking newspaper. Besides, he had just been offered a position by a local township as auxiliary snowplow driver. It was his dream job. He could hardly wait.

Except that winter it hardly snowed. His phone didn't ring once. By spring, he and Ellen had made a decision. Chris was back in the newspaper business.

It wasn't just his disappointment at not getting to drive the plow that had changed his mind. The project had piqued his curiosity. While it was true that he'd sworn never to come near a desk again, this idea felt different. For one thing, he'd be his own boss. For another, the local market research he'd conducted for his friend had revealed that older residents in the community still remembered the weekly that had folded in the mid-'50s and that they still missed it dearly. Here, Chris and Ellen realized, they'd found a way to work for themselves in an interesting and professionally satisfying field while also offering a needed service to their new, beloved community. Chris's string of odd jobs, he realized, had helped him get to know business owners, road crews, farmers, teachers. "You couldn't have designed a better way to spend your time if you were going to start a newspaper,"

he reflected later. "I wasn't coming out of the city to run this paper in this quaint town."

He, Ellen, and the friend decided to restart a weekly. Four decades later, even as print journalism struggles to remain afloat
everywhere, the *Chronicle* is still going strong. It remains the area's newspaper of record.

A few months after starting the paper and committing themselves permanently to the community, Chris and Ellen bought
the yellow house at the T-intersection, halfway between Loudon's
and Entropy.

One of Chris's very first acts as editor-in-chief was to recruit
Loudon to pen a weekly column. Loudon had taken every opportunity to assure Chris that starting a paper was a terrible idea.
But just before the first issue went to press, he showed up with
a sheaf of lined, yellow legal paper containing the column he'd
written, which his wife Arlene had recopied in her fine hand. And
he continued to do the same nearly every week for many years.

Everyone in town already knew to drop what they were doing and listen when Loudon started telling a story, and his style
turned out to translate beautifully into print. Loudon's voice in
the paper was a draw in itself to local subscribers, but he also
offered Chris some public bona fides. "I think it's time you got
better acquainted with the editor of the *Chronicle*," he wrote in a
postscript to his fourth column. "I won't bore you long.

Journalist by trade

Canadian by birth

Optimist by nature

Vermonter by choice

Father of twins by accident."

For many people in the community, Chris and Loudon's friendship stood as an ideal example of the kind of mutual aid and
collaboration between locals and newcomers that would, in the
next decades, become so common in Vermont as to no longer
seem notable. But in a way, Chris and Loudon's story was actually much simpler: they just liked each other. Next to that trust
and mutual admiration, all their differences fell away.

*

The October sun had already started to sink behind the hills before the dome budged again. Chris and Loudon, along with Charlie Barrows, Donald and Donald's brothers, stood with Larry around the drunkenly leaning house, discussing what to do next.

As Donald and Loudon tried out one jerry-rigging idea after another, the other men watched, their hands on their hips.

It was too much for Judy. At first she had tried to keep herself in the discussion about what was happening to her house, but it was exhausting to remain actively engaged, especially when no one else, including Larry, was treating her as a participant. As Norman inched the crawler here and there, the others looping and unlooping chains from the supporting logs, she finally just glazed over and watched blankly from the sidelines.

Larry didn't notice. His whole attention was on the creative problem solving under way. It never occurred to him that Donald and the others would fail to find a solution. "They're going to make this work," he was certain.

Sure enough, hours after it had first crested the hill, Norman's crawler at last teased and tugged the dome delicately into place atop the foundation. Once they were sure it was balanced and stable, Larry and Judy stepped inside to determine the precise direction for the large, triangular front windows. To everyone's delight, it was easy to turn the dome with them inside, one foot this way, just a little more to the left, until they settled on the perfect view.

After everyone had gone home, before the night fell entirely, my parents took one last peek at their new vista: the long, sloping green field below, bordered by fiery maples rising up into rolling, purple hills; behind them, the White Mountains a pale tracery at the edge of the distant sky. It was perfect.

That night, the wind started to blow. The gently-swaying tree-tops at the edge of the field began to lash wildly. Larry and Judy watched leaves whip past the dome's big windows until they turned out the light and lay on the loft bed in the total darkness, the wind howling madly all around them. Gusts buffeted the dome, crashing into the windows in bursts. My parents hardly slept. Larry's mind raced: had they made a terrible mistake? Maybe the snow hadn't melted gently off this ledge, maybe it had been violently blown away. Judy kept imagining the little round house coming loose from its foundation and pitching forward to roll all the way down to the bottom of the hill. All night she waited to feel the first lurch.

But in the morning they woke still in the same place. Larry's relief that the dome had not budged was quickly replaced by euphoria at what they'd accomplished. The house was here and here it would remain. Now he knew what kind of battering the dome was strong enough to withstand.

Judy too woke happy and relieved, but it didn't escape her notice: the weather had changed in the night. The flat, gray sky hung low overhead, and the air had picked up a hint of frost. Yesterday's bright red and yellow leaves had vanished in the wind, leaving the maples stripped and stark.

For some reason, decades later, it was a detail that Judy never forgot.

It took a few more years to get the cabin's walls in place. Measuring and cutting notches in the ends of the logs so they fit snugly on top of one another was fun, careful work, but Judy and Larry only had weekends and summers to make progress.

A Goddard architect had helped them draw up a design for the new, bigger house, with the dome in the center, serving as the living room. To the left of its big triangular windows, one log cabin wing now extended along the ledge, its windows facing the front field; Larry designed a deck to run its full length. On the dome's right side, another wing extended back toward the spruce forest. At the cabin's corners, where the logs crossed one another, Larry wanted a sawed-off, square-cut finish, while Judy preferred the look of axe-cut ends. They compromised and finished the deck wing Larry's way and the back wing Judy's.

Each wing had an upstairs and a downstairs room, totaling three bedrooms, plus Larry's office, which looked out over the deck to the view beyond. In the dome/living room, rugs and bolsters took the place of a couch; the loft remained the master bedroom. On the dome's back wall, opposite the big windows, they'd widened the door, which now opened straight into the kitchen, in the space where the two wings came together. A trap-door at the far edge of the kitchen opened into the cool, dark, cave-like cellar with its earth floor and walls of raw stone, the space basically unchanged since Judy had cleared away the last of its rubble.

Judy finished laying the brick for the kitchen floor the spring she was heavily pregnant with me. By the time I arrived—in the hospital, by emergency C-section—the new house was ready. Which wasn't to say *finished*.

Every year brought a new improvement—and occasionally, a setback. In planning the house, Judy and Larry had decided to include space next to the kitchen for a conventional, indoor bath-room, but they were still using the A-frame outhouse that they'd pried up and carried up the hill the same day as they'd moved the dome. They'd dug a new hole for it fifty yards from the house. Judy's father, Eddie, had carved a dedication for the door, chris-tening it "The R. M. Nixon Memorial Hall." Inside, on a string, as a nod to the Sears catalogs that traditionally took the place of Charmin, hung a copy of the Watergate Papers.

It wasn't until my younger brother was born that they finally installed an indoor commode. The composting toilet they'd cho-sen was a Swedish model called a Toa-throne. The bowl and seat looked like a conventional toilet, but it emptied into a closed, dumpster-sized tank in the cellar. This tank contained absor-bent peat moss and a special enzyme intended to rapidly digest the waste. For a few months, it worked beautifully. Then winter arrived: the temperature at night plummeted and record levels of snow blanketed the fields. The banks lining the shoveled walk-way up to the kitchen door were over Judy's head.

Picking the baby up from where he'd been playing on the floor of the dome one day, Larry noticed that the house had devel-oped a low-lying stench. It turned out that the Swedish enzyme did not thrive in a climate of subzero temperatures. The tank was indoors so it wasn't actually frozen, but it clearly needed to be warmer. Larry tried a few ideas to see if he could coax the temperature upward, but not much had worked. The only one that had seemed to do the trick was hanging a heat lamp down into the top of the basement tank. For a few days, the smell seemed to get better. Then, trying to encourage the enzyme further by eliminating another source of cold drafts, Larry also stretched a sheet of plastic over the bowl itself, closing the lid to keep it in place.

That night, Judy couldn't sleep. Larry had already climbed up into the dome's loft and my baby brother and I were long since in bed—me in a cozy log-walled room behind the big cookstove and him in his cradle on the floor of the dome. But Judy was wired. She still felt hours away from sleep when she finally decided it was late and she needed to go to bed. When she went to use the bathroom, she heard a strange sound, a kind of muted *whup-whup-whup*, coming from the toilet.

She lifted the lid. The loose plastic sheet popped downward with a sudden *whomp*. In a flash, Judy recognized the guttering sound she'd been hearing: fire struggling for oxygen. But it was too late. The puff of air hit the heated gasses in the tank below, and the peat moss burst into flame.

The acrid smell of burning plastic filled the room. Judy ran to get Larry out of bed, trying to convey urgency without waking the baby. "Water," he heard her say as he climbed down the ladder. Still half asleep, he stopped at the kitchen sink and picked up a saucepan. "That's not going to do it!" she hissed. He looked over and saw flames licking up from inside the toilet. He grabbed the fire extinguisher.

Thick, harsh smoke was now pouring out of the bathroom and trailing through the house. Leaving Larry to battle the flames, Judy rushed back and forth between the rooms where my brother and I still slept. Even in the darkened house, Judy could see the thick layer of smoke in the dome, hovering just above the cradle. How much smoke is too much for a baby? Judy found herself wondering. If she picked him up, she'd be bringing him higher, into the smoke. Should she take him out of the crib and set him on the floor? The dome's winter windows were sealed shut against drafts, and opening a door would mean letting in the frigid wind and possibly fueling the flames. How would she know when it was time to flee? And to where? The house was surrounded by waist-deep snowdrifts, and the car was parked a quarter mile away at the bottom of the hill. Judy kept checking the line of smoke above the cradle as she dashed around gathering snowsuits and sleeping bags, ready for Larry's signal that the only safe place left for her children was outside in the 30-below night.

Later they realized that they had so little hope a fire truck could make it up the snow-packed driveway that neither of them had even considered calling the fire department.

In the cellar, Larry aimed the fire extinguisher into the tank. After three blasts, he found to his horror that the canister was empty. For the last time in his life, he didn't have a second one.

But they were lucky: the three blasts were enough. The foam seemed to have smothered the flames. Working quickly, Larry attached a garden hose to the sink and soaked the smoking, sewage-y peat moss with water. He stayed there all night, staring into the tank and spraying down flare-ups, until at last there was no more smoke—just a wretched, burned-plastic cesspool.

For the rest of the winter, Judy and Larry carried chamber pots through the snow to empty into the R. M. Nixon Memorial Hall. In the spring, they installed a conventional flush toilet.

Before long, Larry and Judy began to work out a rhythm to their professional and family lives. Their original plan was to each work a part-time schedule so that they could split childcare. To make this arrangement possible, Larry had quit his full-time dean position at CCV, to his male colleagues' skeptical shock. In the late '70s, after my brother was born, he accepted an exciting new job helping develop a distance-learning program for nontraditional students at a college an hour and a half away. The model he helped invent became the basis for many distance degree programs that followed. The job was still part-time, allowing him to share childcare, but what he'd hoped would be a flexible schedule turned out to be more demanding than he'd predicted. He was away a lot in the evenings, meeting with students, and there were weekend conferences and quarterly residencies when he was gone for weeks at a time.

Judy had also started a job with a demanding commute. Working in health care suited her, but after I was born, she changed her mind about becoming a midwife. Instead, she found nursing jobs, first at a home health agency working with at-risk mothers and then later at a new child health center founded by a rural antipoverty program. She loved this job, though it required a thirty-mile commute over treacherous winter roads. Many of her coworkers were recent Vermont arrivals like herself. Across the state, other back-to-the-landers interested in professional careers were starting other community service programs, from mental health clinics to public law practices.

Neither Larry or Judy had expected to spend so much of their time commuting, but it couldn't be helped. Their weekends and days off were devoted to fixing the house and working on the land.

Larry had started experimenting with making wine. He planted a tiny vineyard, 125 vines of a cold-weather *foch* grape that could withstand harsh winters. Eventually, he produced a pleasant, tannic red wine, along with wines made from apples, plums, and dandelions (his tongue-in-cheek slogan: "We ferment anything too slow to crawl away").

With the neighbors, Nash and Mariel, Larry and Judy decided to put in a huge shared garden in the same meadow where the dome had once stood. Together, they planted lettuce, spinach, carrots, peas, beans, cabbage, corn, tomatoes, squash, and pumpkin. There was a strawberry patch and a rambunctious stand of raspberry canes, and a leafy clump of rhubarb whose ruby stalks Judy cooked into compote and sweetened with maple syrup.

My brother and I were too young to actually help much in the garden, but there was plenty for us to do nearby while the adults worked. We dug for fat earthworms or stripped naked and painted ourselves in mud. I loved to pull sugar-snap pods from the vines, cracking them open and eating the sweet peas one at a time, pretending they were the candy I was rarely allowed to have. The adults seemed to decide we couldn't do much damage in the carrot beds and let us pull up however many we felt like eating. Sometimes I carried these over to the spring bucket to wash them off, but just as often I was too lazy, rubbing the dirt off onto my leg and crunching slowly as I lay on my back between the beds, watching the sky between the lacy, waving carrot tops.

Our half of the garden's bounty was destined for the earth-and-stone cellar below the trapdoor. Descending the ladder into the cellar felt exactly like climbing underground and smelled that way too, rich and damp, laced with the scent of fermenting fruit from the shelves holding Larry's wine. Other shelves held mason jars of home-canned tomatoes, applesauce, jam, and as many kinds of pickles as Judy had had time to make. The big chest freezer held Tupperware boxes of corn, beans, and peas. Across from it was the root cellar—a few square feet of loose, dry soil in which Judy buried potatoes, rutabagas, and carrots to keep them fresh for a few months.

Our milk came from Donald's farm. When we climbed out of the car in the dooryard, the ever-present smell of manure mixed with the scent from the wild chamomile that grew in sunny patches in the dust. Inside the barn's tiny, whitewashed milk storage room, Judy opened the valve of Donald's huge silver pasteurizing tank. But before she filled the glass gallon jar she'd brought, she unscrewed the lid and turned it over like a saucer. This, she filled to the brim with fresh, frothy milk and handed it to me gingerly. My brother and I took turns sipping. The milk was sweet and full of sharp strange flavors that changed completely twice a year—once in the spring and again in the fall when the cows moved between summer grass and winter silage.

I spent a lot of time in that barn. Donald had a granddaughter who, by a stroke of luck neither of us really appreciated until years later, was born exactly eleven days after me. Our kindergarten class had a total of nine children, drawn from a twenty-mile radius around the village school. Nat had brown eyes and curly brown hair and lived with her parents in a tidy ranch house at the edge of a field between her grandfather's farm and our house. It went without saying that we were best friends.

As soon as we were old enough to be trusted to look out for the occasional crevasses that could drop ten feet down between the stacked bales, Nat and I spent every free moment exploring the barn's hayloft, looking for feral kittens. Hours later, our arms covered in ferocious scratches and our hair smelling of dusty, clean hay, we'd climb down the ladder to the low-ceilinged milking room. Here it smelled of hay too, but mixed with manure and milk and the deeper tang of the cows themselves that I recognized in the milk's flavor. If we came down from the hayloft at milking time, we had to stand back as Nat's grandfather, Donald, secured the stanchion that held each cow in place and slipped the silver cylinders of the milking machine over her teats.

At Nat's house, you could sometimes catch a whiff of barn from the work clothes hanging in the mud room, but mostly her house held the warm, comforting smells of dryer sheets and pot roast and potatoes. The living room had a deep, soft carpet, a couch, and a big rectangular window where you could look out and see who was driving by. Her TV was huge and in color and she was allowed to watch shows on channels besides PBS—*Mork & Mindy* and *The Dukes of Hazzard*.

Most of my parents' friends had houses more like ours—smelling of wood smoke and Nag Champa and maybe fermenting fruit from the big crocks in the hallway. They were made of unpainted wood, with ladders and trapdoors and lofts and whole, tarp-draped areas where children weren't allowed to go because the loft lacked a railing or the unfinished walls revealed tempting tufts of cotton-candy-pink fiberglass insulation.

Our closest neighbors, Nash and Mariel, lived in a turreted, window-filled house at the top of a sloping hayfield. A path through the woods led directly from our house to theirs. By the time I was five, I could have walked it in my sleep (and did walk it alone, unbeknownst to my mother, at three—Mariel called to tell her where I was). We shared a phone line with them, as well as with Roger and Blanche Perron, the farm family who had owned the land before we did. The party line meant that when one household got a call, it rang in a neighbor's house too. We only picked up on *ring ring*; a solo *ring* meant it was for the Perrons. Sometimes when you picked up the receiver to make a call, you heard other people already on the line and had to hang up again until they were finished.

For years, Judy had been talking with Nash and Mariel about trying to start a Quaker meeting. When she was still living in Cambridge, she'd briefly worked in a state-run children's home and had met some Quaker men who were working there as part of their Conscientious Objector duties, in lieu of going to Vietnam. She had decided then that if she ever had a son, she would convert. My brother was three when she finally decided it was time. She called up a few other friends and invited them to silent meeting in the dome. Before long, it became a regular, weekly event; thirty years later, the meeting, now formally part of the Society of Friends, still meets every Sunday.

In addition to Nash and Mariel, several other back-to-the-land families helped start the meeting. Vicki (from New Jersey) and Howie (from Flatbush, Brooklyn) lived with their two children, Marinshine and Evan, in a house they were building at the edge of a field in a nearby township. Topher and Marie (Cambridge; suburban Maryland) lived closer by, with their two children Tim and Sarah, almost the same ages as my brother and me. Topher and Marie had built a cozy cabin out of reclaimed barn boards in the woods above an old millstream. The cabin had electricity but no running water and the family of four slept in an open loft above the central living space. Marie was an artist; Topher worked as a contractor but he was very interested in alternative energy, particularly solar cells. In the late '70s, encouraged by a federal tax credit for home solar use, he started a business installing solar panels on people's houses. He and Marie were designing the larger house they'd build next to the cabin and outfit with state-of-the-art solar technology.

It was the fact that everyone was working on their houses and no one could get anything done with children around that led Judy and the other mothers to the idea of workdays. One Saturday a month through the summer, the whole group got together to help one family do whatever large tasks needed accomplishing—not unlike the barn raising Larry and Judy had attended at Loudon's.

While most of the adults helped dig a foundation or put up fence posts around a field, someone volunteered to watch the children. Usually there was some small task for us to help with— picking up nails from the floor of a building site, helping in a bucket brigade, shelling peas for the night's big potluck dinner, or dragging brush into a pile for the bonfire that would follow. The long days were exhausting and fun.

After the festivity of the workdays, our own house felt somber and quiet. On winter days Larry was away, Judy rose before dawn to relight the woodstoves and boil water for a cup of tea. After climbing down to the cellar to retrieve the frozen vegetables for that night's supper, she'd leave them in the sink to defrost and put a pot of beans on the counter to soak. Once she'd woken me and my brother, gotten us washed and quickly dressed in our chilly bedroom, she ladled milk from the big glass jar over our cereal, then hustled us into snow pants, jackets, boots, hats, and mittens. She closed up the woodstoves and turned on the light over the front deck to light our snowy, evening hike home. Already hoping that the car parked at the bottom of the driveway wouldn't be too frozen to start, she loaded me, my brother, our school things, and whatever she needed for work onto a plastic sled at the top of the snow-packed driveway. Together, we zoomed through the frigid morning air to the bottom of the hill.

One Saturday afternoon, a friend took me ice-skating at a local rink. I was by myself in the middle of the ice when my feet slid away from me and I fell. It didn't hurt enough to cry, but when I tried to get up, I couldn't.

It was already dark when the friend dropped me off at the bottom of the driveway, where my mother and bundled-up brother were waiting. When Larry was home, the ride up the hill was fast and fun because he usually drove the second-hand snowmobile they'd bought for this purpose. But its pull cord was designed for a taller person and Judy had a hard time getting it started, so most often, we walked.

The friend told my mother about my fall and that I'd been asking her to carry me. Judy just nodded. When the car's taillights had disappeared around the bend, she asked me if I thought I could walk and when I said no, my earlier calm dissolving into tears, she put me in the plastic sled, a rare privilege. The sled was too heavy for her to haul both of us, so my three-year-old brother walked all the way up the long hill—bravely and generously, I thought even then.

In the house, Judy assumed she was humoring me by splinting my leg with magazines tied on with rags, but after watching me hop around the dome the whole next day without putting weight on it once, she decided I might really be injured. After finding someone to watch my brother, she drove me an hour away to the hospital. My leg was fractured after all. I spent the rest of the winter in a cast, unable to walk without crutches.

My brother's toddler generosity didn't last long; when Larry wasn't home to pick us up with the snowmobile, for the rest of the winter, Judy had to pull both of us up the hill through the frigid darkness by herself.

CHAPTER 19

For Loraine, the adjustment to nuclear family life with LJ had pros and cons. For the most part, she loved having her kitchen to herself, where all her pots remained right where she put them and she could plan a meal ahead without having to worry that a key ingredient would suddenly vanish. But still, sometimes she found herself thinking about that first summer— all those nights telling stories around the fire and then her walking tent to tent with her guitar in the moonlight, singing everyone to sleep. She missed that feeling, the way everyone had looked at each other, their eyes full of love.

Whatever had been the hardships of Myrtle Hill's communal heyday, Loraine had never felt lonely. Even now, she and Hershe and the succession of women who lived in the Big House were in and out of each other's homes constantly—their children even more so. But at night, after Amelia and Rahula and the new baby, Rose, LJ's daughter, were tucked into their beds, Loraine sometimes missed having other women to talk to.

LJ, like the other men, spent two weeks a month on the road, driving for Loaves & Fishes. On the one hand, this schedule was much better than a 9-to-5 because he could get so much building done during the off weeks. But on the other hand, he was gone a lot and Loraine missed him. Plus, their ancient pickup truck was forever breaking down and leaving Loraine and the kids stranded. Finally, LJ taught her how to repair it herself. Very quickly, she learned to tighten the fan belt and change the battery. Now at the end of the day, she was scrubbing grease from her fingernails as often as dough.

It was only later that she noticed the irony. She had spent the whole communal period doing traditional women's work; it was only now, still in the same demanding setting, that she'd been pulled into a new skill set, compelled by the simple need of this puny, two-adult, nuclear-family workforce. Her newfound ability to tinker the truck back into sputtering life remained one of her proudest accomplishments.

Loraine liked feeling her confidence grow as she learned to fend for herself. But with LJ gone, the nights were still lonely. Her eyes weren't strong enough to read for very long by kerosene lamp. When they did finally get electricity, convincing the power company to bury the cables so as not to mar the wildness of the landscape, she liked singing along to the radio as she worked in the kitchen. But it still wasn't the same as listening to Fletcher read aloud or the whole group dissolving in hysterical laughter over a joke that no one could later remember. Or those spontaneous, love-filled, moonlit nights.

It's possible those nights would have vanished anyway—they were all closer to thirty than twenty now, after all. And, nostalgia aside, she had to admit: living apart had lessened tensions in a lot of ways.

Ever since they'd abandoned the need for a unified philosophy, there were many fewer fights over the garden, for example. Loraine had turned over a stretch of earth closer to her house, and Hershe had done the same down by the dome, leaving the upper field gardens to Lilith and Jed. The once-communal supply of spades and pitchforks had long-since gravitated to individual households. The idea that Loraine would ever need to "borrow" a trowel from Hershe would have sounded ridiculous a few years earlier but at least this way if someone left her shovel to rust in the rain, it was her own problem. Except when Hershe returned a borrowed item to Lilith with insufficient gratitude: then the whole hill could hear them screaming.

The men tended to roll their eyes at these conflicts when they were around to hear them, but they had their problems too.

Chiefly, the road. Unlike the garden, the road *had* to be shared, and taking care of it was one of the few remaining vital chores the group had to deal with collectively. A dirt road takes a lot of maintenance, especially a poorly graded former tractor trail like the one winding up Myrtle Hill. Whose job was it to keep up the drainage ridges, without which every rainstorm threatened to wash the whole thing out? Should they pay to resurface it with new load of gravel? Or to plow it in the winter? These questions weren't very different from those facing other groups of neighbors on other shared roads, but Myrtle Hill's communal background contributed some unique complications. To start with: where should the money come from?

The group's legally innovative Land Trust ownership had worked beautifully well. By taking turns with the payments, they'd repaid their mortgage in just a few years. Now "Myrtle Hill Farm," the entity, owned the land outright. It was a huge coup, but the mortgage (and ongoing taxes) were the only expenses they'd agreed to share in this way. They had no other cooperative financial system. When they lived together, the arrangement had actually been quite simple: for every need requiring cash, the money had always simply appeared from somewhere or they'd done without.

Now that finances lay much more within the domain of each family, it became much less clear how they were to determine financial responsibility. For the electricity, they'd made a neighborly arrangement. Those closest to the main road had gotten it first—the Big House, plus Hershe and Terry in the dome. Then the others had each paid to extend the line up the road, first up to LJ and Loraine's, then up to Jed and Lilith. But how should they handle the road? More like this, as any cooperating neighbors might? Or more like the mortgage, as a united group?

And in that case, what would "group" actually mean? Should Craig and Amy and Dennis prove their ongoing membership by helping pay for the road, even while living at Entropy Acres? Should people at the top of the hill pay more than the families at the bottom since they were the only ones who drove its whole length? Especially if it seemed like the people at the very top could afford more since they had good jobs and no children?

The group could not decide. And in their now-erratic meetings, the discussions grew less and less respectful, more and more frustrated. Soon it seemed to Loraine that negotiations about the road had become an excuse to vent every personal slight and resentment.

It was Hershe and Terry who first raised the big question.

Terry had fixed up Myrtle Hill's dome beautifully, dividing the round interior into rooms as best he could, including a sleeping loft for the children—Jethro and the sister to whom Hershe had given birth, there in the dome.

Terry was working for the trucking company and Hershe for the community cannery, but they didn't have much money to invest in badly needed further renovations. When they went to ask the bank about a home-improvement loan, though, they ran into a dismaying problem. Though they might own the house itself (their friends had agreed to sell them the dome for $1), the land it stood on belonged to "Myrtle Hill Farm." Thus, the bank wouldn't help them.

For Hershe and Terry, borrowing from family was not an option. The bank had been their only hope. It was a bitter irony: the commune members' desire to remain at Myrtle Hill had outlasted the group's ability to live together, but now their idealistic, shared ownership structure was creating a serious obstacle to their staying.

When Hershe brought the issue up at a meeting—What if someone needed a mortgage? How flexible were they willing to be about the idea of communal ownership?—everyone else was frankly shocked. Even Loraine, Hershe's most loyal friend, used the word "sacrilege."

As LJ's shock faded, though, it was replaced by empathy for the bind in which Hershe and Terry found themselves. They really needed more financial flexibility than the commune's original ideals had foreseen. And it was not lost on LJ that he was in the same position. No matter how much work and money he put into his own house, which he had recently tripled in size with a new addition, he and Loraine would never be able to sell and move somewhere else unless they found a buyer who was not only willing to own an eccentrically built house on a communally held lot, but who would also be accepted as a member by the entire group. Somehow this did not seem likely.

To Loraine, as painful as it was to think of entirely letting go of the communal ideals in which she had believed so passionately, she didn't want a lack of compromise to drive her friend Hershe away. Part of what Loraine had sought in commune life was to live by ideals, but part of it was friendship too.

Jed and Lilith, though, strongly rejected the idea of changing the commune's founding structure to suit the personal needs of an individual member. If this system isn't working for you anymore, LJ remembered them telling Hershe, "maybe it's time to move on."

Loraine and Jed were now the only founding members of the commune still living at Myrtle Hill. Hershe and Terry's question had forced the two of them into diametrically opposed positions: to Jed, upholding the communal principle of group ownership trumped the individual needs of its members (who were, after all, interchangeable under the banner of "the group"). To Loraine, it was more important to remain flexible to the needs of the commune as it *was*, not as they had hoped it would be. To her, it did not feel like a coincidence that the people who were willing to let go of ideals in the face of hard practical decisions were also the ones who had lived in the Big House through the winter.

A philosophical rift would have been destructive enough. But the arguments over group priorities rapidly entwined themselves with existing, interpersonal dynamics of alliance and hostility. The discussions stopped being productive and started turning nasty.

Finally, Jed and Lilith agreed to at least consider what non-communal land ownership might mean. The others had assumed that splitting the land would mean even shares for each member. But Jed and Lilith had a different idea: they'd contributed more financially over the years, in the form of food, supplies and equipment, so they should get more property.

The others were outraged. Before they knew it, the discussion had turned to an accounting of each member's contributions to the group. The help and mutual support that had been offered freely at the time now underwent a retroactive reckoning: Which counted more? Jed's generator, which had allowed everyone to run power tools while they built their houses? Loraine's endless cooking through all the years of communal living? LJ's magical ability to keep the cars running? Hershe's care of the cows and chickens? Terry's green thumb? It was an impossible and destructive calculation.

Not for the first time, LJ wished the group had long ago adopted a formalized system for conflict resolution. Or honestly, even an accepted practice for civil discourse, other than the ubiquitous encounter session model, which encouraged "honest" interactions that tended to veer toward harsh personality critiques. Now, when they needed it most, the group had no structure to help them step back from the cycle of personal attacks and regain their footing as a group. The loose consensus method that had served them in their early years had relied for its function entirely on shared goals and personal goodwill. Now that their goals were more diffuse and petty sniping had badly damaged their goodwill, the group was adrift. They had no mechanism for deciding how to live together.

And, it would soon become clear, these conflicts over land were only the beginning of the trouble.

One afternoon, LJ and Loraine came home from a few days away to a shocking sight. As best they could put it together later, Jed must have walked down from his house at the top of the hill, cutting through the former communal garden in the upper field across from their kitchen windows, until he reached Loraine's favorite row of ancient maples. Then he had started his chainsaw.

By the time Loraine got home, all that remained of the trees was a row of stumps and a chaos of limbs and mangled branches.

Jed's reasoning, as LJ and Loraine understood it later, was that he needed firewood and the trees, being old, would have required cutting sooner or later anyway. But to LJ and Loraine this logic did not make sense. To them, his act felt personal.

In her shock and grief, Loraine had wanted to rush to Jed's door and demand to know why, of all the acres of forest, he had chosen these beloved trees to fell. What stopped her from doing this was another troubling incident that no longer seemed isolated.

LJ and a new friend, Ronnie, who was living in the Big House, had been cutting firewood in the stand of hardwoods between LJ's house and Jed's. As Ronnie recalled it later, he had just finished a cut when he looked up to see Jed charging toward him through the underbrush. Ronnie was wearing safety earmuffs and the chainsaw was still idling so it took him a moment to register what Jed was shouting at him, something like: *Get off my property! You have no right getting wood here!*

Ronnie's first response was to laugh—they were on commune land. There was no *my* property, for Jed or for any of them. He was still laughing when he noticed that Jed was carrying his .38 pistol. LJ heard the shouting and came over to where they were standing. He looked at Jed in disbelief. "What the hell are you talking about?" he said. "He's helping me cut my firewood." Jed calmed down, but the incident left LJ shaken.

If Ronnie had heard him right, Jed's saying *my property* was disturbing. It was becoming clearer that, in the absence of any formal group decision about whether and how to divide up the commune's shared land, Jed had decided to simply begin taking the action that suited him best. In truth, this approach was not so different from how the group had always proceeded when faced with a decision on which they couldn't come to consensus. The difference this time was that Jed had apparently decided unilaterally to claim a significant portion of the commune's property as his own.

After that, the other families on the hill found themselves avoiding the acres around Jed's house. Loraine missed using the sun-heated outdoor shower, but it just wasn't worth getting yelled at. If she needed to walk up by Jed and Lilith's to gather the ramps or wild ginger that grew up there, she waited until she saw them drive away before slipping into the woods. Without agreeing to any formal boundaries, the rest of the group tacitly ceded Jed the periphery that seemed to keep him satisfied.

Unless they had to, they mostly didn't interact with Jed and Lilith at all. The two of them were gone frequently, particularly in winter, and tended to zoom down the hill, already sealed in their giant, black trucks.

LJ hated leaving his family alone on the hill for long stretches with neighborly relations so tense, but Loraine seemed to be handling it. Things weren't so bad that she'd forbidden the children from coming and going as they pleased, which made him feel better.

In fact, it was a point of pride for the adults to keep the children blissfully ignorant of any trouble between the households. Depending on what new family was staying at the Big House, there might be as many as nine kids on the hill at one time. All the houses, including Jed and Lilith's, remained open to all of them.

Compared to the dome, the cabin, and the Big House, Jed and Lilith's tall, bright home was a luxurious and uncluttered palace. It had windows everywhere, yet was warm and undrafty. They had rugs and throw pillows and built-in shelves full of books and knickknacks. Jethro liked going up there to sit on their soft, comfortable couch (the only one on the hill) and listen to music. Before everyone had electricity, Jed's generator meant that he had the group's only stereo; even now, they still had the biggest music collection, since they or their friends were always bringing new albums from the city. Jed and Lilith had travelled and they had boxes full of shiny treasures, coins and beads, that they let you spill out on the rug. Even their dishes struck Jethro as glamorous—they had tiny glasses, just for juice, but if you asked for water, they gave you a different, bigger glass—and, unlike everything in his own house, they had been bought new.

At first, Jethro even liked the bomb shelter. In his recollection, Jed only showed it to him once: a squat, concrete bunker half buried in the ground a short way from the house. It had a heavy door and steps leading down to a dark, tiny room where Jethro caught a glimpse of shelves crammed full of canned food. He was impressed in a "whoa, cool!" kind of way, though he declined Jed's offer to descend the steps and check it out more closely.

Later, after he'd thought about it some more, what disturbed Jethro wasn't the space itself, though it certainly hadn't looked appealing, or even the fact that Jed had gone to the trouble of installing a bomb shelter in the first place. It was the fact that the shelter was so small, only big enough for two. If something terrible really did happen, a nuclear attack or whatever it was Jed was so worried about, he and Lilith clearly had no intention of saving Jethro or his sister or mother or Rahula or Loraine or any of them. Years later, Jethro recalled following this thought to its logical conclusion: "If they're doing so much to protect themselves and we're not at all part of what they're protecting? Then invariably that makes us a threat." He'd never given much thought to the gun Jed habitually wore, but now he started wondering: "What are you carrying a gun for if you're never going to use it?"

He didn't stop going up to Jed's to hang out, but he didn't stop worrying either.

Though Myrtle's adults weren't fully conscious of it at the time, the children's freedom to treat every house on the hill like their own represented a hope, however faint, that the differences could be mended and the group made whole again. Their friends outside the hill had the same hope. A number of them tried, at various points, to intercede and formally or informally help Myrtle's remaining residents come to an understanding about how to share the land. No one got anywhere. Even if everyone in the group could come around to the idea of splitting land into individual plots, no one could agree on a fair size. People's positions had become too entrenched and the mutual sympathy that might have allowed for flexibility and compromise had entirely vanished.

For Craig, though he normally relished the role of peacemaker, the squabbles among his former commune-mates had pushed him to the point of exhaustion. He'd come to realize that his talents lay in getting projects going more than in running them long-term—he was a "starter," as he put it. Once the co-op had stabilized (permanently, it turned out, though later as a privately owned health-food store), he felt it was time to move on. Eliot, after he and Peg split up, had gotten involved in a group led by a Bolivian spiritual teacher who led trainings in Scientific Mysticism. On Eliot's recommendation, Craig attended an Arica training. By the time Loraine started calling him with complaints about Jed, he had already left Vermont.

Amy listened sympathetically to Loraine, but Jed had been a good friend to her and she did not want to take sides. For Amy, once Craig had left, there was not much keeping her at Entropy. Besides, she was ready for the next step in her life. She too went and did an Arica training and, like Craig, did not return.

Amy's business partner, Craig's sister Melissa, was a city girl through and through and had never felt fully comfortable in Vermont. When she and Dennis finally broke up, she headed for California and did not look back.

Entropy Acres, a.k.a. the Myrtle Hill Annex for People on Their Way Out, had trimmed its steady population all the way down to just one: Dennis.

But Dennis wasn't alone for long. He had met a strong, gorgeous blonde girl named Peggy Day, who had moved to the area on her own and spent her first few months crashing with whoever had space. She had kept Amy company at Entropy during a few winter weeks when everyone else happened to be away, and another few weeks cabin-sitting for Nick while he was gone. She had even spent a couple of days camping at Myrtle Hill before moving back over to Entropy, and eventually, in with Dennis. Forty years later, the two of them would still be living there.

Dennis enjoyed driving trucks for Loaves & Fishes, especially since it meant working with his best friend LJ, but he knew he didn't want to spend his whole adult life on the road. He wanted to have more time at home, on the farm—not to mention more time with Peggy Day. Plus, he wanted to work for himself.

Growing up in New Jersey, Dennis had never had much exposure to horses, but when he first moved to Entropy, helping take care of the two pale Belgians was one of his favorite chores. In particular, whenever the horses needed new shoes, Dennis found himself riveted by the process.

The blacksmith and farrier was Azarias Raoul Caron, the same French-Canadian inventor-genius who had rebuilt Entropy's wooden wagon wheel years earlier. Caron's shop in town was a cluttered marvel of waste-nothing ingenuity. It was divided in two—one side held Caron's crowded woodshop; the other was fitted with a forge and anvil, installed and arranged by Caron to his own, idiosyncratic specifications. The shop had a basement beneath it. To keep the anvil from crashing through the floorboards as he worked, Caron had supported it from below with a huge length of tree stump, two feet wide and tall enough to stretch the whole height of the basement, plus another several feet buried underground.

As Dennis watched Caron work, he found he had question after question for the older man. Though Dennis had been recruited by Columbia University's wrestling program, he had deferred in favor of following his father into a union job as a mechanic on the shipyards of New York. In addition to a knack for creative tinkering, he knew how to weld.

Finally, Dennis asked Caron if he would teach him how to shoe horses. Caron demurred. He wasn't interested in giving lessons—though if someone wanted to buy his whole shop and take over the business, he might reconsider. He was feeling his age and was ready to retire, but his sons all had other jobs and weren't interested.

Dennis wasn't sure. Then one day, a friend of a friend on a visit from New York mentioned casually that he'd heard the blacksmith was considering selling his equipment and that he thought there might be some good antiques that he could buy cheap and resell in the city. Dennis and Peggy Day hated this idea. They also knew that once Caron stopped working, the area would be left without a blacksmith. Dennis made up his mind. He made Caron an offer: he'd buy the whole business on the condition that the older man would stick around and help Dennis learn his craft—a kind of reverse apprenticeship. Caron agreed.

For the next several years, whenever Dennis was working in the shop, Caron came down from his apartment upstairs to help him troubleshoot and offer pointers. At first he tried to just sit in a corner and watch, smoking his pipe, but he invariably jumped up to help. As Dennis put it, "that man couldn't not work."

Dennis realized immediately that the older man didn't respond to people who acted like they already knew what to do and that his best method for accessing Caron's genius was to maintain his own humble curiosity. This wasn't hard.

"You have to *think* like a blacksmith," Caron frequently reminded him. This often meant that tackling a tricky job might begin with inventing and forging yourself a new and unique tool. Dennis loved the way that mastering elemental materials—iron, fire—and the techniques of this ancient skill left him perfectly free for the almost limitless possibilities of his imagination. Plus, he loved living in Vermont and was eager to find a livelihood for himself that might also offer a service to his neighbors. Through Dennis's careful apprenticeship, the area kept its blacksmith— albeit one with a thick New Jersey accent.

Peggy Day too was finding ways to make a living in her new-found home. Almost as soon as she arrived, she became the very first reporter Chris hired to work on his new newspaper. Like Chris, she loved how reporting gave her access to people in the community she might not meet otherwise. But, like Dennis, she was also an entrepreneur.

Her family owned the Florida orange groves that had (not coincidentally) supplied Craig's co-op with fruit. Watching the co-op's trade relationships develop had spurred an idea. At Christmas, her mother's friends always wanted real, fresh-cut trees and balsam wreaths, but those weren't always easy to find down South.

The business that Peggy eventually built drew from her work as a community news reporter, which had helped her understand what might make seasonal wreath-making an appealing job for local women—she supplied wire and tools but had them cut their own balsam, for example, and she guaranteed her orders, paying in cash and picking them up herself so that women living back in the woods with no car might still have a source of income.

Decades later, Northeast Kingdom Balsam still ships thousands of locally made wreaths a year, nationwide.

All across the country, other back-to-the-land entrepreneurs were following a similar calculus, drawing from both a city-person's sense of the available market and a rural-resident's awareness of supply potential. People who had declared themselves ready to overthrow capitalism a few years earlier now found themselves calculating market rates for the products and cash crops whose revenue helped support their families in their new-found homes. The Farm in Tennessee had several profit sidelines, including soy ice cream and a solar-cell manufactory. Twin Oaks made hammocks. A Vermont commune called Mad Brook started an advertising circular called the *Green Mountain Trading Post* that still exists. Other back-to-the-landers found markets for products they'd started out cultivating for themselves—goat cheese, tofu, nut butters.

And, in the same spirit, at least at first, marijuana.

The history of marijuana cultivation in Vermont had a very specific turning point.

Through most of the 1970s, the pot being grown in most parts of America were New World *sativa* strains—Panama Red, Acapulco Gold. While these varieties had no trouble flourishing in California, in the Northeast the short growing season cut short plants' development. Even the most dedicated gardeners couldn't coax a tropical plant to bud-stage maturity in five months. The plants came up all right, but they stayed small—short enough to hide among the tomatoes or in the back of a flower bed—and yielded only the (less-potent) leaves for consumption. Rolled into a joint, "it was like smoking smoke," as one person remembered. You got a headache long before you got high. Among people who took their weed seriously, noted another, "no one wanted to smoke it."

"Ditchweed," as some called it, was the variety that had caused the bus-driving scandal for Entropy Acres. Larry and Judy, like many, many other early-'70s counterculture newcomers, had tried to grow some too. In their case, they had started a few plants from seed in early spring, nestled among tomato seedlings and using their dome's big windows as a greenhouse. One day, Loudon and Donald had dropped by, visiting, and looked up at the contraption Larry and Judy had rigged—the seedling flats laid out on an old door hitched to pulleys on the ceiling so that it could be raised high out of the way or lowered for watering. "Oh, that's clever," one of them remarked. Then, not missing a beat, "You don't have anything funny growing in there do you?" Larry and Judy tried to laugh naturally but they spent the rest of the visit wondering if the men had truly noticed anything.

Later it seemed to Larry that the neighbors' joke had been more a probe about identity. Everyone knew hippies smoked pot. "The question was, were we hippies or not? Did we smoke dope or not?"

Neither Judy nor Larry thought of themselves as hippies, but they did smoke dope when it was offered. They were sufficiently older than everyone at Entropy and Myrtle that they had both graduated college before ever encountering marijuana. Larry smoked for the first time in Kathmandu at the end of his Peace Corps tour, a joint of ganja that made him laugh and laugh and laugh. Judy remembered that her Peace Corps group in 1965 had been threatened sternly with expulsion if any of them were found to have *ever* used marijuana and that by the very next year, this rule had been abandoned because it would have made recruiting college students impossible.

Larry and Judy, whose other drug use extended no further than a failed experiment with peyote (no one hallucinated, everyone barfed), found the idea of growing marijuana appealing in the same way Larry's homemade wine appealed. The pleasure came more from the satisfactions of self-sufficiency than from the intoxicant quality of the product itself.

Whatever their motivations, Larry and Judy did not get very far with their cultivation efforts. Though they did transplant the half-dozen pot seedlings into a secluded clearing in the woods, every single plant was eaten by deer. They never bothered trying again.

For others more serious about their dope, the insufferable quality of northeastern ditchweed meant that homegrown never really cut it. For a decent high, you still had to rely on more po-tent strains, grown elsewhere.

Until 1978. That year, someone—by some accounts a guy from Goddard, by others someone going by the name Douglas Fir—returned from Afghanistan with marijuana seeds sewn into the hems of his clothes. The variety he imported from the Hindu Kush was an *indica* strain, producing a much stronger, more brain-melting high than the floaty, previously ubiquitous *sativas*. Best of all, at least as far as northern growers were concerned, it was a cold-weather plant requiring only a few short months to grow to maturity. Suddenly Vermont growers could get the same kind of crops as their friends in New Mexico and California, with ten-foot high plants yielding sticky, fragrant buds.

For the first time, "Vermont Green" meant a product that peo-ple actually wanted to smoke. And were willing to pay for.

As Dennis explained it years later, "All of a sudden you could be a hippie living back in the woods and make a lot of money. And some people got nutty about it."

It took Loraine longer than she could later explain to notice that Jed's marijuana cultivation seemed to be of a bigger, more seri-ous intensity than her own. Jed's paranoia, which they'd teased him about since the first summer, now seemed, in some ways, to be justified.

But back then, that paranoia had always been directed out-ward, at the world. Now, his neighbors feared, he had begun to see them the same way.

One night LJ and Loraine were returning home with the chil-dren after a few days away. As soon as they turned onto the long commune road, they noticed that something looked odd. As they passed the Big House and headed up toward their own home, they saw a beam of light blazing across the upper field and into their eyes. They all squinted, stunned, as LJ steered the car, nearly blind, out of the beam and into their own driveway. LJ and Loraine hurried inside to put the girls to bed. It wasn't until they themselves went to their own room to sleep that they real-ized that the beam coming from a spotlight positioned at the top of the upper field was shining directly through their curtain-less window. Their bedroom was lit like a sports stadium.

Loraine was in her third trimester with her fourth child, and LJ was home between long-haul runs. Sacrificing sleep was simply not an option. LJ grabbed some lopping shears and headed up through the field. A few minutes later, the light vanished, leaving the room in blissful darkness. LJ climbed in bed without a word.

They were just drifting off when they heard shouting. LJ got up and went outside once again. As he recalled it later, Jed and Lilith were standing in the road. "You can't do that! It's my light! It's my land!" Lilith was screaming, indignant. Jed stood next to her, saying nothing, but holding a baseball bat. LJ was never one for physical confrontation, but he knew that in a fistfight, Jed, slight and wiry and never without his glasses, would be no match for him. Facing Jed now, though, he was acutely aware of his own bare hands and feet. In the darkness, he couldn't see whether or not Jed had his gun but the thought of it—and of his daughters and pregnant wife watching from the windows—kept him from responding with the full fury he felt. Eventually, he turned and went back inside, leaving the other couple on the lawn, still fuming.

Later, it occurred to LJ that Jed and Lilith hadn't intended the light as a deliberate provocation as much as a security measure, to blind any cars coming up the road. But this was almost more troubling from a communal point of view: it wasn't that Jed had intended to destroy his neighbors' quality of life, it was just that he didn't care.

CHAPTER 20

The next incident came just a few weeks later.

Loraine was getting ready for the arrival of the new baby. She'd be doing things a little differently this time. With her previous birth, her first child with LJ, there had been complications. She'd assumed she'd have another, easy, quick home birth but the labor had been excruciating and, after twenty-four hours, showed no signs of progressing. Finally the friend acting as Loraine's midwife took LJ aside. "Look, this is not going right," she told him. "You've got to go to the hospital. She'll only listen to you, you've got to talk her into it." He did, and just in time. It turned out that the baby was in a posterior position with the umbilical cord wrapped around her neck. The doctor was upset with Loraine for having waited so long to come in, but he managed to turn the baby, sparing her a Caesarian. Rose had been born healthy, big and strong.

With this, her second pregnancy with the six-foot-two LJ, Loraine could tell already that the baby would be equally large. She had no interest in repeating that panicked rush, so this time she planned to deliver at the hospital.

The plan was that Amelia—now a teenager and an experienced babysitter—would watch her younger sisters with Hershe and some other friends looking in, for the hours Loraine and LJ would be gone. Loraine planned to labor at home as long as she could.

And so, the afternoon her labor started, she was in the upstairs bedroom of her house, Amelia helping her time her contractions, when she heard shouting outside.

Terry had chosen that same afternoon for a conversation with
Jed. The speed with which he and Lilith drove their trucks up
and down the road was driving Hershe crazy. She and Terry had
two little daughters in addition to Jethro, and the family in the
Big House had kids too—all of whom liked to ride their bikes on
the flat stretch of road near the dome. Those big trucks zooming
past freaked Hershe out, but it was the apparent indifference of
the drivers to the safety of her children that really infuriated her.

Until the land disputes got bad, Terry and Jed had always
gotten along well. As Terry explained it later, his goal that day
was to go have a reasonable conversation with Jed about the importance of keeping children safe. He went up to Jed's house,
knocked on the door, and said, "I gotta talk to you." When Jed
came out, the two men sat down near the woodpile. But it wasn't
long before the conversation became heated; when Lilith overheard and joined in, the volume kicked up another notch. Finally Terry decided he'd had enough. The thought of Jed's guns
kept him calmer than he otherwise might have been. But as he
walked away down the road back toward LJ's cabin, Jed and
Lilith followed him, still shouting.

It was this commotion that Loraine heard from the upstairs
bedroom. She knew that for a healthy labor to progress she
needed to stop listening and concentrate on her contractions,
but she couldn't focus on anything but the angry voices of her
former commune-mates. At last, Hershe arrived to pick up Loraine and take her to the hospital. After firing off a few choice
words of her own, she sent the others away and went upstairs to
fetch Loraine and help her down to the car.

The baby, Loraine's fourth daughter, was born a few hours
later, big and healthy (and posterior again). But when Loraine
brought Jessie home, it was to a community in tatters.

Loraine herself had hoped that the land disputes might be resolved and everyone could go back to working together and getting along. For her, that hope was now gone. What had shaken

her, as she'd labored in the upstairs bedroom, listening to her former friends—former *family*—shouting at each other below, was the look on Amelia's face. Loraine could see that her daughter didn't want to be left alone on the hill in charge of her sisters because she was afraid they would not be safe. And Loraine couldn't reassure her because she was scared too.

The adults had not succeeded, as they had hoped, in keeping the children out of their conflict. Worse, instead of creating a utopia in which their kids could thrive, free of the hang-ups and poisons of their own childhoods, they'd somehow fostered a climate that was actually worse. How had things gotten this bad?

In idealistically stripping away so many layers of societal norms and expectations, Loraine realized later, the group had also inadvertently stripped away a number of important protections. The families on the hill who feared Jed's volatility and his guns had no system in place for restricting his behavior or for asking him to leave. Their only option would be to leave themselves, abandoning the houses and gardens into which they'd invested years of work, not to mention ceding control of land that was still legally and morally theirs. Even if they'd had money to move or rent, which none of them did, they weren't prepared to take this step.

Later, Loraine, LJ, Hershe, Terry, and the families in the Big House identified the summer Loraine's fourth daughter was born as, in Terry's words, "the point of no coming back."

"I don't think we were ever close to each other after that," Hershe said later. The question of whether and how to split up the land remained as undecided and contentious as ever, but any hope of empathy or compromise between Jed and Lilith and the other families had gone.

For their fellow Myrtleites living elsewhere, this latest development was excruciating. They listened to both sides explain the conflicts and did not know what to believe. Craig and Amy were busy with their lives elsewhere, so they mostly kept out of the fray. Dennis and Peggy Day, closer by, were working hard to integrate themselves into the local community and were also the first stop for complaints from both sides. They had tried hard to mediate with no success. They were exhausted. Very quickly their attitude about everything to do with the mess on the hill became, "Don't get us involved. We want nothing to do with it." Dennis and LJ, best friends and lifelong neighbors, found they could not talk about it, to their own mutual sorrow and disappointment.

For Loraine, often alone with the children when LJ was gone trucking, her sense of isolation was compounded by another realization: if something truly bad were to happen, she would not be able to go to the police.

The reason for this was growing in little plots back in the woods.

For Loraine, that summer became another, different kind of turning point. For her, the decision to grow a cash crop of pot had stemmed in large part from her frustration with living so eternally close to poverty. She'd managed to free herself, as planned, from the tyranny of 9-to-5 jobs, but perpetual financial insecurity, it turned out, was exhausting. A little more money, she had hoped, would buy a little more freedom.

Now she saw that this line of logic too had a fatal flaw—felonious money wasn't freedom at all. It was its own kind of trap.

For her, the decision was clear. Her short career as a cash-crop pot farmer ended as suddenly as it had begun.

By then, there were other good reasons to get out of the business.

By all accounts, the early, carefree days of potent, profitable "Vermont Green" were exciting times. One local communard, a native Vermonter, remembered a group of friends meeting in a hotel bar and all pulling trimmed buds out their pockets to compare with pride. It reminded him of the way sugarmakers held their little amber jars of syrup to the light to show off its quality. The outlaw elements of pot-growing felt consistent to him too with the long, local border-region history of playing cat-and-mouse with law enforcement: poaching deer out of season, herding cows through the woods to avoid import tax, or the bootlegger past that made certain Prohibition-era houses among the region's finest.

But the profits from marijuana proved too enticing for its production to remain at a farmers' market scale. At the time, a pound of trimmed buds could fetch $1,600 with each plant yielding as much as half a pound. "What started out as a couple plants in the garden and then becomes an industry—as soon as you get money involved in it, then it gets weird," explained one former grower. As another put it, the huge sums "brought out the worst in everyone."

First came the rip-offs. Mature plants were tall, but they were light as goldenrod. Anyone who could make off through the woods with a mere armload of someone else's crop could find themselves thousands of dollars richer. The outraged grower could not go to the police, of course, so they had to find other recourse. "It became like these little wars in the hills," one person recalled. "There was gunfire and sabotages." For many counterculture growers, the moment they found themselves procuring arms to potentially use against another human was the moment they realized they'd gone too far. For others, though, the immense profits still justified risking a little product loss—or a little gunfire.

Then came the Reagan administration's War on Drugs. States received enforcement funding if they agreed to cooperate by adopting federal prosecuting guidelines, including the confiscation of property for those convicted of cultivation.

In one early, well-publicized case, a grower was convicted of raising a large number of marijuana plants concealed inside a cornfield. He was sentenced to several years in prison, but it was the fact that he also lost his family farm that convinced huge numbers of casual pot growers to rip out their plants cold turkey. No homegrown self-sufficiency was thrilling enough to risk losing your land.

But for other growers, whose motivation had now turned toward the hundreds of thousands of dollars to be made in a single season, the rewards still outweighed the risks.

It wasn't until 1984 that federal drug enforcement funding arrived in Vermont in earnest. By then, according to later court transcripts, Jed was the only resident of Myrtle Hill still growing marijuana. In fact, he and Lilith and their new baby were practically the only residents at all.

The Big House had lain empty for several years since the last family staying there had left. A decade of winters had not been kind to its speed-driven construction, and its changing roster of families had not bothered to invest much in improvements. And too, there were simply fewer people around these days willing to live in such austere conditions. Or desperate enough to remain in the tense, anxious atmosphere of Myrtle Hill.

To friends outside the hill who still interacted with the funny, generous Jed they'd always known, it was hard for Hershe and Loraine to convey that their dominant feeling toward their neighbors wasn't anger but fear. Any time Jed and Lilith went away, if it was during growing season, Jed hired local kids to "check in" on his place, a job for which Loraine had seen them carrying guns. Jed himself, as had been the case for years, even when he went into town, was never without his holstered .38.

Then one day, LJ and Loraine came home from a few days away to find a sight that would have felt impossible during the commune's first years together.

Jed had put up a fence. Four strands of barbed wire now emerged from the woods and encircled the entire upper field: the former gardens, the stone wall, the chopped-down maples, and the spot where the buck deer emerged—all of it. Every time Loraine looked out her kitchen windows at the fenced-in field, she felt a stab of anger and fear. Where the fence ran across the road a few yards up from LJ and Loraine's, its gate held a giant, orange sign: "No Trespassing." Later, following the barbed wire into the woods as it circumscribed the territory Jed had definitively claimed, they found another sign. "Trespassers will be prosecuted," it read. And then handwritten underneath: "Or shot.—Jed."

Without needing to be told, the hill's remaining kids gave the barbed-wire fence a wide berth, even when playing on Rahula's lawn, within a ball's easy bounce of the "No Trespassing" sign. To the younger children who couldn't remember visiting their home, Jed and Lilith seemed less like real people and more like an ominous, threatening force, appearing only dimly through the rolled-up windows of their big trucks. For all the children, no matter where they were or what project they'd undertaken, the sound of Jed and Lilith's trucks turning into the driveway—distinctive in part because the motors ran smoothly, unlike the beaters their own parents drove—became their cue to run and hide. It was a game that was not a game.

Outside of Jed's boundary, though, life for Myrtle Hill's children could still be idyllic. They had total freedom to explore the hill's unfenced stretches of woods and fields, to build forts and fairy houses and tend their own gardens alongside their mothers'.

For all of them it was also what Amelia later called "a working childhood." Their chores were assigned to them not just to build character (though they did) but also out of simple workforce necessity. All of them spent endless hours in the garden, weeding and filling yogurt containers with plucked-off potato beetles (a vestige of the land's former life as potato fields) and then later in the season, harvesting and helping can and freeze the vegetables that would keep them fed all winter. One of Jethro's nightly tasks was to pump the next day's water so it would be ready for breakfast and bathing in the morning. He hated this job, but as he remembered it, "There was very little arguing about chores. There was a very clear understanding that if the chore wasn't done, we would be cold, or we would be hungry."

Jethro was the only boy on the hill (and, when the men were away, often the only male). As the oldest in his family, he had more responsibilities than his two younger sisters—and even more after Hershe and Terry's relationship fell apart and Terry moved away. Hershe took to calling Jethro her "right-hand man." Though decades later when he became a father himself he would take pains to ensure that his own children wouldn't have to shoulder the same level of responsibility, it was a role that twelve-year-old Jethro took very seriously. And never more seriously than the late-spring day his mother's sheep escaped their pen and made a dash up the road—straight for Jed and Lilith's.

Loraine was in her kitchen when she looked out and saw Hershe's sheep charging up the road toward her. She knew that as soon as they passed her house and hit the gate across the road, they'd have to stop. But then she looked at the fence itself, running along the edge of the upper field and realized for the first time: even though it was barbed wire, it had been built with humans and not animals in mind. The sheep would be able to duck right under. Loraine didn't know exactly where in the woods Jed had located his crop, but she knew that if he discovered sheep rampaging across his property he would go ballistic. She dashed outside to try to head them off.

Within a few minutes Hershe appeared, followed by her children and her new boyfriend. Just as Loraine had feared, a couple of the sheep had managed to push under the wire. While Hershe rounded them up, the others tried to keep the rest from following. Hershe had just gotten the two escaped sheep back onto the road when Jed and Lilith came charging down. Lilith was holding their baby. As Hershe recalled, Jed was shouting, "If any sheep are on our property, we're going to kill them all."

Hershe, never one to back down, responded with a torrent of profanities.

Jethro was glad Loraine was there. Of all the adults, to him she always seemed like the most likely peacemaker. He knew his mother well enough to see that she was not planning to walk away from this one quietly. As Jed ducked under the fence and advanced toward her, visibly fuming, Hershe suddenly turned to Jethro. "Take your sisters and go home," she said. "Run, and don't look back." Jethro didn't need to be told twice. He grabbed his sisters' hands and took off down the road but not before he saw Jed shove Hershe, hard. As he ran, Jethro's mind raced—what exactly was he supposed to do? Would he and his sisters be safe in the house? Should they hide in the woods instead? All of them had seen it: Jed was wearing his gun. About this, there wasn't a doubt in Jethro's mind. If he heard a shot, it would mean that his mother was dead.

Up on the road, Jed had Hershe around the throat, his fingernails digging into the back of her neck. Hershe's boyfriend had
gone ahead herding the sheep, but now he ran back to intervene.
His punch sent Jed's glasses flying. Jed and Hershe toppled to
the ground still struggling. The gun fell into the dirt. Blinded,
Jed managed to hastily kick it into the bushes before Hershe
could grab it. "Lilith, Lilith, my glasses! Where are my glasses?"
he shouted.

The next thing Loraine knew, Lilith was saying "Here, Loraine, hold the baby," and thrusting the now-screaming child into
her arms.

It wasn't until much later—after the sheep were back in their
pen, after everyone had returned to their own kitchens to put
ice on their wounds; after the gun had been retrieved from the
ditch, blessedly unfired; after the terrified children had been reassured that, despite Hershe's bleeding scalp and bruised neck,
everyone was okay; after Hershe had decided that enough was
enough and Myrtle Hill was no longer a safe place to live—that
Loraine realized the irony in Lilith's gesture. Loraine and Lilith
were supposedly mortal enemies, but in the heat of the moment,
Lilith hadn't even hesitated before handing her only child into
Loraine's keeping. It was a testament to Loraine's inherent Earth
Mother steadiness, but it was also a tattered shred left from the
time when no one on Myrtle Hill would have thought twice about
entrusting one another with their children. This one last vestige
of mutual trust had revealed itself in the exact moment it was
permanently destroyed.

By that fall, Hershe and her children were living in a new
house, in another town. Jethro's sisters had spent their entire
lives in the dome—Annalei was born there—and, though they
were glad to feel safer, for them, leaving Myrtle Hill was nothing
short of traumatic.

One August afternoon the next year, a prop plane flew over Myrtle Hill, low. By then, the mid-'80s, these were common enough
that all the kids in the area knew how to identify them—I distinctly remember playing with friends over on our own hill and

all of us stopping to point and shout gleefully, "Narc plane! Narc plane!"

At two in the morning, Loraine was awoken by the sound of trucks driving up and down the road outside of her house. She did not get out of bed to look.

The next afternoon, police acting on a neighbor's tip found a pile of fresh, green marijuana plants dumped in the woods off a back road a mile from Myrtle Hill. There were nearly five hundred plants, some ten feet tall, with the roots still attached. Later the State's Attorney estimated that this pile at full maturity would have fetched over a quarter-million dollars.

The police cars swarmed up Myrtle's road a few days later. According to the officers, Jed met them as they got out of their cars in his driveway. His hands were covered in engine grease. He was not surprised to see them, he explained, because he'd seen the plane go over. "I knew you were coming," he told them.

The officers spread out. One later testified that he found a faint path leading from Jed's driveway through the woods toward a field one hundred yards away. The field had clearly been recently torn up. The officers found uprooted stalks "with roots that were shook free of soil" that they suspected were marijuana.

In their report, the officers noted the "No Trespassing" sign and the barbed wire. They also found a pressure hose buried under the driveway and attached to a bell, like the ones used at gas stations. Around the edge of the torn-up field they found strands of fishing line hung with cowbells. Nearby was a shooting target. It was "strategically located," the report noted, in such a way that one "could pretend to miss to in fact shoot people at the marijuana patch."

At the start of the search, the officers asked Jed if he had any weapons in the house. He led one of the officers to his bedroom. From the wall next to his bed, he pried free a few nails and reached into a hidden compartment behind the wall. From inside, he pulled out a bullet-proof vest, a machete, a gas mask, and a fully loaded Uzi. He disarmed the gun and handed his hardware over to the police. He stored it next to the bed, he explained, so that his toddler wouldn't find it. He needed the Uzi, he told them, to protect his family from wild animals.

The trial took place over a year later. Jed had been charged with cultivation, along with possession for the five ounces of marijuana the police had found inside his house.

In a move that would have been unthinkable years earlier—and remained, for many in the wider, local counterculture, unforgivable—three of Jed's former commune-mates agreed to testify against him. Summer came back from Texas to tell the jury how Jed had frightened her then-teenage daughter Leecia with a gun when she was walking in the woods on a visit to Myrtle; Summer's ex-husband August described a boundary dispute during which Jed had threatened him too. August was afraid of Jed's gun, he testified, but he also felt "sorrow," he said, "like I was sort of ashamed that he felt like he had to relate in this way." The third witness was Loraine.

It was around the time she agreed to testify that Loraine learned some horrifying news. She called Craig in a panic. Craig had remarried and moved to Pennsylvania to work for Rodale Inc., helping publish *Organic Gardening & Farming*. It had been a while since he'd been in touch with anyone at Myrtle. Now he asked Loraine to slow down so he could understand what she was telling him.

Because Jed faced a cultivation charge and because Vermont had adopted federal sentencing guidelines, a guilty verdict would mean that the state would seize Jed's land—except that it wasn't Jed's land, it was land owned by "Myrtle Hill Farm." The group had never been able to agree enough to formally legalize the property divisions they'd been living by all these years. If the state went ahead with the seizure, they'd take Myrtle Hill's entire property.

Craig agreed to do what he could. Establishing the land trust with its beautiful, simple, idealistic structure had been one of his proudest accomplishments. There were now hundreds of them across the country, in varying forms, and he felt like he'd helped to pioneer a radical new form of ownership. The group's original idea had been that they'd own the land together, forever. If they, collectively, decided not to live there anymore, they'd imagined, the land would simply be reabsorbed, ownerless, into the primordial earth.

But the legal system did not see it this way. The nonprofit commune was the property's owner, and therefore responsible for what happened there. Now Craig, Loraine, and the others had to hope that the State's Attorney might consider the fact that only one commune member was on trial and had, the others asserted, acted alone (Jed's defense was arguing the opposite) and that this might convince him to be lenient, even though it meant forgoing a major, federal sentencing requirement. As it was, Jed's felony charge threatened to place the land for which they'd all worked so hard into the worst place they could have imagined— the unfeeling hands of the state.

For Loraine, the dilemma was acute: a verdict of innocent would mean that she might still be living next door to a person whose volatility she'd already feared *before* she testified against him at trial; with a guilty verdict, she would likely lose her home.

The days in court were long and stressful for everyone. Making it all the more surreal for Loraine was the fact that it had been years—almost since the commune had split into nuclear families—since she had spent unbroken lengths of time with Jed. Her fear of him had been a powerful presence in her life for years, but she'd almost forgotten that he was someone she'd once known well. Now, they sat across the courtroom from each other all day.

And then, though neither LJ nor Loraine could think of it later without shuddering, each day of intense courtroom drama ended with Loraine and LJ and Jed and Lilith climbing back into their separate cars and heading home, up the same driveway, past each other's houses, two hundred yards apart in the middle of nowhere.

One afternoon, Loraine was on her way to the witness waiting room when she poked her head into a half-open door to ask the officer inside for directions. On the table was a huge pile of guns— rifles, pistols, a short machine gun. She had inadvertently walked into the evidence room. "What's this?" she asked the officer.

"This was all from your neighbor's house," he told her. She started to shake.

The trial lasted ten days. After five hours of jury deliberation, the verdict came back: guilty.

Craig had called everyone he could think of. One friend, a local Vermonter named Emory Hebbard, had been one of the impartial mediators they'd brought in to try and resolve the commune's property dispute. Now Em was the state treasurer. Craig called him. "Have you heard about what's going on at Myrtle Hill?"

"Yeah," Hebbard said, "I've heard something but I don't know the details, I'll call you back." When he called Craig back he sounded grim. "They want to attach the land. It's part of federal drug policy." There had been a lot of busts locally, and the State's Attorney was ambitious. "They want to make a case out of it," he told Craig. "They want to make an example and they're going to target these hippie communes."

"What can you do?" Craig asked him. Hebbard had found a good lawyer for them, and would do what he could higher up. "Thanks," Craig said.

It took a long time. To pay the endless legal fees, the remaining commune members agreed to raise some money by having the backwoods sections of the land logged. None of them liked it, but there didn't seem to be much choice. Even Jed, when Craig talked to him, agreed to this.

At long last, Hebbard and his colleagues prevailed. Myrtle Hill's land did not become the property of the state.

After everything they'd been through, the final decision to break the land into individually owned pieces seemed almost simple. Which isn't to say painless. Each family who had been living there, including Jed and Lilith, got the twenty acres surrounding their homes; the rest—mostly the swampy woods now torn up by logging—they kept in one piece. Craig, Amy, and Fletcher took responsibility for this section, calling it The Block.

"It was clear to me by then I was not going to live on a commune there," Craig explained later. "I didn't want to live on the land. But I wanted to keep together some sense of it." To him, the land had not lost an ounce of potential. "We thought, 'Well, maybe something else will evolve. Maybe our children will want to go back there someday.'"

But they didn't. The three of them paid taxes on the land for years until finally their spouses called a reality check: "Enough already! We're paying all this goddamn money and we never see it!"

"But I would have paid on it forever," Amy said. "It was a real wrench to let it go." Those three fields and surrounding woods had been the first place she'd ever lived where she felt perfectly safe. She hated the idea of not having a formal connection to those acres. But then she realized: Myrtle Hill, the place she'd loved, the communal family who had saved her, had already vanished. She could grieve for that loss. And then, if she still wanted the security of owning a piece of the earth, some small green place to which she could escape, "I could buy land some-place else. It didn't have to be Myrtle Hill. Myrtle Hill was gone."

Jed and Lilith had moved their family to the West Coast almost as soon as the trial ended. Jed returned to Vermont only to serve his two-year sentence. They sold their twenty acres as soon as they could and left Myrtle Hill behind forever.

When she knew at last that Jed had truly gone, his barbed wire fence pulled down and thrown away, Loraine took a walk, exploring the sections of woods and fields that had been off-lim-its to her for so long. She ended up near where she'd built her sapling-and-plastic shelter that first summer, next to the old stone wall that flanked the upper field, just behind the line of ancient maples that Jed had felled. The maples' stumps were all still there, the wood still scarred and stark. She was about to turn away when she noticed something—behind the stumps, a whole new grove of saplings had started to grow. She stared at them for a moment, then sank down and began to sob.

When she stood up again and wiped her eyes, it was with a new clarity. "That energy is gone from here now," she said out loud. "It's safe now and it's ok." She felt a wave of relief, like a sigh from the trees.

CHAPTER 21

When the 1984 election returns came in, announcing that not only had Ronald Reagan won a second term, but that he'd won in a landslide, Larry was not surprised. But the news still made him so furious he pulled the television off its shelf, carried it outside to the front deck of the dome house, and heaved it into the snowy field below. From Larry's point of view, Reagan's first term had already been devastating. He had gutted the EPA, rolling back some of the hard-won environmental regulation that had followed the first Earth Day. One of his first acts as president was to remove Jimmy Carter's solar panels from the roof of the White House. When he repealed the tax credit that supported home solar installation, our friend Topher's solar business went under immediately. Other social programs met the same fate: Hershe's community cannery lost funding and closed, as did the child health center where Judy worked. She found another job in a town thirty miles from the dome, this time as a hospice nurse, which required her to spend hours on the road each day, driving to the homes of the sick and dying.

The night Larry threw the television off the deck, he was alone in the dome. The summer before, Judy had moved out, taking my brother and me with her.

Our new apartment in town, closer to Judy's job, had flat walls with floral wallpaper and rectangular windows through which you could see straight into the house next door. When the weather turned cold, the weak, dusty heat rose out of vents in the floor. Even sitting right on top of them, you never got toasty like you would after even a few minutes near a woodstove. Living in town did have advantages—we lived walking distance from the library, and my bike went much faster on pavement than dirt roads. But other differences unnerved me. We didn't know our neighbors, but we could hear their television through the thin walls. At night, strangers' cars roared by outside, the headlights racing across the bedroom ceiling, keeping me awake.

My brother and I only lived at the dome house on the weekends now when we visited our father. When he got a teaching job in Boston, he, and soon my stepmother Sharon, a fellow academic, began commuting biweekly. At the dome, my brother and I still awoke in the morning to the creak of our father easing down the ladder from the loft bed and rattling the lids on the cookstove as he lit the day's fire. We still watched cartoons sprawled on our bellies in the dome's big triangular sunbeams. We jumped up during commercials, ran out to the woodshed in our pj's, gathered a heavy armload of split cordwood, then clomped back to the house, hooking the kitchen door open with a toe before tumbling the whole pile into the wood box and racing back to the television. We went to Quaker meeting on Sunday and pressed apples from the old orchard for cider and spent hours in the woods inventing games with our friends. But it wasn't the same. We felt our mother's absence acutely, but it was something more—not just for us, but for everyone. Some sense of urgency had lifted.

For my family, my parents' divorce marked a clear turning point in our back-to-the-land experience, but many other families underwent a similar shift around the same time for reasons of their own.

"Not every person's timetable was identical, of course," writes Eleanor Agnew in her memoir, *Back from the Land*, "but throughout the eighties a transition took place in the lives of back-to-the-landers." The apocalyptic future that had felt so near in the late '60s had not materialized. For many, the endless toil of the "simple" life stopped feeling like a solution or an antidote and started feeling like a problem itself. "Anyone who has actually tried to live in total self-sufficiency . . . knows the mind-numbing labor and loneliness and frustration and real marginless hazard that goes with the attempt," Stewart Brand admitted in 1975. "It is a kind of hysteria."

Young back-to-the-landers who had felt reassured by the "real" skills of growing their own food and building their own shelter were now also experiencing what their farm neighbors and forebears had long known: relying strictly on yourself and on the land for your livelihood puts you frighteningly at the mercy of chance. An early frost, a slipped saw blade, a hot-selling market vegetable suddenly passing out of vogue—one stroke of bad luck could be devastating. Many were shocked to discover that poverty—even romantic, "turned-on" poverty—was defined not by a lack of material possessions but by a lack of control. Mortgages and health insurance and the other systems their parents had counted on to provide stability suddenly made a lot more sense.

For a lot of people, the endless grind was simply no longer worth it. "I don't *want* to make my own Grape-Nuts or grow my own mustard seed," back-to-the-land memoirist Linda Tatelbaum declared in 1987. "I've stopped reading *Mother Earth News* and other back-to-the-land magazines that extol the 'simple life.' Call it enough to eat from your garden year 'round. Call it enough to be minimally responsible for the world's pollution. I've come to believe in compromise. I believe that conforming to anything warps a life, that keeping up with the Nearings is just another form of rat-race."

"We were tired," Agnew says. Many rural communards and homesteaders permanently returned to the cities and suburbs. Many others, notes Agnew, "remained on the land but eased back into a more traditional agenda, one jettisoned principle at a time." Before Reagan had even left office, the biggest, most widespread and radical communal and back-to-the-land movement in American history had wound to a close.

But the story does not stop there.

It's only recently, since the dawn of the 21st century, that the real impact of the 1970s back-to-the-land movement has begun to make itself known.

It's undoubtedly true that, with some notable exceptions, very few rural communards and homesteaders still live exactly according to the principles and under the conditions they set for themselves forty years ago. But this is a narrow definition of what constitutes a movement's "success."

The tendency has been to lament this shift as a failure of ideals—to see the decision by parents of young children to seek out good-paying jobs or to install phones, electricity, or bedroom doors as "jettisoning principles" and not just responding honestly to the changing needs of a changing life. It should not be shocking that people who had the option to escape a stressful, physically taxing existence into financial security and physical comfort took advantage of that option. To fault them, or anyone, for choosing a more stable life for their children holds on to a romantic idea about the "purity" of poverty.

And too: back-to-the-landers who returned to cities or suburbs did not, for the most part, fully abandon the underlying ideals that had led them to build cabins and plant gardens, even after they no longer lived in those cabins or raised their organic veggies themselves. Their time in the woods and in communes had changed them. And when they went back to Middle America, they changed it.

Every last leaf and crumb of today's $39 billion organic food industry owes its existence in part to the inexperienced, idealistic, exurbanite farmers of the 1970s, many of whom hung on through the '80s and '90s, refining their practices, organizing themselves, and developing the distribution systems that have fed today's seemingly insatiable demand for organic products.

Every YouTube DIY tutorial, user review, and open-source code owes something to the *Whole Earth Catalog*'s contention that our most powerful resource is connection to each other and access to tools.

Every mixed-greens salad; every supermarket carton of soy milk; every diverse, stinky plate of domestic cheese; every farm-to-table restaurant, locavore food blog, and artisanal microbrew has a direct ancestry in the 1970s' countercuisine.

They may have been wrong about the timing of the apocalypse, but the '60s' counterculture was right to worry about the destructive limits of fossil fuels and the need to develop alternative energy. One researcher in the 1990s found that the level of environmental activism among back-to-the-landers was four times that of the general population. Some worked toward conservation efforts in their own, newly chosen rural homes, while others spent decades tinkering with and refining their alternative energy designs. Others rose to positions of environmental leadership in the nation, setting policy or agitating from the outside—the urgency with which they'd once responded to a nuclear threat now focused instead on combatting climate change.

Due in part to the slow, steady presence of this environmental leadership, the public's demand for green innovations have pressured even huge corporations to get involved. Who, even in the '90s, would have imagined the early-21st-century reality of compost bins at Yankee Stadium? Or organic food on the menu at McDonald's? Or solar panels on the roof of Walmart?

The internal, generational confidence that had allowed so many of America's privileged young people to risk an unknown future by going back to the land had proven correct—in "dropping out" and "getting back," they had not forfeited their place as inheritors of the earth. But by rejoining the mainstream, bringing this newfound experience, skills, and perspective with them, many of them helped to bend the mainstream in their own direction.

And it's not at all clear that the majority of back-to-the-landers even left their newfound homes. Many of the rural counties that saw a surge in the 1970s did not see a corresponding decline a decade later, even as demographic statistics nationwide trended back toward urbanization.

In the back-to-the-land community of my own upbringing, I notice this: forty years later, almost everyone is still there, living lives much closer to their '70s incarnation than to the conventional American middle-class lives they'd left.

*

In our Quaker/workday community, my parents' friends spent the next decades commuting from their professional jobs as teachers, nurses, and social workers to the remote hayfields where they continued to plant huge organic gardens and build and repair their eccentric houses. Those houses all have indoor plumbing, phones, electricity, and high-speed internet now, but every family whose house we helped build during those Saturday workdays is still living in them today.

After the demise of his solar business, Topher got a job teaching science at a local, alternative private school. For over a decade, he taught students to build solar cars that they entered in a national race, the Tour de Sol; one year his middle schoolers placed second, after MIT. Several of his students went on to become scientists and engineers. Topher and Marie have spent the last twenty years building, by themselves, a gorgeous full-sized house next to their tiny cabin. It's only recently, thanks to Vermont's new solar energy policy, that Topher's hand-built panels have reduced their electricity bill to zero. Marie recently retired from her job as a state social worker. Their daughter, Sarah, is the executive director of a Vermont nonprofit called The Center for an Agricultural Economy, which offers, in part, an industrial processing kitchen—an updated, professional version of Hershe's community cannery—for use by the region's thriving number of small farms and food businesses. Her brother, Tim, is a professor of ecology.

Nash and Mariel, our closest neighbors through the woods, continued working on their beautiful, turreted house and commuting to their jobs as a guidance counselor and nurse practitioner, respectively. When Nash passed away in 2011, Loraine sang a song at his memorial. Mariel still lives in the house and tends her large, organic garden, aided by her daughters Reeve, a teacher, and Kit, a chef specializing in local, seasonal, farm-to-table cuisine.

Our other neighbor, Nick, still lives in the same valley, in a bigger house near his cabin. For years he has been a member of the volunteer fire department and an EMT. He has spent the last forty years working for himself as a logger and now, in his 70s, he is saving up money to retire.

His friend Charlie Barrows, the banker-selectman, passed away recently. Lois still lives in her historic brick house in town. Toward the end of his life, Charlie noted that at Town Meeting, you could no longer tell the difference between the locals and the newcomers—the locals might have long hair and the hippies no longer dressed quite so eccentrically. Nick, Nash, and Topher all served on the select board at various times, and Nick has been the town moderator for many years.

Hershe too, served on her town's select board, the first woman ever to do so. She still lives on the 72-acre farm where she moved with Jethro and his sisters after fleeing Myrtle Hill. She has since remarried, to a man from a Vermont dairy farming family. Her home is equipped with a professional-grade food processing center and every year, she cans hundreds of pounds of produce—tomatoes, strawberries, beans—from her immense organic gardens and orchards. Recently, she began raising organic raspberries for a local company that produces artisanal fruit liquors.

Pancake, after he left Myrtle Hill, settled back in Connecticut. He eventually remarried and spent a long career teaching and working with at-risk kids.

When Jethro was a teenager, at the urging of his grandmother, Pancake's mother, he attended boarding school on a scholarship. At UVM, he became a debate champion and went on to coach Cornell's policy debate team to a top ten national ranking. When his children were born, he found that the coaching job interfered too much with his family life, so he left academia in favor of returning to Vermont. He and his wife and three kids now live a few miles from Myrtle Hill. Aided by his sister Annalei, a graphic designer, Jethro runs a successful web design business. As he puts it, "I work with people all over the world, but I get to live here." Of Hershe's six grandchildren, five were born at home.

Dennis and Peggy Day still live at Entropy Acres, and Dennis still works as a blacksmith and farrier. He has served the town as a lister for several decades, as well as working on the ski patrol of a local mountain. Peggy Day wrote for Chris and

Ellen's newspaper for many years and, in addition to running her wreath business, is now the director of the county history museum. Their oldest daughter teaches English in a nearby town; their younger two are currently living in Maui.

When Dennis and Peggy Day offered to buy Entropy Acres from Peg and Eliot, Peg was glad to know the farm would be in good hands. After leaving Vermont, Peg developed a career in counseling, organizational consulting, and journalism. Since retiring, she has become active on the board of her local food co-op. She still makes her own yogurt now and then, but she finds she can get excellent goat cheese at Trader Joe's. She and her husband, an environmentalist and cabinetmaker, live in rural New York State in an old farmhouse they've painstakingly restored and where she cultivates a big organic garden. They just finished building a solar-heated outdoor hot tub. Peg's son lives in a state that recently legalized recreational marijuana; he obtained a growers' license and is currently struggling with the many challenges of becoming a farmer.

While still living at Entropy Acres, Eliot had an experience that turned out to shape the rest of his life. One of the goats fell ill with an ailment that the vet was certain would prove fatal. Eliot decided to try a cure he'd found in one of his books: "the raw juice of cucumbers, squeezed into the eyes." The remedy worked and the goat survived. For Eliot, the experience of successfully using plants for healing proved transformative. After leaving Vermont, he studied acupuncture and Classical Chinese Medicine; in the mid-1980s, according to his website, "he was initiated as a medicine man" in the shamanistic tradition of the Huichol people of the Sierra Madres in Mexico. Now he runs a retreat center in the Catskills where he teaches a practice he calls Plant Spirit Medicine.

Craig spent most of his career as a magazine publishing executive at values-driven companies. He worked at Gardenway and Rodale Inc., helped start *Harrowsmith* and *Eating Well*, and served as the publisher of the *Utne Reader*. He and his wife of thirty-six years, Patricia, live in Minneapolis and now run an executive leadership program aimed at helping groups and corporations communicate and collaborate. He recently got back in touch with his friend Cro, from Franklin, and they now talk almost every day.

Craig and Amy also remain very close. After leaving Vermont, Amy spent twenty-five years running a catering company that specialized in artisanal, "healthy gourmet" cuisine. In her late thirties, she earned a master's in English literature from the University of Sussex in England. She is now the global director for an international nonprofit, where she works to help people form meaningful communities through online mediums. She and her husband live in Northern California, where they see Fletcher regularly.

Both Fletcher and Nancy settled in California. Nancy remarried and worked for many years in a local cannery. Today, she and her husband drive an electric car, belong to their local CSA, and recently installed solar panels on their roof. Now retired, Nancy makes art full-time. In her paintings, she incorporates materials that would otherwise go to landfills, a process directly inspired by the "art from nothing" approach of Drop City.

Fletcher—no longer looking like Woody Allen, with a silver beard so long he wears it braided—spent several decades selling his homemade jewelry on Telegraph Avenue in Berkeley. More recently, he taught digital art to college students before retiring to focus on his own photography. Through his wife, Barbara, he is also now the brother-in-law of Drop City's John Curl.

Once or twice over the last few decades, Jim the Bear has dropped in on Fletcher or Nancy, unannounced, before disappearing again. The last they heard, he was still living free in Mexico.

Rahula has also settled in the Bay Area. She has spent her whole adult life as an activist, most recently as a mediator and facilitator in an antiracism organization. In 1999, when she was twenty-seven, she spent six months in jail for pelting the mayor of San Francisco in the face with a pie. Until very recently, she lived exclusively in collective houses; when her daughter was born, Rahula's whole household was with her and her partner in the hospital birthing room.

Rahula's sister Amelia also lives in California. She and her husband own a small homestead farm near Santa Cruz, where they raise vegetables and eggs. Amelia recently fitted her pickup truck with a solar-powered coffee roaster that she drives to farmer's markets. An award-winning beer maker, she recently published her first book, *Sustainable Homebrewing: An All-Organic Approach to Crafting Great Beer.*

Rahula and Amelia's two younger half-sisters, who were born after the end of the communal era, have chosen more conventional careers. Rose went to Harvard and is now a veterinarian in Los Angeles; her sister Jessie is a surgeon.

When they visit their father, LJ, they visit him at Myrtle Hill. LJ has spent the past several decades driving trucks and construction equipment for a local contracting company. His and Loraine's marriage didn't survive the stress brought on by the trial and by the demise of Myrtle Hill; they divorced in the late 1980s. LJ has since remarried. His wife, Theresa, is the daughter of the farmer whose land my parents and their friends bought, with whom we shared a party line for years.

LJ's cabin—now a roomy, open house, which he continues to improve—is one of the last buildings left from Myrtle Hill's communal era. The Big House sat unoccupied for years until it finally became dangerous and had to be knocked down; after Hershe left, the dome suffered vandalism and also never recovered.

The house built by Summer's ex-husband August still stands back in the woods behind LJ's, and Leecia and her family spend a lot of time there. Summer, retired from a long career as a librarian, now splits her time between Vermont and her native Texas. She is still politically radical and still ferociously antibourgeois.

The only other house left from the Myrtle Hill era is Jed and Lilith's. After passing through several owners, the house sat empty for years. Very recently, it was bought by a couple from the city who are fixing it up.

In the years after the trial, freed from the fear she'd lived with for so long—her whole life, really—Loraine felt her confidence continue to grow. She went back to school, earning a degree through one of the distance-learning programs my father Larry had helped design. She also became certified in conflict mediation—a skill set she wished she'd acquired years earlier.

Though recently she has begun working with troubled youth through the local justice center, most of Loraine's career continued to be centered around food, as a caterer and cook.

As she's gotten older, Loraine has lost a lot of height to osteoporosis, which she treats by drinking organic eggshells dissolved in lemon juice. Now when she goes on long herb-collecting walks, she takes along two ski poles for balance. She has never stopped honing her herbalist skills or asking what happened to her first teacher, the mysterious Herb Mary—recently a friend told her about a plant nursery on the other side of the state, run by a British woman called Mary. Loraine lives alone, but she talks to Hershe and Summer almost every day. Her brother, who came home from Vietnam into a counterculture life not unlike Loraine's, is now a licensed marijuana grower in Washington State; he is finding it difficult and expensive to keep up with all the regulation. Loraine still writes songs and plays them on her Martin guitar—no longer shy, she performs whenever she feels moved. Recently, she wrote a new song for her friend Bernie Sanders's presidential campaign. She plans to record it on video and have Jethro help her post it to YouTube.

Judy still lives in the town where she moved with my brother and me after leaving the dome. In the late '80s, she left her hospice job and became a school nurse. The house she bought in town—the second home she'd owned as an adult, but the first she had not built herself—came with an above-ground pool, which she immediately removed and replaced with an organic garden. She installed a woodstove in the living room and filled the back pantry with canning jars of homemade pickles and applesauce.

When my brother and I were in high school, she would come watch us play sports, slipping away from the lacrosse field at halftime to walk the short distance over to the now-overgrown lot where Hatch's Natural Foods had once stood. David Hatch died of cancer suddenly in 1976—his friend Ram Dass delivered his memorial eulogy—and the house burned down not long after. But twenty years later, Judy could still find the remains of Ira Hatch's organic gardens. She gathered the hardy perennials—comfrey, lovage—that still thrived among the weeds. For all her other whole-foods ingredients, she could now shop at the co-op or the natural food store or the farmer's market.

Larry and his wife Sharon commuted between Boston and Vermont for more than a decade. When my brother graduated from high school, they moved to Whidbey Island, near Seattle, to help found an institute dedicated to promoting environmental leadership, located on the site of a 19th-century homestead farm-turned 1970s' intentional community-turned retreat center. Since Larry retired, he has dedicated himself fully to climate change activism. He has also returned to Vermont, to the dome house.

Last summer, my brother Todd and I, with our families, were visiting our dad and stepmother at the dome.

My brother lives in Montpelier in an old farmhouse on four acres just outside of town. He and his wife heat with wood and keep chickens and have a big organic garden; their electricity now mostly comes from the solar panels on their roof. Todd can ride his bike into the capital where he is assistant attorney general. Susie was born in Brooklyn but fell in love with farming— she is now director of UVM's Farmer Training Program, where every year she receives more and more applications from young people hoping to one day run their own small farms.

That afternoon at the dome, we sat outside on the deck, holding glasses of sweet, amber wine—apple, Larry's own, one of the last, dusty bottles from the cellar. The view remained almost unchanged from forty years before—the long, sloping, tree-bordered meadow; the perfectly round hills, with their tidy green fields; the White Mountains in the distance. But a few things had changed. The forty-foot spruce that had grown plentifully enough to supply my parents with a house had started to tumble and be replaced by birch and maple, the next species in the steady churn of forest succession. More dramatically, to the east, the hills in the distance now sport a line of huge, energy-producing windmills.

Watching my children and my brother's chase each other through the field below, I suddenly thought of a story Larry had told me.

*

One morning in the mid '70s, he was driving from the dome to his job in Montpelier when he passed a long-haired hitchhiker and decided to pick him up. They started chatting on the long drive. The man was coming from Myrtle Hill. The group was no longer living together, the man explained. "I'm sorry the commune failed," Larry said. "It was an interesting experiment."

The man responded immediately. "It wasn't a failure," he said. "We learned a lot of things and it's going to go on and evolve and continue and become something different than it was, but we always knew that would happen." Larry was listening. "There's no such thing as failure," the man said. "Just because we didn't end up with what we thought we were going to end up with doesn't mean we ended up with nothing. We ended up with something else. Which is also beautiful."

Notes

This book contains no composite characters or locations. The chronology of events appears as accurately as possible, drawing from documented sources and individuals' recollections. For specific scenes, I gathered details from as many participants as I could, as well as from newspaper articles, videos, photographs, and other sources. All dialogue or thoughts that appear in quotation marks are rendered verbatim as related to me by the speaker or someone present at the time, or as reflected in letters, transcripts, or other written materials; for more general insights and reflections, I have used paraphrase. Where appropriate, I used a character's commune name in lieu of their given name. A few names have been changed to protect privacy, including the name of the commune.

Chapter 1

4 **There's a definite panic on the hip scene in Cambridge:** Raymond Mungo, *Total Loss Farm: A Year in the Life* (New York: E. P. Dutton, 1970), 22.

5 **a million young Americans:** This number comes from Terry A. Simmons, "But We Must Cultivate Our Garden: Twentieth-Century Pioneering in Rural British Columbia" (PhD diss., University of Minnesota, 1979), cited in Jeffrey Jacob, *New Pioneers: The Back-to-the-Land Movement and the Search for a Sustainable Future* (University Park, PA: The Pennsylvania State University Press, 1997). Historian Dona Brown notes that Simmons's figure was "extrapolated from a small area in British Columbia . . . an excellent scholarly study, but hardly adequate to the task of calculating an entire continent's efforts," Brown, *Back to the Land: The Enduring Dream of Self-Sufficiency in Modern America* (Madison, WI: University of Wisconsin Press, 2011). To date, the actual number of back-to-the-landers in this period

remains unclear, especially since many scholars interested in historic rural simplicity movements tend to emphasize only the single-family, homesteading iteration of the 1970s' back-to-the-land movement, ignoring or overlooking its important, influential, communal manifestation.

6 **Writing in 1968:** Kenneth Keniston, *Youth and Dissent: The Rise of a New Opposition* (New York: Harcourt Brace Jovanovich, 1971), 252.

6 **The feeling—to be very Superkids!:** Tom Wolfe, *The Electric Kool-Aid Acid Test* (New York: Farrar, Straus & Giroux, 1968), 39.

6 **But parents who'd lived:** For a thoughtful treatment of the 1950s' potent combination of affluence and fear, see Todd Gitlin, *The Sixties: Years of Hope, Days of Rage* (New York: Bantam Books, 1987), chap. 1.

7 **Our work is guided by the sense:** "'The Port Huron Statement,' 1962," in *Takin' it to the Streets: A Sixties Reader*, Alexander Bloom and Wini Breines, eds. (New York: Oxford University Press, 1995), 50.

7 **The Bomb had receded:** Gitlin, *The Sixties*, 220.

7 **Never before have so many:** Keniston, *Youth and Dissent*, ix.

7 **When I left the city I felt:** Elaine Sundancer, *Celery Wine: The Story of a Country Commune* (Yellow Springs, OH: Community Publications Cooperative, 1973), 167.

7 **The move to the country is a doomsday decision:** Mark Kramer, *Mother Walter and the Pig Tragedy* (New York: Alfred A. Knopf, 1972), 7.

7 **It turns out that a farm with friends:** Kramer, *Mother Walter*, 5.

8 **The 1970s remain the only moment:** Jacob, *New Pioneers*, 21.

8 **Only afterward was it called a movement:** Robert Houriet, *Getting Back Together* (New York: Avon Books, 1972), 9.

8 **The HIP Merchants:** Chester Anderson, "Uncle Tim$ Children" (broadside, 4/16/1967), in Kristine McKenna and David Hollander, *Notes from a Revolution: Com/Co, The Diggers & the Haight* (Foggy NotionBooks, 2012), 161.

9 **a number of older hands realized:** Peter Coyote, *Sleeping Where I Fall: A Chronicle* (Washington, DC: Counterpoint, 1998), 80.

9 **its most widely read issue:** Jean-François Bizot, *200 Trips from the Counterculture: Graphics and Stories from the Underground Press Syndicate* (London: Thames & Hudson, 2006), 229.

9 **The main message:** "Interview with Timothy Leary," *San Francisco Oracle*, "Politics of Ecstasy" (October 1967), 26.

9 **mass upsurge of nationwide interest:** Richard Fairfield, *Communes USA: A Personal Tour* (Baltimore, MD: Penguin Books, 1972), 284.

9 **By one contemporary count:** Hugh Gardner, *The Children of Prosperity: Thirteen Modern American Communes* (New York: St. Martin's Press, 1978), 7.

9 **as many as ten thousand:** Judson Jerome, cited in Gardner, *Children of Prosperity*, 7; Gardner finds this number high and puts the figure closer to 3,000 in 1970, with several thousand more arriving in the next few years. Again, hard figures prove incredibly difficult to come by for scholars of all eras. As Timothy Miller puts it: "How many communes existed during the 1960s era? Thousands, probably tens of thousands. How many people lived in them, at least briefly? Tens of thousands, conceivably a million. Could you please be more precise? No, I can't." Miller, *The 60s Communes: Hippies and Beyond* (Syracuse, NY: Syracuse University Press, 1999), xviii.

9 **on kicking off the biggest:** Gardner, *Children of Prosperity*, 249.

9 **Not since the fall of Babylon:** Richard W. Langer, *Grow It! The Beginner's Complete in-Harmony-with-Nature Small Farm Guide* (New York: Avon Books, 1972), xi, in Brown, *Back to the Land*, 208.

10 **immediately sold fifty thousand copies:** Brown, *Back to the Land*, 205.

Additional sources: Theodore Roszak, *The Making of a Counterculture: Reflections on the Technocratic Society and its Youthful Opposition* (Berkeley, CA: University of California Press, 1968); Charles A. Reich, *The Greening of America* (New York: Random House, 1970); Philip Slater, *The Pursuit of Loneliness: American Culture at the Breaking Point* (Boston: Beacon Press, 1970); Timothy Miller, *The Hippies and American Values* (Knoxville, TN: University of Tennessee Press, 2011); *Imagine Nation: The American Counterculture of the 1960s and '70s*, Peter Braunstein and Michael William Doyle, eds. (New York: Routledge, 2002); Raymond Mungo, *Famous Long Ago: My Life and Hard Times with Liberation News Service* (Boston: Beacon Press, 1970); Annalei McGreevy, "Persistence of Communal Living" (BA Thesis, Environmental Studies; University of Vermont, 2000).

Chapter 2

11 **find their soul in their automobile:** Herbert Marcuse, *One Dimensional Man* (London: Sphere Books, 1968), 9.

18 **You've had this idea too, right?:** Stewart Brand, "Earth People's Park," *Whole Earth Catalog*, January 1970, 28–29.

19 **The rap that rang truest:** Hugh Romney, *The Hog Farm and Friends, By Wavy Gravy as told to Hugh Romney and Vice Versa* (New York: Links, 1974), 107.

20 **breathe pure air:** "Mood Is Joyful as City Gives Its Support: Millions Join Earth Day," *New York Times* (April 23, 1970), 1.

20 **On the evening news:** *CBS Evening News* (April 22, 1970), http://www.youtube.com/watch?v=nEmARFci__I.

Chapter 3

36 **I went to the woods; I say, beware; In proportion:** Henry David Thoreau, *Walden, Or, Life in the Woods* (1854).

37 **securing the greatest degrees; how to make the getting:** David E. Shi, *The Simple Life: Plain Living and High Thinking in American Culture* (New York: Oxford University Press, 1985), 142–143.

38 **simplicity and clear perception:** Shi, *Simple Life*, 140.

38 **Our objects:** "George Ripley to R.W. Emerson" (November 9, 1840), in *In Search of the Simple Life*, David E. Shi, ed. (Salt Lake City, UT: Peregrine Smith Books, 1986), 151.

39 **great-aunt of Buckminster:** Fred Turner, *From Counterculture to Cyberculture: Stewart Brand, the Whole Earth Network, and the Rise of Digital Utopianism* (Chicago: The University of Chicago Press, 2006), 55.

39 **I had rather keep:** Shi, *Simple Life*, 144.

39 **This morning I have done wonders, etc:** Shi, *In Search*, 156.

39 **were happy:** Shi, *In Search*, 155.

40 **parental protest:** Geraldine Brooks, "Orpheus at the Plough," *The New Yorker* (January 10, 2005), 62.

40 **insufficiently ideal:** Shi, *In Search*, 159.

40 **miserable, joyous, frivolous manner:** in Brooks, "Orpheus," 63.

40 **interesting and deep-searching conversation:** Shi, *In Search*, 160.

40 **Neither coffee, tea, molasses, nor rice:** Charles Lane, in "Fruitlands," accessed November 2, 2015, http://www.alcott.net /frame.html.

41 **sported an enormous beard:** "Fruitlands."

41–42 **I only took a little bit; Are there any beasts; With the first frosts:** Louisa May Alcott, "Transcendental Wild Oats," *The Independent* (December 18, 1873).

42 **They look well in July; I hate her:** Brooks, "Orpheus," 64.

42 **were so busy discussing; are always feeling of their shoulders; Miss Page made a good remark:** Shi, *Simple Life*, 137–138.

43 **put their life back together:** As Brooks tells it, the Alcotts succeeded: "Back in Concord by 1844, Bronson renovated a house that had been literally a pigsty and turned it into the cozy retreat, Hillside, that Louisa May would lovingly describe in *Little Women*" ("Orpheus," 64).

43 **To live for one's principles:** Alcott, "Wild Oats."

Chapter 4

48 Sources for Drop City (here and throughout): Peter Rabbit, *Drop City* (The Olympia Press, 1971); *Drop City* (documentary, 2012), dir. Joan Grossman, 82 min.; John Curl, *Memories of Drop City: The First Hippie Commune of the 1960s and the Summer of Love* (iUniverse, Inc., 2006); Mark Matthews, *Droppers: America's First Hippie Commune, Drop City* (University of Oklahoma Press, 2010); Alastair Gordon, *Spaced Out: Crash Pads, Hippie Communes, Infinity Machines, and Other Radical Environments of the Psychedelic Sixties* (New York: Rizzoli, 2008); correspondence with Gene Bernofsky and Tom McCourt; Miller, *The 60s Communes*; Fairfield, *Communes USA*; Gardner, *Children of Prosperity*.

49 **It was extremely exciting:** *Drop City* (documentary).

51 **It was dangerous:** Rabbit, *Drop City*, 44.

52 **Angular, unearthly, demented:** William Hedgepeth and Dennis Stock, *The Alternative* (New York: Collier Books, 1970), 153.

52 **Seeing Drop City:** Gordon, *Spaced Out*, 178.

55 **Blissful state of positive paranoia:** Gardner, *Children of Prosperity*, 243.

Chapter 5

Sources for People's Park: *Berkeley in the 60s* (documentary, 1990), dir. Mark Kitchell, 117 min.; Bloom and Breines, *Takin' it*; Gitlin, *The Sixties*.

61 **Your people ripped off the land:** Frank Bardacke, "Who Owns the Park?" (broadside, 1969), reprinted in Bloom and Breines, *Takin' it*, 473.

61 **We're using the land:** *Berkeley in the 60s* (documentary).

62 **Work on the Park was joy:** Gitlin, *The Sixties*, 355.

62 **The Park was a little island:** Denise Levertov, "Human Values and People's Park," in Bloom and Breines, *Takin' it*, 474.

62 **A way of saying, 'If we had control':** *Berkeley in the 60s* (documentary).

62 **Following in the protest style:** "That was the definitive movement style, squarely in the American grain, harking back to Thoreau's idea of civil disobedience, to the utopian communards' idea of establishing the good society right here and now—but also to the pragmatists' insistence that experience is the measure of knowledge, and the do-it-yourselfers' (and entrepreneurs'!) belief in getting down to business" (Gitlin, *The Sixties*, 85).

63 **In a down-to-earth way:** *Berkeley in the 60s* (documentary).

63 **The Park has brought:** John Oliver Simon, "The Meaning of People's Park," in *Takin' it*, 648.

63 **The park issue is not the issue; Don't you simply explain:** *Berkeley in the 60s* (documentary).

64 **Communist sympathizers:** Seth Rosenfeld, "The Governor's Race," *San Francisco Chronicle* (June 9, 2002).

64 **Amid rampant disbelief:** Gitlin, *The Sixties*, 357.

64 **400 other protestors:** Tim Findley, "I Was a Prisoner at Santa Rita," *San Francisco Chronicle* (May 24, 1969).

65 **We're going to be shot at:** *Berkeley in the 60s* (documentary).

65 **reports revealed that Reagan:** Gitlin, *The Sixties*, 358.

66 **People's Park ended the movement:** Gitlin, *The Sixties*, 361.

67 **What we have in mind:** *Woodstock* (documentary, 1970), dir. Michael Wadleigh, 184 min.

Chapter 6

73 **A 1975 *New York Times* article:** Roy Reed, "Rural Population Gains Now Outstrip Urban Areas," *New York Times* (May 18, 1975).

73 **Communal societies:** Miller, *The 60s Communes*, xiii.

Sources for utopian communal experiments of the past: Charles Nordhoff, *The Communistic Societies of the United States* (New York: Harper & Bros., 1875); Mark Holloway, *Heavens on Earth: Utopian Communities in America 1680-1880* (New York: Dover Publications, 1966); Arthur Bestor, *Backwoods Utopias* (Philadelphia, PA: University of Pennsylvania Press, 1970).

74 **In a period of just a few years:** Miller, *The 60s Communes*, xiii.

74 **sense of common purpose:** Miller, *The 60s Communes*, xxii.

74 **At least twice as many:** Gardner, *Children of Prosperity*, 3.

75 **A number of scholars give credit:** Benjamin David Zablocki, *The Joyful Community: An Account of the Bruderhof, A Communal Movement Now in its Third Generation* (Baltimore, MD: Penguin, 1971), 300; Gardner, *Children of Prosperity*; Miller, *The 60s Communes*.

75 **urban communes numbered in the thousands:** Zablocki, *Joyful Community*, 300.

75 **fifty communes in Vermont:** Houriet, *Getting Back Together*, 390; Miller, *The 60s Communes*, xix.

75 **Hippy groups a few country miles apart:** Houriet, *Getting Back Together*, 8.

Sources for Johnson's Pasture fire: "Four Die in Guilford Blaze," *Brattleboro Daily Reformer* (April 17, 1970); "Guilford Hippie Colony Swept by Fire; Four Dead," *Rutland Herald* (April 17, 1970); "Scene of Tragedy"; Grady Holloway, "Hush Pervades Stricken Colony," *Brattleboro Daily Reformer* (April 18, 1970); George Spangler, "Fire Sweeps Commune, 4 Die," *Burlington Free Press* (April 18, 1970); Norman Runnion, "Pasture Normal Again," *Brattleboro Daily Reformer* (April 24, 1970); "Commune Victims Idents Confirmed," *Brattleboro Daily Reformer* (April 28, 1970).

81 **Would they come home with us:** Mungo, *Total Loss Farm*, 140; Andrew Kopkind writes that a "leaky stovepipe" led to the fire, but contemporary news reports and eyewitness accounts point to a kicked-over lantern or candle (Kopkind, "Up the Country: Five Communes in Vermont," *Working Papers for a New Society* 1, no. 1 (1973): 44–49).

Chapter 7

Sources for The Farm: Stephen Gaskin, *Hey Beatnik! This is the Farm Book* (Summertown, TN: Book Publishing Co., 1974); *Birth Story: Ina May Gaskin & The Farm Midwives* (documentary, 2012), dirs. Sara Lamm and Mary Wigmore, 95 min.; http://thefarmmidwives.org/our-history/; Miller, *The 60s Communes*.

Sources for Short Mountain, Radical Faeries, women's land collectives: Alex Halberstadt, "Out of the Woods," *New York Times Magazine*, 8/6/15; Heather Jo Burmeister. "Rural Revolution: Documenting the Lesbian Land Communities of Southern Oregon," MA Thesis, History, Portland State University, 2013; Scott Herring, *Another Country: Queer Anti-Urbanism* (New York University Press, 2010).

Sources for Morningstar and Wheeler's Ranch: The richest, most detailed source on the two communes is written by many of the communards themselves (in particular, Ramon Sender, Bill Wheeler, Gwen Leeds, and Near Morningstar): *Home Free Home: A History of Two Open-Door California Communes*, accessed April 25, 2013, http://www.diggers.org/homefree/hfh_int.html; Ian A. Boal, Janferie Stone, Michael Watts, and Cal Winslow, eds., *West of Eden: Communes and Utopia in Northern California* (Oakland, CA: PM Press, 2012); Miller, *The 60s Communes*; Fairfield, *Communes USA*; Gardner, *Children of Prosperity*; Gordon, *Spaced Out*; Houriet, *Getting Back Together.*

91 **Stewart was talking about having a 'back-forty':** *Home Free Home*, chap. 1.

91 **Sender was an avant-garde composer:** details about Sender's biography in *Home Free Home*, chap. 2; also Miller, *The 60s Communes*, 12.

93 **the manifestation of all mother-love:** *Home Free Home*, chap. 2.

93 **Could we send a detachment up to take care of the orchard:** *Home Free Home*, chap. 3.

93 **The Diggers are starting up a farm:** "The Diggers Do Not Sell" (broadside, 3/3/1967), in McKenna and Hollander, "*Notes*," 156.

93 **a two-column, handwritten wish list:** "Digger Farm Needs" (broadside, 1967), in McKenna and Hollander, "*Notes*," 154.

94 **The new-found trip of work and responsibility; Morning Star Diggers will swap work and organic vegetables for what have you; I was charmed:** *Home Free Home*, chap. 3.

94 **One sociologist found that 70 percent:** Lewis Yablonsky, *The Hippie Trip* (New York: Pegasus, 1968), 26.

95 **Lou, there aren't any black people here:** *Home Free Home*, chap. 2.

95 **Morningstar is remedy; suffering from various degrees of urban sickness:** Houriet, *Getting Back Together*, 168.

95 **Society's problems were coming:** *Home Free Home*, chap. 3.

96 **Open land means simply that God is the sole owner:** Fairfield, *Communes USA*, 242.

96 **Shitting in the garden:** Houriet, *Getting Back Together*, 139.

97 **Please don't come up to Morning Star:** *Home Free Home*, chap. 5.

97 **the wandering hippie girl:** *Home Free Home*, chap. 4; Miller, *The 60s Communes*, 220.

97 **Grow your hair long and don't take a bath:** *Home Free Home*, chap. 6.

97 **Lou Gottlieb was formally served:** *Home Free Home*, chap. 4.

97 **If you can find any traces of 'organization' here:** Gardner, *Children of Prosperity*, 134.

98 **The county officials were patient:** *Home Free Home*, chap. 4.

98 **five times the originally-estimated cost:** *Home Free Home*, chap. 17.

98 **He owed her for damages:** Miller, *The 60s Communes*, 51.

99 **Whatever the nature of the Divine:** Miller, *The 60s Communes*, 55.

99 **There will be no more Morningstars:** *Home Free Home*, chap. 9.

99 **Why don't you open your land?; I never closed it:** Boal et al., *West of Eden*, 132.

99 **I wanted a place in history:** Miller, *The 60s Communes*, 51.

Sources on Morningstar East/Reality Construction Company: Fairfield, *Communes USA*; Gardner, *Children of Prosperity*; Houriet, *Getting Back Together*; Hedgepeth and Stock, *The Alternative*.

102 **mystics, winos, runaways, and hermits; nowhere had I found such diametrically different communes:** Houriet, *Getting Back Together*, 195.

103 **When we don't have any gas to get out:** Houriet, *Getting Back Together*, 198.

Sources on New Buffalo: Fairfield, *Communes USA*; Gardner, *Children of Prosperity*; Rabbit, *Drop City*; Arthur Kopecky, *New Buffalo: Journals from a Taos Commune* (Albuquerque, NM: University of New Mexico Press, 2004); Robbie Gordon, interview; Robert Houriet happened to be present for an important turning point at New Buffalo, dramatically captured in his book, *Getting Back Together*.

104 **How can you get any further from white middle-class America:** Houriet, *Getting Back Together*, 169.

105 **one chapter in a long history of white Americans:** Philip Deloria, "Counterculture Indians and the New Age," in Braunstein and Doyle, *Imagine Nation*, 159; also Deloria, *Playing Indian* (New Haven, CT: Yale University Press, 1999).

105 **They're city kids:** *Easy Rider* (1969), dir. Dennis Hopper (95 mins.).

Sources for Libre: Roberta Price, *Huerfano: A Memoir of Life in the Counterculture* (Amherst, MA: University of Massachusetts Press, 2006); Rabbit, *Drop City*; Houriet, *Getting Back Together*; Fairfield, *Communes USA*; Miller, *The 60s Communes*; Coyote, *Sleeping Where I Fall*.

106 **Drop City was continually overcrowded:** Rabbit, *Drop City*, 147.

106 **four-fused exploded rhombic dodecahedron:** Houriet, *Getting Back Together*, 236.

Chapter 9

Sources for Hatch's: Jack Cook, "By the Bag, Barrel or Ounce," *Blair & Ketchum's Country Journal*, January 1976, 58–63 Carol Maurer, "On the Trail of Lost Granola," *Vermont Life*, Winter 2001, 83–86; William Shurtleff and Akiko Aoyagi, *History of Erewhon—Natural Foods Pioneer in the United States (1966–2011)*, http://www.soyinfocenter.com/books/142.

Sources for Howard and Rodale: Andrew N. Case, "Looking for Organic America: J.I. Rodale, the Rodale Press, and the Popular Culture of Environmentalism in the Postwar United States" (PhD diss., University of Wisconsin, 2012); Warren J. Belasco, *Appetite for Change: How the Counterculture Took on the Food Industry* (Ithaca, NY: Cornell University Press, 1989); Samuel Fromartz, *Organic, Inc: Natural Foods and How They Grew* (Orlando, FL: Harcourt, 2006).

128 **The impact on me was terrific!:** Case, *Looking for Organic America*, 34.

129 **They are the hippies, the student rebels:** Robert Rodale, "The New 'Back to the Land' Movement," *Organic Gardening and Farming* (September 1969), 21, in Case, *Looking for Organic America*, 285.

129 **The circulation of Organic Gardening and Farming:** Case, *Looking for Organic America*, 258, 300.

129 **unless he was run down by a sugar-crazed cab driver:** Case, *Looking for Organic America*; Dick Cavett, "When That Guy Died on My Show," *New York Times Opinionator*, May 3, 2007.

132 **The potato crop, such as it was:** Chris Braithwaite, "If I'm a Nutty Food Faddist, Then You're a Sickly Half-Poisoned Victim of the Agro-Chemical Complex," *The Globe Magazine*, ca. 1970, 10–13

134 **You don't need to know that much:** in Gordon, *Spaced Out*, 178.

Sources for Brand and the *Whole Earth Catalog*: Turner, *From Counterculture to Cyberculture*; Andrew G. Kirk, *Counterculture Green: The Whole Earth Catalog and American Environmentalism* (Lawrence, KS: University of Kansas Press, 2007); correspondence with Stewart Brand.

134 **Useful as a tool:** "Function," *Whole Earth Catalog*, Fall 1968.

135 **The WHOLE EARTH CATALOG got started in a plane over Nebraska:** Stewart Brand, *The Last Whole Earth Catalog*, June 1971, 439 (NB: this was not actually the last *Whole Earth Catalog*; another issue came out in October 1974 called *Whole Earth Epilog*).

135 **I had the idea that the higher you go:** Turner, *From Counterculture to Cyberculture*, 69.

Chapter 10

Sources for *Domebooks*, Kahn, Pacific High School: Lloyd Kahn, *Domebook 2* (Bolinas, CA: Pacific Domes, 1971); Gordon, *Spaced Out*.

156 **The whole process is clumsy:** in Gordon, *Spaced Out*, 216.

Chapter 11

Sources for the Nearings: Helen and Scott Nearing, *Living the Good Life: How to Live Sanely in a Troubled World* (Schocken Books, 1970); Rebecca Kneale Gould, *At Home in Nature: Modern Homesteading and Spiritual Practice in America* (Berkeley, CA: University of California Press, 2005);

Jean Hay Bright, *Meanwhile, Next Door to the Good Life* (Dixmont, ME: BrightBerry Press, 2003); Greg Joly of the Good Life Center, interview/correspondence; *Living the Good Life with Scott and Helen Nearing* (documentary, 1976), dir. John Hoskyns-Abrahall, 30 mins.; Brown, *Back to the Land*.

172 A couple, of any age from twenty to fifty: *Good Life* (paperback), 4.
173 Today very many young people: *Good Life* (hardcover), ix.
174 The society from which we moved: *Good Life* (paperback), x.
174 On any other basis: ibid., 199.
174 unattached, uncommitted; raised in comfort: Brown, *Back to the Land*, 206–7.
175 No man is free who has an animal: *Good Life*, 27.

Chapter 13

Sources for the "Hippie-Chicano War:" Iris Keltz, *Scrapbook of a Taos Hippie: Tribal Tales from the Heart of a Cultural Revolution* (El Paso, TX: Cinco Puntos Press, 2000); Elia Katz, *Armed Love* (New York: Holt, Rinehart & Winston, 1971); Miller, *The 60s Communes*; Price, *Huerfano*; Coyote, *Sleeping Where I Fall*; Gardner, *Children of Prosperity*; Houriet, *Getting Back Together*.

201 Every time a white hippie comes in: Gardner, *Children of Prosperity*, 113.
201 They just left everything sitting there: *Drop City* (documentary).
202 Hillary Rodham: though she read the article, "Jamestown 70," in her role as editor, she was not a fan, reportedly dismissing it as "mental masturbation."
202 another, more widely read piece: Richard Pollak, "Taking Over Vermont," *Playboy* 19, no. 4 (1972).
202 We have not invited them: Gov. Deane Davis, press release, May 19, 1971, courtesy of the Vermont State Archives and Public Records.

Chapter 14

206 the annual number of American runaways: Christine Chapman, *America's Runaways* (New York: William Morrow), 31.
214 We want to drop out, but we're buying our food: Sundancer, *Celery Wine*, 135.
215 The Governor threatened to raise state taxes: Houriet, *Getting Back Together*, 72.

215 **one community in Hawaii:** *The Source Family* (documentary, 2012), dirs. Maria Demopoulos and Jodi Wille, 98 min.

215 **Snakepit Eddie successfully convinced officials:** *Home Free Home*, chap. 21.

216 **You have no right to be poor:** Rabbit, *Drop City*, 63.

216 **The poverty of your hip commune or household:** Mungo, *Total Loss Farm*, 93.

216 **poverty is sensual, poverty is turned on, poverty is thrilling:** "Interview with Timothy Leary," 24.

216 **It said how strong and beautiful and honest:** Rabbit, *Drop City*, 112.

Chapter 15

Sources for Ina May Gaskin and The Farm Midwives: Samantha M. Shapiro, "Ina May Gaskin and the Battle for At-Home Births," *New York Times Magazine* (May 23, 2012); *Birth Story: Ina May Gaskin & The Farm Midwives* (documentary, 2012), dirs. Sara Lamm and Mary Wigmore, 95 min.; Katie Allison Granju, "The Midwife of Modern Midwifery," *Salon.com* (June 1, 1999), accessed November 4, 2015, http://www.salon.com/1999/06/01/gaskin/; Ina May Gaskin, interview, "The Brian Lehrer Show," 93.9 WNYC FM, January 17, 2013; Ina May Gaskin, *Spiritual Midwifery* (Summertown, TN: Book Publishing Co., 1975); The Farm Midwives, "Our History," http://thefarmmidwives.org/our-history/.

236 **I learned by listening to women:** *Birth Story* (documentary).

Chapter 16

248 **Our experiment was a colossal failure:** Kit Leder, "Women in Communes," *The Last Whole Earth Catalog*, June 1971, 222.

248 **none of the women . . . wanted to be liberated:** Houriet, *Getting Back Together*, 157.

249 **everyone does what they enjoy doing:** Herbert A. Otto, "The Communal Alternative," in *Utopia USA*, Richard Fairfield, ed. (San Francisco, CA: Alternatives Foundation, 1972), 12.

249 **Even though the women may have embraced and enjoyed their tasks:** Coyote, *Sleeping Where I Fall*, 288.

249 **I was really quite tired of kitchen work:** Vivian Estellachild, "2 Hip Communes," in Fairfield, *Utopia, USA*, 189.

249 **His hands moved so slowly:** Sundancer, *Celery Wine*, 48.

250 **Hey, look, you can't leave all the *kids* here:** Coyote, *Sleeping Where I Fall*, 289.

Chapter 17

257 **Everywhere, a screaming need for privacy:** Houriet, *Getting Back Together*, 26.

257 **We have very little sense of community here:** Ken Kesey, "All Asshole Farm Exposé," *The Last Whole Earth Catalog*, June 1971, 181.

258 **For Kesey, the last straw came:** Terry Gross, "The Fresh Air Interview: Ken Kesey" (1989), in *Conversations with Ken Kesey*, ed. Scott F. Parker, (University of Mississippi Press, 2014).

258 **several thousand fewer rural communes in operation:** Gardner, *Children of Prosperity*.

258 **While everyone is working together on actual construction:** Rabbit, *Drop City*, 147.

258 **how strongly they built commitment, etc.:** Rosabeth Moss Kanter, *Commitment and Community: Communes and Utopias in Sociological Perspective* (Cambridge, MA: Harvard University Press, 1972), 64.

Sources for co-ops: Craig Cox, *Storefront Revolution: Food Co-ops and the Counterculture* (New Brunswick, NJ: Rutgers University Press, 1994); Daniel Zwerdling, "The Uncertain Revival of Food Cooperatives," in *Co-ops, Communes & Collectives: Experiments in Social Change in the 1960s and 1970s*, John Case and Rosemary C. R. Taylor, eds. (New York: Pantheon Books, 1979), 91–111; Jim Higgins, "The Plainfield Co-op (1971-1975)," courtesy of the author; Belasco, *Appetite for Change*.

Sources for "counter-cuisine" and organic food movement: Belasco, *Appetite for Change*; David Kamp, *The United States of Arugula: The Sun-Dried, Cold-Pressed, Dark-Roasted, Extra Virgin Story of the American Food Revolution* (New York: Broadway Books, 2006); Samuel Fromartz, *Organic, Inc: Natural Foods and How They Grew* (Orlando, FL: Harcourt, 2006); Michael Pollan, *The Omnivore's Dilemma* (Penguin, 2006); Lucy Horton, *Country Commune Cooking* (New York: Coward, McCann & Geoghegan, 1972); Robert Houriet, interviews.

262 **hypochondriac food faddists:** Cox, *Storefront Revolution*, 38.

262 **Dipping desiccated wheat germ crackers into yeasty carrot juice cocktails:** Belasco, *Appetite for Change*, 16.

267 **Whiteness meant Wonder Bread, White Tower, Cool Whip:** Belasco, *Appetite for Change*, 48–49.

268 **An idealistic, 24-year-old grad school drop out:** http://www.cascadianfarm.com/our-farm/the-farm, accessed October 24

2015; for a critique of Cascadian Farms and Big Organic generally, see Pollan, *Omnivore's Dilemma*.

268 **The founder of Silk first learned:** Fromarz, *Organic, Inc.*, 161.

271 **We don't want a commune, we want a community:** Kesey, "All Asshole Farm Exposé."

Chapters 18–19

Sources for marijuana history: Eric Schlosser, *Reefer Madness: Sex, Drugs, and Cheap Labor in the American Black Market* (New York: Houghton Mifflin, 2003); Emily Brady, *Humboldt: Life on America's Marijuana Frontier* (New York: Grand Central Press, 2013); "Vermont Intensifies Raids on Marijuana Growers," *New York Times*, 9/22/85; background interviews with several former Vermont marijuana growers.

287 **they installed a conventional flush toilet:** a slightly skewed, heard-through-the-grapevine version of this story appears in Don Mitchell, *Moving UpCountry: A Yankee Way of Knowledge* (Dublin, NH: Yankee Books, 1984), 184.

Chapter 20

Sources for surveillance, bust, trial: public documents including newspaper articles, police reports, and court briefs.

Chapter 21

326 **Not every person's timetable was identical; we were tired; eased back into a more traditional agenda:** Eleanor Agnew, *Back From the Land: How Young Americans Went to Nature in the 1970s and Why They Came Back* (Chicago: Ivan R. Dee, 2004), 198–199.

326 **Anyone who has actually tried to live in total self-sufficiency:** Turner, *From Counterculture to Cyberculture*, 121.

327 **I don't *want* to make my own Grape-Nuts:** Linda Tatelbaum, *Carrying Water as a Way of Life* (Appleton, ME: About Time Press, 1997), 4, in Gould, *At Home in Nature*, 54.

329 **One researcher in the 1990s:** Jacob, *New Pioneers*, 179.

Acknowledgments

First and foremost, my deepest thanks go to the people who made this book possible by sharing so much of themselves: Loraine, Craig, Hershe, Amy, Fletcher, Nancy, LJ, Pancake, Summer, Terry, Amelia, Rahula, Leecia, and Jethro; Chris, Ellen, Eliot, and Peg; Dennis and Peggy; Cro and Jblu; Charlie and Lois; Nash and Mariel, Nick, Topher and Marie; Larry, Judy, and Todd. I can't thank you enough for your thoughtfulness and patience during many hours of interviews and conversation, and for your generosity in allowing your personal stories and experience to offer others a deeper understanding of this complex, exciting moment in American history.

Though they don't appear as characters in this book, I'd also like to thank those who provided important context: Penny Patch and David Martin, Mary Mathias, Paul Lefebvre, Anita Landa, Edward Hoagland, Theresa Perron, Evan Perron, Darlene Young, Janice Urie, and John Campbell. Robert Houriet helped in every possible way—as an astute, historical observer and the author of my most valued source text, as a Vermont communard and friend of Myrtle Hill, as a leader in the organic farming movement, and as a fellow writer tackling the problems of narrative. I am deeply indebted to Annalei McGreevy for her generosity with her time and scholarly materials and for her exceptional undergraduate thesis, which offered vital perspective into Myrtle Hill itself and into the communal era as a whole.

For providing me invaluable insights into this period, both in print and in interviews, I would like to thank Timothy Miller, Stewart Brand, Peter Coyote, and Wavy Gravy; as well as Robbie Gordon, formerly of New Buffalo.

The many months of research that went into this story would not have been possible without the work of librarians, archivists, and researchers, in particular the Interlibrary Loan offices of Columbia University and Baruch College (CUNY), the Berg Collection of the New York Public Library, and the Stewart Brand archive at Stanford University. Greg Joly of the Good Life Center was especially generous. The wonderful people of the Vermont Law Library, in particular Paul Donovan and Vance Asselin, went above and beyond in answering my every question and helping me locate important resources. I am also very grateful for the enthusiasm and collaborative spirit of Jackie Calder and Leslie Rowell of the Vermont Historical Society.

I have found myself thinking constantly of the many teachers whose wisdom and encouragement led in a straight line to this book. Jackie Dadourian, Kitty Toll, Mike Lumbra, Judy Kelley, and Tom Lovett instilled a lifelong curiosity about history and a passion for good sentences. Nancy Dye, Steve Volk, Len Smith, and David Young offered me the opportunity to discover how much I loved the archives and the challenge of putting together a long-form, narrative historical story. Cris Beam, Mike Janeway, Stephen O'Connor, Richard Locke, Lis Harris, Samuel G. Freedman, and Darcy Frey showed me what it means to work at the top of one's craft. To Patty O'Toole, I am forever indebted. Her support on the page, in person, of this project and of my career has been nothing short of life changing.

To Ron Chernow, Stacy Schiff, and Brenda Wineapple—thank you for your advice and friendship and for allowing me to see up close how to turn towering stacks of research materials into the story of people's lives.

Many smart readers helped bring these chapters to life along the way, in particular, Michelle Legro, Alexander Landfair, Sue Mendelsohn, and Carin White. Special thanks to Brook Willensky-Lanford, Matt Lombardi, Ed Herzman, Todd Daloz,

Susie Walsh Daloz, Weezie Sachs, Pam Parker and John Kilbane. Thanks also to Mike Dimpfl, Lacey Clarke, Jesse Robinson, Abby Rabinowitz, Beth Raymer, Kim Tingley, Hannah Merriman and Sohrob Nabatian, Joyce Slayton Mitchell, Victoria Mills, and Schecter Lee for support of all kinds.

This book would not be the same without the tireless efforts and enthusiasm of the incomparable Paloma Contreras, best research assistant ever.

Thank you to my agent, the extraordinary Kris Dahl, for good counsel at every turn. My editor, Clive Priddle, through patience, humor, and well-timed insight helped me produce the exact book I always wanted to write. Thank you.

To my family, Judy Daloz, Larry Parks Daloz and Sharon Daloz Parks, Todd and Susie Walsh Daloz, Ron and Ellen Herzman, Suzanne and Chad Paeglow, and Paul Herzman for everything, from taking care of my children to opening up your homes and offices; to your patient listening, excellent questions, and thoughtful contributions; to your pride and enthusiasm for me and for this project—I can't thank you enough. Todd, Larry, and Judy, thank you for trusting me to tell our story.

Hannah and Ben, thank you for your patience and for the joy you bring to my life every day just by being your awesome selves.

And last but not least, Ed. This book would not exist without your generosity, bravery, good ideas, and good faith. I am lucky beyond words to have such an amazing partner in life and love.

Kate Daloz received her MFA from Columbia University, where she also taught undergraduate writing. She lives in Brooklyn, New York.

PublicAffairs is a publishing house founded in 1997. It is a tribute to the standards, values, and flair of three persons who have served as mentors to countless reporters, writers, editors, and book people of all kinds, including me.

I. F. Stone, proprietor of *I. F. Stone's Weekly*, combined a commitment to the First Amendment with entrepreneurial zeal and reporting skill and became one of the great independent journalists in American history. At the age of eighty, Izzy published *The Trial of Socrates*, which was a national bestseller. He wrote the book after he taught himself ancient Greek.

Benjamin C. Bradlee was for nearly thirty years the charismatic editorial leader of *The Washington Post*. It was Ben who gave the *Post* the range and courage to pursue such historic issues as Watergate. He supported his reporters with a tenacity that made them fearless and it is no accident that so many became authors of influential, best-selling books.

Robert L. Bernstein, the chief executive of Random House for more than a quarter century, guided one of the nation's premier publishing houses. Bob was personally responsible for many books of political dissent and argument that challenged tyranny around the globe. He is also the founder and longtime chair of Human Rights Watch, one of the most respected human rights organizations in the world.

·   ·   ·

For fifty years, the banner of Public Affairs Press was carried by its owner Morris B. Schnapper, who published Gandhi, Nasser, Toynbee, Truman, and about 1,500 other authors. In 1983, Schnapper was described by *The Washington Post* as "a redoubtable gadfly." His legacy will endure in the books to come.

Peter Osnos, *Founder and Editor-at-Large*